Paint Shop Pro 8
explained

Books Available

By the same authors:

BP546   Microsoft Works Suite 2004 explained
BP545   Paint Shop Pro 8 explained*
BP544   Microsoft Office 2003 explained
BP538   Windows XP for beginners*
BP525   Controlling Windows XP the easy way*
BP522   Microsoft Works Suite 2002 explained
BP514   Windows XP explained*
BP513   Internet Explorer 6 and Outlook Express 6 explained*
BP512   Microsoft Access 2002 explained
BP511   Microsoft Excel 2002 explained
BP510   Microsoft Word 2002 explained
BP509   Microsoft Office XP explained
BP505   Microsoft Works Suite 2001 explained
BP498   Using Visual Basic
BP493   Windows Me explained*
BP491   Windows 2000 explained*
BP487   Quicken 2000 UK explained*
BP486   Using Linux the easy way*
BP465   Lotus SmartSuite Millennium explained
BP456   Windows 98 explained*
BP448   Lotus SmartSuite 97 explained
BP433   Your own Web site on the Internet
BP341   MS-DOS explained
BP284   Programming in QuickBASIC
BP258   Learning to Program in C

If you would like to purchase a Companion Disc for any of the listed books by the same authors, apart from the ones marked with an asterisk, containing the file/program listings which appear in them, then fill in the form at the back of the book and send it to Phil Oliver at the stipulated address.

Paint Shop Pro 8 explained

by

**P.R.M. Oliver
and
N. Kantaris**

**Bernard Babani (publishing) Ltd
The Grampians
Shepherds Bush Road
London W6 7NF
England
*www.babanibooks.com***

Please Note

Although every care has been taken with the production of this book to ensure that any projects, designs, modifications and/or programs, etc., contained herewith, operate in a correct and safe manner and also that any components specified are normally available in Great Britain, the Publishers and Author(s) do not accept responsibility in any way for the failure (including fault in design) of any project, design, modification or program to work correctly or to cause damage to any equipment that it may be connected to or used in conjunction with, or in respect of any other damage or injury that may be so caused, nor do the Publishers accept responsibility in any way for the failure to obtain specified components.

Notice is also given that if equipment that is still under warranty is modified in any way or used or connected with home-built equipment then that warranty may be void.

© 2004 BERNARD BABANI (publishing) LTD

First Published - May 2004

British Library Cataloguing in Publication Data:

A catalogue record for this book is available from the
British Library

ISBN 0 85934 545 9

Cover Design by Gregor Arthur
Printed and Bound in Great Britain by Cox & Wyman Ltd, Reading

About this Book

This book *Paint Shop Pro 8 explained* was written using Paint Shop Pro 8.1 running under Windows XP. It is meant for both the beginner and those upgrading from an earlier version of Paint Shop Pro, or PSP as it is familiarly known. The material in the book is not really presented for the reader to start at the beginning and go right through to the end. An attempt has been made to follow a logical sequence, but the more experienced user can start from any section, as they have been designed to be as self-contained as possible. The book does not, however, describe the workings of Microsoft Windows, or how to set up your computer hardware. If you need to know more about these, then may we suggest that you refer to our other books, also published by BERNARD BABANI (publishing) Ltd, and listed earlier in this book.

This book is intended as a supplement to the on-line Help material, and to the fairly detailed user manual that comes with the package. If you don't have a user manual, we even tell you how to get one free of charge! The book will provide the new user with a set of examples that will help with the learning of the most commonly used features of Paint Shop Pro 8, and hopefully help provide the confidence needed to tackle some of the more advanced features later.

The first chapter looks briefly at the history of PSP and where version 8 fits in. The initial installation is covered, as is how to download the User Guide and keep the program up to date.

The next two chapters spend some time explaining the PSP user interface, especially toolbars, palettes and dialogue boxes. Unless you understand these you are literally lost.

Chapters follow on working with selections and images, and using the many electronic painting tools available. Next we cover layers and masks, and please don't just skip this. You will really find the effort here to be worthwhile.

We follow with sections on how to use text in your images, on enhancing photographs, an introduction to vector images and tools, using scripts or macros to automate your work, how to customise PSP your own way, and finally how to optimise your images for use on the Internet.

The book is rounded off with a fairly extensive glossary and five appendices of reference material. These include such things as, all the keyboard shortcuts, the PSP file types and where they are stored, the graphic file types that you can use in PSP, and some background on colours and colour models. We included the material that we often have to search around for ourselves!

Good luck with the book and we hope you enjoy reading and using it with Paint Shop Pro.

About the Authors

Phil Oliver graduated in Mining Engineering at Camborne School of Mines and has specialised in most aspects of surface mining technology, with a particular emphasis on computer related techniques. He has worked in Guyana, Canada, several Middle Eastern and Central Asian countries, South Africa and the United Kingdom, on such diverse projects as: the planning and management of bauxite, iron, gold and coal mines; rock excavation contracting in the UK; international mining equipment sales and international mine consulting. He later took up a lecturing position at Camborne School of Mines (part of Exeter University) in Surface Mining and Management. He recently retired, to spend more time writing, consulting, and developing Web sites.

Noel Kantaris graduated in Electrical Engineering at Bristol University and after spending three years in the Electronics Industry in London, took up a Tutorship in Physics at the University of Queensland. Research interests in Ionospheric Physics, led to the degrees of M.E. in Electronics and Ph.D. in Physics. On return to the UK, he took up a Post-Doctoral Research Fellowship in Radio Physics at the University of Leicester, and then a lecturing position in Engineering at the Camborne School of Mines, Cornwall, (part of Exeter University), where he was also the CSM Computing Manager. At present he is IT Director of FFC Ltd.

Acknowledgements

We would like to thank the following. All of our friends and colleagues, for their helpful tips and suggestions which assisted us in the writing of this book. Various graphic designers for taking the trouble to post excellent PSP tutorials on their Web sites. Some of these gave us inspiration, but they all helped our knowledge base. Ron Lacey for his superb Web site and for his permission to use the vector image in Fig. 10.35, and of course, Jasc Software Inc for producing this superb version of Paint Shop Pro.

Trademarks

Arial and **Times New Roman** are registered trademarks of The Monotype Corporation plc.

HP and LaserJet are registered trademarks of Hewlett Packard Corporation.

Microsoft, **MS-DOS**, **Windows**, are either registered trademarks or trademarks of Microsoft Corporation.

Paint Shop, **Paint Shop Pro** and **Jasc** are either registered trademarks or trademarks of Jasc Software Inc.

Photoshop, Acrobat and PostScript are registered trademarks of Adobe Systems Incorporated.

All other brand and product names used in the book are recognised as trademarks, or registered trademarks, of their respective companies.

Contents

1

Getting Started

If you are reading this book you are obviously interested in mastering the very powerful graphics program Paint Shop Pro (PSP). Hopefully, in the chapters of this book we can help you get to grips with it. When it is opened for the first time the new PSP version 8 can look very daunting. Starting with the next chapter, we will try and clarify this by first exploring the working environment and tools of the program, and then by explaining in more depth its main features, using examples where possible. With perseverance and a little patience, by the time you get to the end of the book you should be quite happy working with Paint Shop Pro. Good luck - but first a little background.

Versions of Paint Shop Pro

Paint Shop Pro began life in 1991 as little more than a simple shareware image viewer and file format converter. Over the years, maybe due mainly to the popularity of the Internet, it has evolved into a fully featured image editor with a following of millions. It is no longer available as shareware, but you can download a trial version from the Internet and have 30 days to try it out. At the time of writing, the latest version Paint Shop Pro 8.1, offers a really superb combination of features and ease of use at a very reasonable price.

The first serious version, Paint Shop Pro 5.0, introduced layering capabilities to the program (making it possible to separate an image into individual components and layers), texture and gradient fill capabilities, floating and customisable toolbars, picture tubes, OLE 2 support, image arithmetic options, emboss and clone brushes, and TWAIN compliant scanner support. Also introduced with Paint Shop Pro 5.0 was Animation Shop, an excellent GIF Animation program, and the Picture Tube tool allowing you to paint with a variety of objects without having to actually draw them.

Paint Shop Pro 6.0 added a variety of important new features such as: GIF and JPEG Exporters for the easy optimisation and output of Web graphics, multiple-level Redo and a Command History, Editable text with character-level formatting, Text bending to circles, lines, or any other shape; Vector object tools for creating editable shapes and lines, a Gradient Editor for creating, editing and saving custom colour gradients, and automatic palette roll-ups to maximise workspace.

The next major release, Paint Shop Pro 7.0, provided some more new additions including a collection of extremely helpful tools for enhancing digital photographs. These included: Automatic Contrast Enhancement, Colour Balance, Saturation Enhancement, and Fade Correction commands, Automatic Small Scratch Removal and Salt and Pepper Filter tools; JPEG Artifact Removal and Moiré Pattern Removal commands; Red-eye Removal, Rapid Scratch Removal and Clarify tools; An Overview Window for navigating around an image in zoom mode, an Autosave option for preventing data loss in the event of a crash, Direct Digital Camera Support, PNG Optimizer function for previewing and optimising PNG type Web images, a Repeat Command, and an Effects Browser for previewing PSP effects.

What's New in Version 8

In version 8 Paint Shop Pro has been completely redesigned and includes new icons, palettes, and menu displays which when mastered make using the software much more intuitive. The Color palette for instance has been replaced by the Materials palette which includes controls for selecting colours, patterns, gradients, and textures. Daunting at first, but as we shall see, superb once you get used to it.

The tools on the Tools toolbar are now grouped into related categories organised on 'flyouts'. They are now controlled from a new Tool Options palette separated into bands, which can be rearranged and resized to suit your working style. The new Layer palette allows you to better manage and view image data and now supports layer groups.

A new Learning Center palette guides you around Paint Shop Pro with Quick Guides to lead you through a variety of common projects to help you get up to speed. There is a new Product Tour, with some 50 topics showing you the many results you can achieve using PSP for all of your photo and graphics projects.

You can create and save custom 'Presets' for all filters and effects in PSP 8. These include Brush Presets which you can use to paint with creative brush effects such as crayon, charcoal, pencil, and more. You can not only choose from many included Presets but create and save your own as well.

There is a new Scripts (or Macros) feature which lets you repeat any series of commands or steps on any image. You can choose from dozens of Preset scripts, or record your own custom series of steps to save and replay, or share with others. These can all be modified using the editor.

The Batch Processing procedure has many new enhancements, such as the ability to rename multiple files or to apply a script to a series of images in a folder.

Most of Paint Shop Pro's native file formats now have new file extensions to make them easier to recognise. PSP 8 images are now saved as **.PspImage** files; gradients as **.PspGradient** files; scripts as **.PspScript** files, and so on. Of course PSP 8 also reads file formats from previous versions of the software.

Standard dialogue boxes are now resizable and remember their window positioning. You can switch off their preview panes and do all proofing right on the main image. Randomize buttons, and the ability to save and load presets, have been added to most effects dialogue boxes.

Holding down the shift key while selecting any toolbar button or menu item now by-passes any command dialogue box, and runs the command with the last used settings. A Reset Preferences dialogue box lets you reset various aspects of PSP 8 to the original configuration, without requiring editing of the registry.

The Effect browser has been completely redesigned, and generates a page of thumbnails. Each one shows the effect of applying a preset for any given effect. Thumbnails are generated for each preset of every effect. You can apply the preset directly right there, or launch the dialogue box to edit and tweak further. As you save presets from effect dialogue boxes they will automatically be added to the effect browser.

PSP 8 supports extensive customisation of the user interface. You can move, add, or remove buttons on toolbars and menus. You can create your own menus and toolbars and assign your own hotkeys. All palettes can be either floating or docked. Docking can be enabled for each palette in the general program preferences, or by right-clicking on any toolbar. Workspace files now store the state of all toolbars, menus, palettes and windows, so you can create and save multiple workspaces that are optimised for specific tasks that you carry out. Very cool.

These are only a few of the new program features and most of them will be covered in more detail in later parts of the book. Perhaps it is worth quoting Jasc Software, the manufacturers:

'Paint Shop Pro, a part of the Paint Shop family of digital imaging and photography products, is the most complete, easy-to-use software for creating professional digital imaging results. By combining automatic and precision tools with an integrated learning system, Paint Shop Pro helps you produce professional results with power and ease.'

We certainly have no problems with this statement. PSP is a great program that gets better with every release.

System Requirements

The minimum system requirements for Paint Shop Pro 8 are: a PC with a Pentium processor or equivalent, Microsoft Windows 98 SP2 or 98 SE SPI, Windows NT4 SP6a, Windows 2000, Windows ME or Windows XP, at least 128 MB of RAM and 200 MB of free hard disc space. A 16-bit colour display adapter with at least a resolution of 800x600 and Microsoft Internet Explorer 5.0 or later.

The recommended configuration is at least a 1.0 GHz or better processor, at least 256 MB of RAM and a 32-bit colour display adapter set at 1024x768 resolution, and Microsoft Internet Explorer 6.0 or later.

PSP 8 is a very powerful software program which needs as much computing speed and power, RAM memory and hard disc space as possible. Even with well in excess of the above specifications we still get our systems hanging up, or slowing down. We recommend you save your work every few minutes, just in case.

Getting the Software

At the time of writing you could get three versions of Paint Shop Pro. Version 5, available free of charge on some PC magazine CDs such as PCPlus. Version 7, advertised at 'knock down' prices in the same magazines, or the latest version 8 at a full price of between £90 and £100.

Downloading a Trial Version

If you have a network or Broadband Internet connection, or are very, very patient, you can download a fully working trial version of PSP 8 from the manufacturers Jasc Software. Their UK site is probably the fastest for this and the URL address is:

http://uk.jasc.com/catalog.asp

as shown in Fig. 1.1 on the next page.

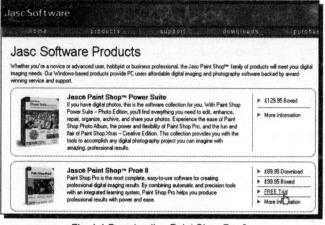

Fig. 1.1 Downloading Paint Shop Pro 8

Be warned though, you will be downloading a very large file of some 61.6 MB. To continue, go to the above page and click the **FREE Trial** link pointed to in our Fig. 1.1 above. Click the Save button in the box that opens and choose a location on your hard disc for the downloaded file **psp810ietr.exe** and then just sit and wait. These download instructions were accurate when the book went to the printers, but Web sites can change. If this happens, you may have to follow your nose a little.

When you have received the complete file you simply have to locate it in a My Computer window and double-click it to start the installation procedure.

You will, of course, have to pay for the program when the 30-day trial period is ended. As they say, 'there is no such thing as a free lunch'!

Downloading the PSP User Guide

If you follow the above downloading procedure you will also need a copy of the program User Guide, as this book is written to complement this, not to replace it! You will need to go to Jasc's US site for this, at:

www.jasc.com

From their home page select the **Downloads** menu item. This takes you to the Jasc Products page. Look for the Paint Shop Pro 8 section and click its **FREE Trial download** button. Complete the short registration form that opens and click on **Continue**. If a File Download dialogue box opens at this stage, click the **Cancel** button, to stop the whole of PSP 8 being downloaded! Unless of course, that is what you want.

From the page that opens (part of which is shown in Fig. 1.2 below) you can download Resource Packs and the 450-page User Guide in a PDF file, for you to read in Acrobat Reader. This is well worth the wait for the 6.1 MB to download.

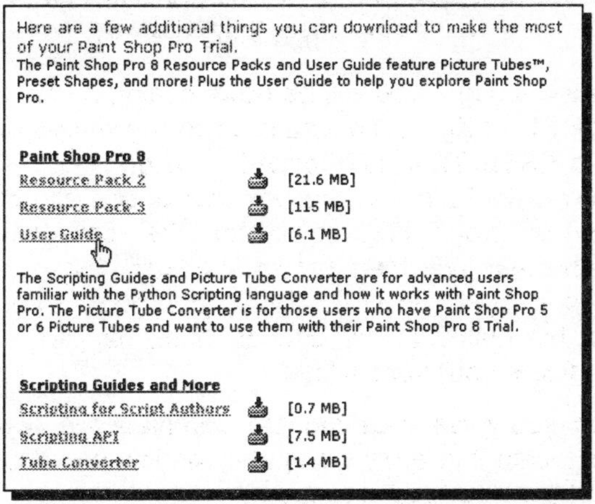

Here are a few additional things you can download to make the most of your Paint Shop Pro Trial.
The Paint Shop Pro 8 Resource Packs and User Guide feature Picture Tubes™, Preset Shapes, and more! Plus the User Guide to help you explore Paint Shop Pro.

Paint Shop Pro 8

Resource Pack 2   [21.6 MB]
Resource Pack 3   [115 MB]
User Guide   [6.1 MB]

The Scripting Guides and Picture Tube Converter are for advanced users familiar with the Python Scripting language and how it works with Paint Shop Pro. The Picture Tube Converter is for those users who have Paint Shop Pro 5 or 6 Picture Tubes and want to use them with their Paint Shop Pro 8 Trial.

Scripting Guides and More

Scripting for Script Authors   [0.7 MB]
Scripting API   [7.5 MB]
Tube Converter   [1.4 MB]

Fig. 1.2 Part of the Resources and Components Page

If the **.pdf** file loads into your Web Browser and opens in Adobe Acrobat Reader, make sure you click the **Save a Copy** button on the Reader toolbar. This works with version 6 of the free Acrobat Reader.

As we said earlier, these download instructions were accurate when the book went to the printers, but Web sites can change. The Jasc Software site has just been completely overhauled, so hopefully will stay the same now for a while longer.

Installing Paint Shop Pro

Installing Paint shop pro is very easy. Placing the program CD into your CD drive should automatically open the screen shown in Fig. 1.3 below.

Fig. 1.3 The CD Installation Menu

If the installation program does not start automatically, don't panic, simply double-click the My Computer icon, then double-click on the CD-ROM icon. When the window opens displaying the contents of the CD, double-click **Setup.exe**.

As shown in Fig. 1.3 you have four menu options. To install PSP 8, to have a look at another Jasc program, the Photo Album (maybe you will have time later), to Browse the CD, or finally to Exit the whole procedure.

Once started, the installation is very painless. If you have a previous version of Paint Shop Pro, it will not be overwritten, so you will still be able to use it as a fall-back.

The first screen tells you that the installation is being carried out by the InstallShield Wizard. Click **Next** to move to the License Agreement box in which you must agree to the licence terms shown in the text window. You do, of course, read such things, don't you? Click **Next** when you are ready.

In the next box complete your Customer Information questions, if this hasn't already been done for you. Click **Back** to return to the previous box, or **Next** to continue to the Custom Setup box shown in Fig. 1.4 below.

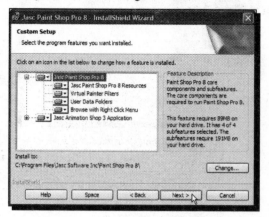

Fig. 1.4 Selecting the Components to Install

Here you can control what features are installed and where on your hard disc they will be placed. You can click the **Change** button if you don't like the default location. Unless you are short of disc space on that drive, it is probably better to accept the default option. To find out what disc space you have on your system click the **Space** button. Clicking **Next** and then **Install** starts the procedure of copying hundreds of files to your disc.

When the copying is complete, the User Options box appears in which we suggest you select to **Place an Icon for Jasc Paint Shop Pro 8 on the Desktop**. As we shall see, it makes opening the program very easy in the future.

After this, the next colourful box is for you to register the software online. This is probably a good idea, in which case clicking the **Next** button will step you through the process. If you don't want to register, simply click the **Skip** button to open the Wizard Completed box shown in Fig. 1.5.

Fig. 1.5 Installation Successfully Completed

Lastly, clicking the **Finish** button, pointed to above, will exit the installation and you should now be able to start getting to grips with Paint Shop Pro.

Updating Paint Shop Pro

PSP 8 is a large and complex package and is being 'improved' all the time. It is a good idea to regularly check to make sure you have the latest version, with the **H̲elp, J̲asc Software Online**, **C̲heck for Updates** menu command.

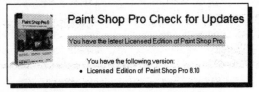

Fig. 1.6 The Result of an Update Check

The last time we did this we received the message shown in Fig. 1.6 above. If an update is available and you purchased a CD copy of Paint Shop Pro 8.0, you can download a patch from the above Web page. We found PSP 8.10 very much faster and more stable than the original PSP 8, even though only a few weeks separated their release dates in the UK.

2

Getting to Know the Program

In this chapter and the next we will describe how to start and stop the Paint Shop Pro program and explain the general user interface and the main components that make up the package.

Starting Paint Shop Pro

 Like most Windows programs there are several ways to start PSP. Initially the easiest is to double-click the shortcut icon, shown here, that was put on the Desktop when the program was installed.

The other way is to use the Windows cascading menu system that opens when you select *start*, **All Programs** from the bottom left corner of the Windows screen. This is shown in Fig. 2.1 below.

Fig. 2.1 The Cascading Menu System

But by far the easiest way of launching the program is from the Windows Quick Launch bar, located just to the right of the *start* button. To do this you must first place the PSP icon on the bar. This is very easy; with the mouse select the **Jasc Paint Shop Pro 8** menu option as shown in Fig. 2.1 above, hold the right mouse button down and drag the pointer over the Quick Launch bar. The menu system will close and a black marker will appear in the bar. Move the pointer left or right until this marker is in the position you want the PSP icon placed and release the right mouse button. A menu will open and select the **Copy Here** option, to copy a shortcut to PSP onto the Quick Launch bar. At any time you can just click this new icon (shown in Fig. 2.2) to open PSP.

Fig. 2.2 Using the Windows Quick Launch Bar

File Format Associations

The first time you open Paint Shop Pro the File Format Associations dialogue box will open, as shown in Fig. 2.3.

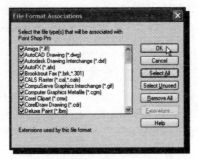

Fig. 2.3 Setting PSP File Format Associations

In this box you can control what file types are automatically opened by Paint Shop Pro in the future. We just clicked the **Select All** to let PSP handle all of our graphic files. If you only want to use certain file types with the program, you can manually click the mouse in the small box to the left of each file type you want included.

In our case above, all the file types selected will show a PSP icon in My Computer windows and will open into PSP whenever their file names are double-clicked. At any time in the future you can re-open this box with the **File**, **Preferences**, **File Format Associations** menu command.

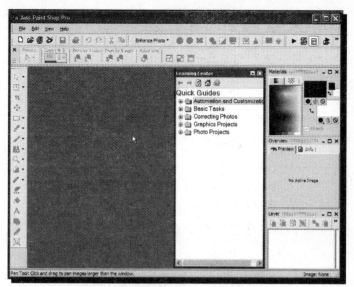

Fig. 2.4 PSP's Default Opening Layout

Paint Shop Pro 8's rather daunting new initial screen layout is shown here in Fig. 2.4. As there is no image open, the available menu and tool options are reduced to those that allow you to modify the screen layout, or to open, create or acquire a graphic image for the program to work with.

Closing Down Paint Shop Pro

Whenever you have finished using the program, click the x close button in the upper right-hand corner of the Paint Shop Pro window to exit.

Clicking the Paint Shop Pro icon in the upper left-hand corner of the title bar and choosing **Close**, using the **File**, **Exit** main menu command, or the **Alt+F4** key combination, are other ways of closing down the program.

With all of these methods you will be given the option to save any files that have been altered since they were opened or last saved.

The User Interface

The illustration below shows the Paint Shop Pro 8 window with an image open in its own window and with the default Toolbars and Palettes showing.

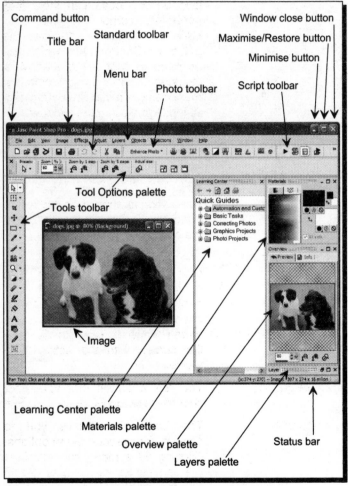

Command button

Title bar

Standard toolbar

Menu bar

Photo toolbar

Window close button

Maximise/Restore button

Minimise button

Script toolbar

Tool Options palette

Tools toolbar

Image

Learning Center palette

Materials palette

Overview palette

Layers palette

Status bar

Fig. 2.5 The Paint Shop Pro User Interface

It is definitely worth spending some time looking at the various parts that make up the PSP interface window, which is subdivided into several areas with the following functions:

Area	*Function*
Command button	Clicking on this program icon button, located in the upper-left corner of the main PSP window, displays the pull-down Control menu which can be used to control the window. It includes commands for restoring, maximising, minimising, moving, sizing, and closing the window.
Title bar	The bar which displays the name of the currently active image.
Minimise button	The button you point to and click to reduce an application to an icon on the Windows Taskbar at the bottom of the screen.
Restore button	The button you point to and click to restore the window to its former size. When that happens, the Restore button changes to a Maximise button which is used to fill the screen with the active window.
Close button	The red X button that you click to close the window.
Menu bar	The bar which allows you to choose from several menu options. Clicking on a menu item displays the pull-down menu associated with that item. If a menu item is not currently available it will be greyed out.

Standard toolbar	A bar of icons that you click to carry out some of the more common PSP actions.
Photo toolbar	Shows icons used for very rapidly enhancing digital photographs.
Script toolbar	Displays command icons, or buttons, used for creating and running PSP scripts, or macros.
Tool Options palette	Lets you select and modify options (such as brush shape and size for a painting tool, or line width for a drawing tool), for the currently selected tool.
Tools toolbar	Lets you click an icon to select which PSP tool to use. Once selected, use the Tool Options palette to control how the tool works.
Learning Center	Called a palette by PSP. This window gives you rapid access to tutorials and Quick Guides for common tasks.
Materials palette	Where you can easily select and control the use of colours, gradients, textures and patterns, for your images.
Overview palette	Shows a thumbnail of the active image as well as information about it. Very useful when you are working with large images.
Layers palette	Where you control the layers that can be used to make an image.
Status bar	The bar that shows useful text about the current menu option or active tool; as well as information on the currently active image.

As is now becoming a standard feature with the better Windows programs, when you move the mouse pointer over a tool or menu bar the options 'light up' when they are active and a brief description is shown on the left side of the Status bar. If you 'hover' the pointer over a toolbar icon a yellow flag opens showing its function.

The Menu System

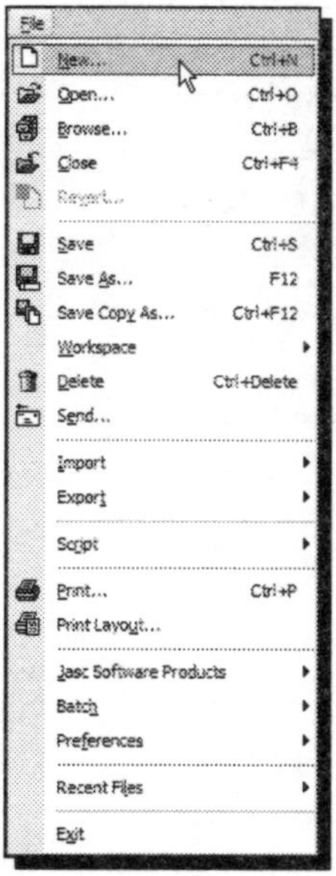

Fig. 2.6 The File
Sub-menu

Each option on the menu bar has associated with it a pull-down sub-menu. This follows the normal Windows convention, so to access the menu, either click the mouse on an option, or press the **Alt** key, which highlights the first option of the menu (in this case **File**), then use the arrow keys to highlight any of the options in the menu. Pressing either the **Enter** key, or the left mouse button, reveals the pull-down sub-menu of the highlighted menu option. The sub-menu of the **File** option is shown here in Fig. 2.6. Note the toolbar icons are also shown to the left of the option list.

Menu options can also be activated directly by pressing the **Alt** key followed by the underlined letter of the required option. Thus pressing **Alt+F**, opens the **File** sub-menu.

You can use the up and down arrow keys to move the highlighted bar up and down a sub-menu, or the right and left arrow keys to move along the options in the Menu bar. Pressing the **Enter** key selects the highlighted option or executes the highlighted command. To leave the menu system with the keyboard, press the **Esc** key enough times to close the menu.

Note that those commands which are not available at any specific time will be inactive and appear on the menu in a lighter colour. In our example on the previous page the **Revert** option is not available.

Keyboard Shortcuts

Many of the menu options have keyboard shortcuts attached to them. These are very useful for people who are more used to the keyboard than the mouse. In fact if you take the trouble to learn these shortcuts you will find they are far faster than using the menu system or the toolbar icons. In the **File** sub-menu shown in Fig. 2.6 there are several. For example, pressing **Ctrl+N**, the 'N' key with the '**Ctrl**' key also depressed, will open the New Image dialogue box.

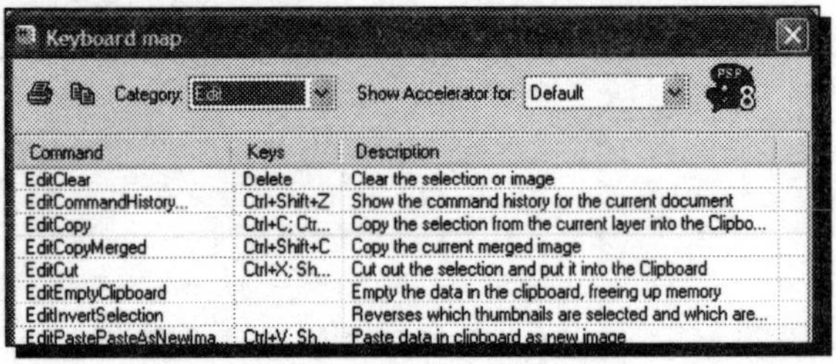

Fig. 2.7 The PSP Keyboard Map

For a complete list of all the standard keyboard shortcuts you can use the Keyboard Map which is opened with the **Help**, **Keyboard Map** menu command. We have also listed the default keyboard shortcuts in Appendix A.

In the next few pages we briefly describe the command structure of the PSP main menu system. This may be useful for new users, but for those upgrading it should help to point out some of the items that have moved around with this version of PSP. We only describe the commands themselves and at this stage make no attempt to explain the meanings of the many specialised words involved. Please don't worry, the explanations will follow later in the text and in the Glossary in Chapter 14. We suggest you go through these pages with PSP 8 open and look at each menu in turn. If you don't understand something just pass to the next item. At least you will get a look at most of PSP's features.

The File Menu

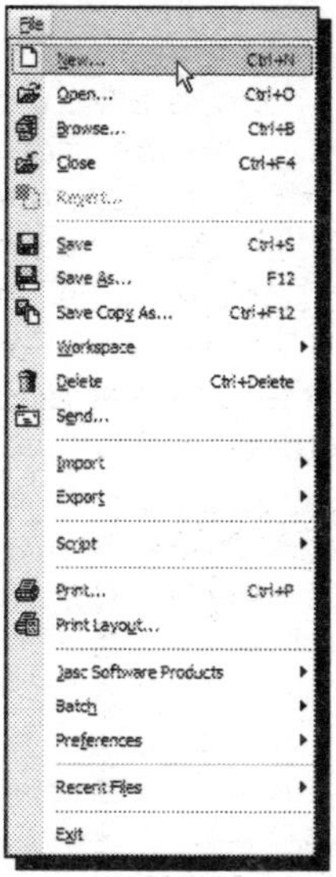

Fig. 2.8
The File Menu

The **New** option opens the New Image dialogue box, **Open** will open an existing image, **Browse** lets you browse the images on your hard drive. **Close**, closes the current image and **Revert** scraps any unsaved changes and reloads the original image.

Save, **Save As** and **Save Copy As** all save an image to disc. Notice the right-arrow beside the **Workspace** option, this means that there is another sub-menu available with options to **Load** an existing workspace, **Save** a new workspace or **Delete** unwanted ones.

Delete will delete the current image from your hard disc and **Send** allows you to e-mail an image. The **Import** sub-menu has options to import a **Custom Brush**, carry out **Screen Capture** and import images from **TWAIN** devices and **From Scanner or Camera**. The **Export** sub-menu has options for image slicing and mapping, for optimising **.jpg**, **.gif** and **.png** files for your Web sites; and for exporting custom tubes, brushes, frames and shapes. You can **Print** the current image and **Print Layout** gives you control over the layout of multiple images.

Jasc Software Products lets you open any other Jasc programs you have. **Batch** allows you to **Process** or **Rename** multiple images at the same time. **Preferences** opens a sub-menu with options to control exactly how PSP works for you. **Recent Files** lists the most recent files you have worked on and **Exit** closes the program.

The Edit Menu

Fig. 2.9
The Edit Menu

The **Undo..** option cancels the last operation you made, whereas **Redo..** reinstates it. **Repeat..** lets you repeat the last command used which allows you to apply the same effect or correction without opening a dialogue box each time. **Command History** shows all the things you have done to an image since it was opened which allows you to undo several steps back.

The **Cut** option cuts out a selected area from an image or layer, moves it to the clipboard and replaces it with the selected background colour or transparency. **Copy** copies a selection or a layer to the clipboard without changing the original, whereas **Copy Merged** copies a merged version of all the layers in a selection to the clipboard. **Paste** offers a sub-menu allowing you to paste the contents of the clipboard into the same image or another image in a variety of ways. **Clear** deletes the current selection without putting it on the clipboard and **Empty Clipboard** clears the Windows clipboard to save memory.

The View Menu

Fig. 2.10 The View Menu

This menu lets you control the visual interface and how you view your images. **Full Screen Edit** opens a full screen view showing only the current image and your current toolbars and palettes. **Full Screen Preview** opens a full screen view showing only the current image. With the latter option you press the **Esc** key to close the preview. **Zoom** opens a sub-menu which lets you zoom your image by different steps. **Preview in Web**

Browser will open the current image in your default browser showing its size and the time it will take to download at different modem speeds.

The **Grid**, **Rulers**, and **Guides** toggle on/off options are used to align and arrange artwork and image elements on the canvas. The **Snap to Grid** and **Snap to Guides** options align objects or brush strokes precisely to the nearest grid line or guide, **Change Grid, Guide & Snap Properties** lets you exactly control all these features. You can toggle on and off the **Toolbars** and **Palettes** you want to use by selecting them in the opened sub-menus. The **Magnifier** option toggles on and off a small window which lets you view the area around the selection point at a 500% magnification. **Docking Options** opens the PSP Preferences dialogue box so you can choose which palettes you want docked. **Customize** allows you to completely customise your toolbars, menus and keyboard shortcuts.

The Image Menu

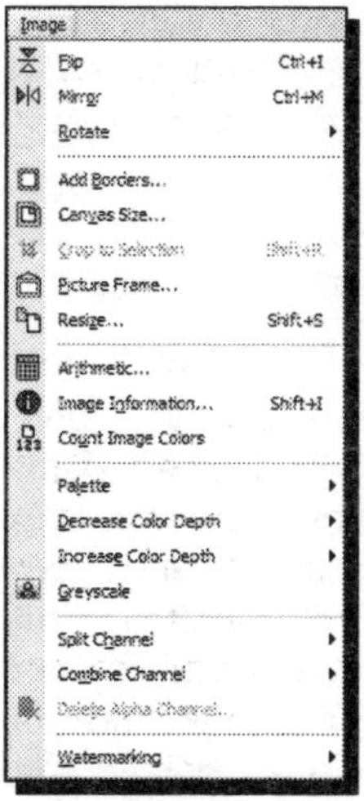

Fig. 2.11
The Image Menu

Most of the features on this menu are for image manipulation. You can **Flip** your image upside down, create a **Mirror** image, or **Rotate** it whichever way you like. **Add Borders** allows you to add a coloured border to your image. **Canvas Size** will show you the size properties of your image and allow you to increase or decrease the canvas size. **Crop to Selection** allows you to crop an image once you have made a selection. **Picture Frame** brings up a dialogue box for adding pre-made frames to an image. **Resize** opens a dialogue box so that you can resize the entire image, not just the canvas as above.

Arithmetic allows you to create a new image by combining two existing ones using arithmetical settings to control the final colour settings. **Image Information** opens a box with detailed information on the current image, you can also add data about the image. **Count Image Colors** will show how many different colours are used in an image.

For images with colour depths of 16 to 256 colours you can control the image **Palette** that contains the colours that are used. You can **Decrease Color Depth** or **Increase Color Depth** of an image. The **Greyscale** command converts a coloured image into a greyscale image with a palette that contains black, white, and 254 shades of grey. **Split Channel** lets you split the colour channels of your image to RGB, HSL or CMYK, and **Combine Channel** does the opposite. **Delete Alpha Channel** deletes any alpha channels in the current image, where an alpha channel is a data storage area in an image that holds selections and masks. **Watermarking** lets you watermark your images, or read a watermark on an existing image.

The Effects Menu

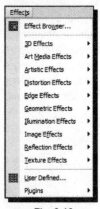

Fig. 2.12
The Effects Menu

Paint Shop Pro has many special effects (or filters) that you can apply to your images, including 3D, artistic, geometric, illumination, reflection, and texture effects as can be seen in the listing in Fig. 2.12.

The **Effect Browser** has been completely redesigned, and generates a page of thumbnails showing the result of applying these effects to the current image. **3D Effects** are used to create buttons, drop shadows, cutouts and bevels. **Art Media Effects** produces a range of stroke type options. **Artistic Effects** offers different artistic filters. **Distortion Effects** offers ways to distort an image like twirling, warping and waving, etc. **Edge Effects** give different ways of enhancing the edges in an image.

Geometric Effects gives a series of geometric shape distortions and skewing options to use on an image. **Illumination Effects** offers the **Sunburst** and **Lights** effects. **Image Effects** allows you to create image **Offsets**, **Page Curls** and **Seamless Tiling** for use as Web page backgrounds. **Reflection Effects** options can produce startling pattern effects. **Texture Effects** offers many options to add depth and texture to your images.

With the **User Defined** option you can create your own effects or filters, or use any of the pre-loaded preset ones. **Plugins** opens a sub-menu containing any plugins you have installed to work with PSP. A sample and a demo plugin were loaded with our version.

The Adjust Menu

Fig. 2.13
The Adjust Menu

This menu contains options which are mainly used for improving digital photographs. **Color Balance** includes a range of options for mixing, balancing and correcting the colours of an image. **Brightness and Contrast** opens a sub-menu of options to control these features, including **Gamma Correction** and **Histogram Adjustment**. There are ways for you to adjust an image colour's **Hue and Saturation**.

The three **Lens Correction** options are, **Barrel Distortion Correction**, **Fisheye Distortion Correction**, and **Pincushion Distortion Correction**. The **Add/Remove Noise** options include **Automatic Small Scratch Removal** and **JPEG Artifact Removal** amongst others. The **Blur**, **Sharpness** and **Softness** options let you adjust the 'focus' of an image. **Red-eye Removal** is used to almost automatically return eyes showing red flash reflection colours to their natural colours. The last menu option reverses the colours and brightness in an image making it a **Negative Image**.

The Layers Menu

Fig. 2.14
The Layers Menu

This menu has the options for controlling layers and masks. The first options all create **New Raster**, **New Vector**, **New Mask**, **New Adjustment Layer**s, or a **New Layer Group**.

You can **Duplicate** or **Delete** the layer which is active in the layers palette. **Ungroup Layers** will ungroup any layers that you may have grouped. **Properties** opens the Layer Properties box in which you can adjust a layer's name, layer grouping and linking, opacity, blending, transparency protection, and layer icon highlight colours. **Matting** cleans up the border of a selection by removing ragged pixels. There are three sub-menu commands, **Remove Black Matte**, **Remove White Matte**, and **Defringe**. These are used when the selection is from an image with a black, white or coloured background respectively.

Arrange and **View** contain options for moving layers around, such as **Bring to Top**, **Send to Bottom**, etc. **Merge** contains the sub-menu with four ways of merging the layers in an image. The next set of options are used for editing and loading or saving Mask layers.

Convert to Raster Layer converts a vector layer to raster. **Promote Background Layer** promotes the background layer to a full layer, which is important as many functions cannot be performed on a background layer itself. **Count Layer Colors** counts the colours within the current layer only.

The Objects Menu

Fig. 2.15
The Objects Menu

This menu contains commands for working with Vector objects, where an object is anything you create with the Pen or Preset Shape tool. Version 8 of PSP has very powerful vector handling features. When used on a vector layer, vector objects are created that can be edited later by changing their properties.

Align and **Distribute** control how the vector objects are placed on the canvas and **Make Same Size** will take all selected objects in the layer and make them all the same size. **Arrange** allows you to send objects to the bottom or bring them to the top, etc.

Group allows you to group several objects to make one shape that can be moved independently or exported and saved for future use. When objects are grouped, you can move, resize, reshape, and change their lines and materials all at once. You can also group several groups of vector objects. **Ungroup** simply ungroups anything you have grouped. **Properties** brings up the Vector Property dialogue box in which you can change an object's colours, patterns, size, etc.

The **Fit Text to Path** option creates text that fits along any vector object such as a line or shape. **Convert Text to Curves** converts the entire text object into one vector object, or each letter into a separate vector object with its own path.

The last group of options, **Edit**, **Node Type** and **Transform Selected Nodes** are all for manipulating object nodes. In PSP each object contains one path made up of contours and nodes and a node is a point on a contour that defines the contour's shape at that point.

The Selections Menu

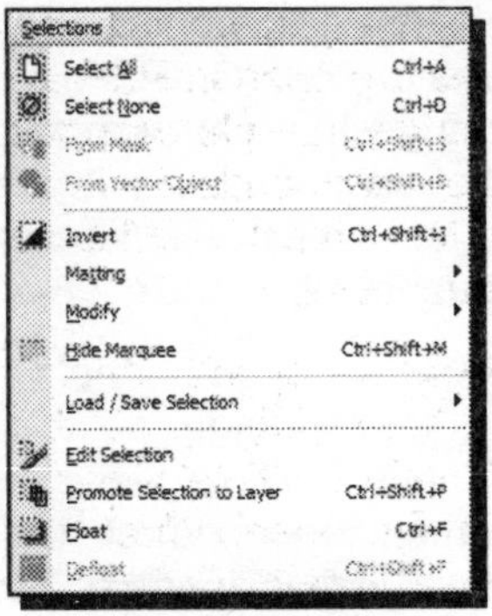

Fig. 2.16
The Selections Menu

Selecting the parts of an image to edit is often the first step in modifying images. Once created, a selection can be edited leaving the rest of the image unchanged. The border of a selection is identified by black and white dashes called a marquee. The **Selections** menu gives different options for selecting various parts, or all, of an image and for handling selections.

Select All will select the entire layer, or the entire image if it only has one layer. **Select None** will deselect any current selections. The **From Mask** option creates a selection from a mask by selecting all the non-masked (non-black) areas and omitting all the masked (black) areas. **From Vector Object** converts vector objects to a raster selection which you can copy and paste into another layer or image.

Invert reverses your selection so that the rest of the image or layer is selected. **Matting** offers the same options as in the **Layers** menu. The **Modify** option lets you edit a selection. You can add to or subtract from a selection, change the feathering, add or remove colours, clean up the edges of a selection, remove specks and holes, smooth the boundary, and recover or apply anti-aliasing. **Hide Marquee** lets you hide the selection marquee. The area will still be selected but the black and white dashes will be removed. **Load / Save Selection** gives you selection loading and saving options from or to a disc or an image alpha channel.

Edit Selection creates a selection from a brush stroke, or applies an effect only to the selection marquee. **Promote Selection to Layer** promotes a copy of a selection to its own layer. You can **Float** a selection to create a copy that you can move or modify without changing the original image. When you finish editing it use the **Defloat** command.

The Window Menu

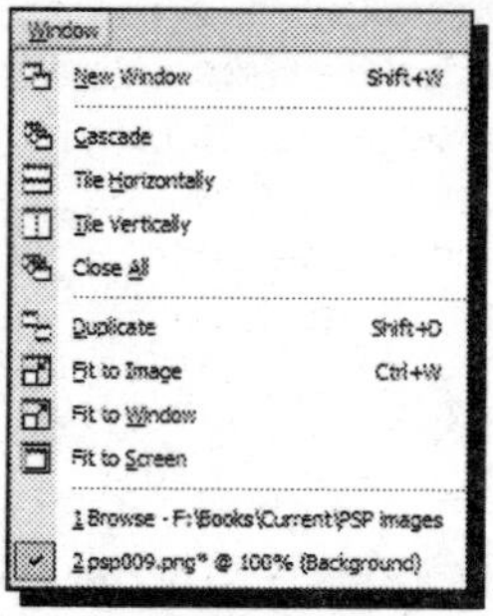

Fig. 2.17
The Window Menu

This menu gives you control over what windows are open in PSP and lets you arrange multiple windows. Many of the commands in it are standard to most Windows programs, but not all.

New Window opens another view of the active image, so it is possible to have multiple views of the same image open. When you make changes in one window, the others are all updated.

Cascade displays multiple windows stacked and cascading from the upper left to the lower right of the workspace. **Tile Horizontally** or **Tile Vertically** display windows side by side horizontally or vertically. They are all resized to fit within the workspace. **Close All** closes all open windows after prompting you to save the files if necessary.

The **Duplicate** option opens an unnamed copy of the current image. This is useful when you want to use one image as the basis for another. After making the duplication you should close the original so as not to accidentally corrupt it. **Fit to Image** fits the window to the image, **Fit to Window** zooms the current image to fit the window size, **Fit to Screen** fits the window and image to the PSP window frame.

All open windows display at the bottom of the Window menu numbered in the order they were opened. The current window has a tick box to the left of its name, as shown in Fig. 2.17 above.

The Help Menu

The last menu which gives access to various off-line and online Help options.

Help Topics accesses the PSP Help system opening screen. **Context Help** gives a query pointer which you can click on buttons, menu items or windows to open the PSP Help system at a relevant page.

Fig. 2.18
The Help Menu

Learning Center opens or closes the Learning Center palette, which gives access to a range of Quick Guides. **Product Tour** opens a 'movies tour' of PSP's main features. **Keyboard Map** displays all of PSP's keyboard commands in the window shown in Fig. 2.7 earlier in this chapter. If you want you can **Register Product Online**.

The **Jasc Software Online** option can be very useful. It gives you access to their Web site, to **Online Support and Services**, **User Forums**, allows you to **Check for Updates**, to access **Resources and Components** and a good range of **Online Tutorials**.

Lastly the **About Paint Shop Pro** option opens a very colourful window with general details about the package, and access to a system info report.

Mouse Right-click Menus

As with most Windows programs, you can use your right mouse button to click objects on the screen and see a drop-down shortcut, or context, menu with contents that depend on what you click. Fig. 2.19 shows the options that were available to us when the mouse was right-clicked on an open image. As usual, unavailable options are shown in grey.

Fig. 2.19 A Right-click
Context Menu

Getting Help

If all else fails with Paint Shop Pro, don't worry too much. As we saw on the last page there are many sources of Help available, as well as the User Guide. If you don't have a User Guide have another look at page 6 and get one online.

The Product Tour

Probably the best place to start is the Product Tour which you access with the <u>**Help**</u>, <u>**Product Tour**</u> menu command.

Fig. 2.20 The Product Tour

This gives quite a good overview of PSP 8. You can run through the whole series of 'movies' by clicking the **Start the Product Tour** link pointed to in Fig. 2.20 above, or select an option to view in the menu system on the left side of the window.

Clicking the ❷ Help button at the bottom of the window explains the other buttons. Enjoy.

Using Quick Guides

Fig. 2.21 Quick Guides in the
Learning Center Palette

The Learning Center palette gives access to a range of useful Quick Guides, as shown here in Fig. 2.21. If you have closed this palette you can use the **Help**, **Learning Center** menu command, or more simply just press the **F10** key, to re-open it.

Even if none of the topics are what you are looking for, it is still worth spending half an hour working your way through them. Make sure you investigate the projects at the end of the listings. Some of them could save many hours of struggle!

Using the Help System

 If you press the **F1** function key when you have an image open, or click the **Help Topics** toolbar button shown here, or use the **Help**, **Help Topics** menu command, the Paint Shop Pro Help window will open, as shown in Fig. 2.22 on the next page. Don't worry if you can't find the toolbar button shown as it is not on the bar by default. But as we shall see later, any of PSP's menu commands can be added to existing or new toolbars.

The Help System includes much of the information contained in the paper User Guide, but is a little lacking in graphic content.

The opening window shown has a listing of 'hypertext links' to some of the help topics a new user is most likely to use first. Clicking any of these opens the relevant Help page, without you having to look for the item itself.

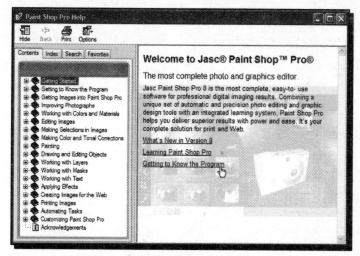

Fig. 2.22 Paint Shop Pro Help

As can be seen here, the left pane of the Help window has four tabbed sections.

Fig. 2.23 The PSP Help
Contents List

The **Contents** tab opens up an impressive list of topics relating to the PSP program. Clicking a '+' at the left of an item, or double-clicking a closed book icon, opens a sub-list; clicking a '—', or double-clicking an open book icon, will close it again. Clicking a list item, with the 🔖 mark as shown, opens the help text in the right-hand pane.

When you want to search for specific words in the index list, you click the **Index** tab and start typing the keyword into the text box as shown in Fig. 2.24. As you enter each letter of the word the list below is automatically updated.

In Fig. 2.24 we started to enter the word colour, but it only took two letters to find the right section, albeit with the American spelling! Then just select what you want from the list and click the **Display** button.

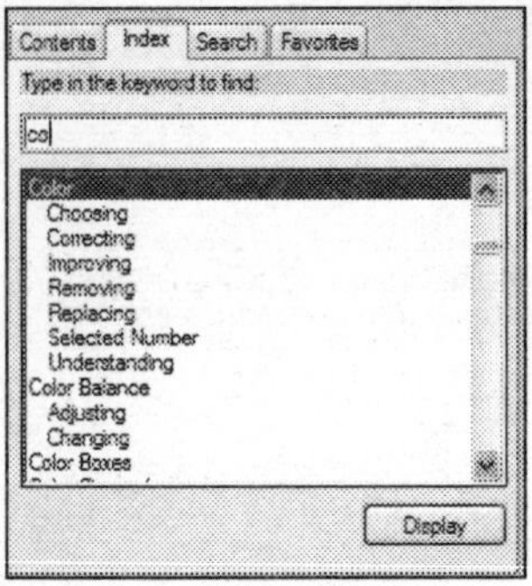

Fig. 2.24 The Help Index    Fig. 2.25 Searching PSP Help

The **Search** tab button opens the pane shown in Fig. 2.25 above in which you can search for text in the body of the Help pages themselves. You type the word required in the top text box, click the **List Topics** button, select from the list below and finally click the **Display** button to open a Help page. In this case searching for 'colour' will find nothing!

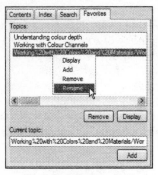

When you find a Help page that you will need again, with the page open click the **Favorites** tab to open the pane shown in Fig. 2.26.

Here we have just clicked the **Add** button and right-clicked on the new 'rubbish' topic name that was added to the list. Selecting the **Rename** drop-down menu option allows us to give the topic a more meaningful name. In the future

Fig. 2.26 Creating a Help Favorite Item

we can just open this pane, select the saved item and click on **Display** to go straight to its Help page. Quite a useful feature we think.

The Help Toolbar

You can control the Help window with the four buttons on the toolbar, as follows:

 Hide - Closes and re-opens the left pane of the Help window, giving more room for the Help text.

 Back - Opens the last Help page viewed in the current session list.

 Print - Prints the current page, or all of the topics in the selected heading. Make sure you have lots of paper in your printer for the latter option!

 Options - gives a sub-menu of all the other toolbar options, as well as allowing you to hide the Help tabs.

The PSP Help system is quite comprehensive and it is usually easy to find the information you are looking for. Do spend some time here to learn, particularly what is new in the program. Other topics can always be explored later.

Screen Tips

If you want to know what a menu command or button does you can also get Screen Tips help. These can be accessed in two ways:

• For help with a menu command, toolbar icon, or a screen region, click **Context Help** on the **Help** menu, or **Shift+F1**, and then click the feature you want help on.

• To see the name of a toolbar or palette button, rest the mouse pointer over the button and its name and keyboard shortcut will appear. At the same time a short description of the option is shown on the status bar at the bottom of the PSP window.

Using the Jasc Learning Center

Once you are familiar with the basics of Paint Shop Pro it may help to look at some on-line tutorials to get to know some of its more powerful features. There are many hundreds of sites on the Internet offering such tutorials. Some are better than others.

A good place to start is on the JASC Web site. They did produce PSP after all. An easy way there is with the **Help**, **JASC Software Online**, **Online Tutorials** menu command.

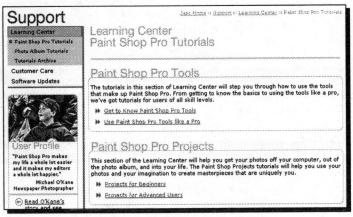

Fig. 2.27 The JASC Learning Center Web Page

At the time of writing, this opened the Learning Center and the page in Fig. 2.27 above could be accessed by clicking the *Learn More* link in the Paint Shop Pro Tutorials section.

When you have finished the Tools and Projects section, make sure you look in the **Tutorials Archive**. Here you will find well over a hundred excellent tutorials. Most of these were written for PSP 7, but they could all be used for PSP 8 as well.

3

Toolbars and Palettes

As we saw in the last chapter, many of PSP's operations are controlled from a fairly complex menu system. Many more, however, are controlled by clicking buttons and selecting options from toolbars and palettes. For most of these options to be active you need to have an image open in PSP.

Opening an Image

You can create a new image from scratch, work with an existing image, capture one off the screen, or import one from a scanner or digital camera. We will only look at the first two options in this chapter. Once an image is open, all the tools will be available for you to use. When no image is open, tools will not be active on the toolbars.

Opening a New Image

 To open a new image use the **File, New** menu command or click the **New** icon on the Standard toolbar, shown here. Both of these open the New Image dialogue box shown in Fig. 3.1 on the next page. This box makes it very easy to set what options you want for the new image.

Now before we click OK, let's explore this window a little bit. We have set both the **Width** and **Height** for the new image to 300 Pixels. The **Units** for computer graphics are usually Pixels, but you can use Inches or Centimeters to force the image to print at a certain size. As for **Resolution**, the default is 200 Pixels/inch, but for graphics that are going to be used in a Web page or sent by e-mail then 72.00 Pixels/inch is the best choice. The file size is much smaller for the same result.

Fig. 3.1 The New Image Box

If you are working mostly with photos that you want to print leave it at 200. For now keep the defaults of **Raster Background** (Vector Background is new in PSP 8), and **Color depth**. Don't worry, these terms will all be covered later on in the book.

You can leave the **Transparent** box checked to give a transparent background to your new image, or click this box to uncheck it and select from the **Color** box to set a colour background for the image. In our example here we right-clicked in the **Color** box and selected white from the colours that were offered.

Last Used
1024 x 768
120 x 240 vertical
1200 x 800
125 x 125 Square Button
234 x 60 Half Banner
3.5 x 5 in horizontal
3.5 x 5 in vertical
4 x 6 in horizontal
4 x 6 in vertical
468 x 60 Full Banner
5 x 7 in horizontal
5 x 7 in vertical
640 x 480
72 x 392 Full Vertical Navbar
8 x 10 in horizontal
8 x 10 in vertical
800 x 600
88 x 31 Micro Button
Business Card horizontal
Business Card vertical
CD Insert
Japanese Postcard horizontal
Japanese Postcard vertical
Panorama
Postcard horizontal
Postcard vertical
Square

Fig. 3.2
Our Preset List

There are a number of Presets available with PSP 8 which automatically give you different types of new images. Just click on the down-arrow in the **Presets** box to view them, as shown in Fig. 3.2. If you double-click an option on this list all the New Image settings will be suitably completed for you.

Another new feature in this dialogue box is the ability to save the current settings as a new Preset. Just click on the ▦ Save Preset icon beside the **Presets** box, type a suitable name and click **OK**. To delete a Preset first select it from the list and then click on the ▩ 'dustbin' icon.

When you have finished exploring this New dialogue box click on **OK** to create the new image. A new window will be opened in the PSP working area, called 'Image 1' and all the tools will be available for you to use.

Opening an Existing Image

There are two main ways to open images that are already saved on disc, you can use the PSP Browser, or the Open dialogue box.

 Clicking the **Browse** button on the Standard toolbar, or using the **File**, **Browse** menu command will open the Image Browser shown below.

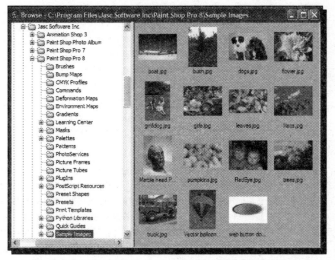

Fig. 3.3 The Image Browser showing the PSP File Structure

The first time this is used it will probably open into the Sample Images folder created by the installation program, as shown in Fig. 3.3. These images are available for the tutorials, etc., but you can obviously use them for learning the program, or for generally playing around with. This of course is the best way to learn, just try out all the options you can find (on a copy of an image) and see what they do!

You navigate through your folders in the left pane of the Browser, select a folder by clicking on it and the images present in that folder will be displayed as 'thumbnails' in the right pane of the browser. To open the required image, either double-click on the thumbnail or drag it onto your workspace.

Clicking the **Open** button on the Standard toolbar, or using the **File**, **Open** menu command will open the Open dialogue box shown in Fig. 3.4 below.

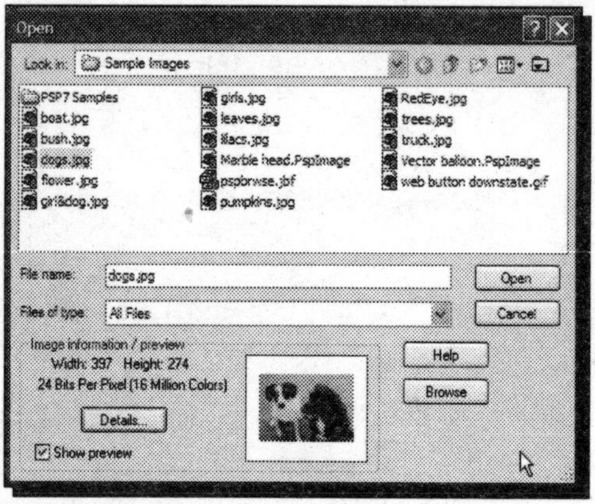

Fig. 3.4 The Open Dialogue Box in List View

This is all standard 'Windows stuff', we can hear you saying, but in PSP 8 dialogue boxes have some interesting extras. You can re-size them by dragging the ▧ handle in their bottom right-hand corner, and the View Menu ▦▾ icon lets you choose how the files will display in the box including a Thumbnails option, as shown in Fig. 3.5 below.

Fig. 3.5 The Open Dialogue Box in Thumbnails View

Unfortunately PSP's own image format **.PspImage** is not supported in Thumbnail view, but as long as the **Show preview** option is selected you can preview a file when it is selected in the listing. Alternatively, you can click the **Browse** button, pointed to in Fig. 3.5, to open the PSP Browser straight into the selected folder.

Another useful feature in most of PSP's file handling dialogue boxes is the **List of favorite paths** button ⬚. Clicking this opens a listing of the folders you are likely to want to go to (Fig. 3.6). When you click on a folder in the list it is placed straight into the **Look in** box. To add any other of your file storage locations to the list, first navigate to the folder with the the **Look in** box, click the **List of favorite paths** button and select **Add Current**. We use this feature a lot.

Fig. 3.6
Favorite
Paths

Once you have selected the file you want, click the **Open** button and the image will open as a new window. You can select multiple files to open by keeping the **Ctrl** key depressed as you select each one.

Once you have been working with PSP for a while you can open one of the four most recently used images with the **File**, **Recent Files** menu command.

As with all Windows programs, you can have numerous windows open at once. Only one of these image windows will be the active image at any one time. You can, of course, only work on the active image, but you can make another open image active by clicking on its Title bar whenever you want to.

Within the PSP working environment, image windows can be manipulated in the usual Windows ways (by moving and re-sizing them or using the window control buttons explained on page 15) but if you minimise an image it is shown as a small title bar at the bottom of but inside the PSP workspace.

The Toolbars

PSP 8 has seven toolbars by default, (not including the status bar). All of these are completely customisable and you can also create your own. In this chapter we outline all the toolbars, but only describe the default icons of the two toolbars that are essential for the basic use of the program. More detail on the tools themselves and the other bars is included where relevant in later chapters.

You open and close PSP toolbars by clicking their options on the menu shown in Fig. 3.7. This can be opened with the **View**, **Toolbars** menu command, or by right-clicking on the toolbar area and selecting **Toolbars** from the context menu. When a bar is selected a blue 'square' is placed around it, as with the **Standard** and **Tools** options in our example here. The **Ctrl+Shift+T** keystroke combination will also open all of the toolbars and palettes.

Fig. 3.7 PSP
Toolbars
Sub-menu

You can place toolbars wherever you like in your PSP working window. If they are floating (away from the window edge) you drag them by the title bar. If they are 'docked' on a workspace edge you can drag them by their ▦ handle. If you hold the **Ctrl** key down while dragging a bar, it will not dock on an edge.

The Standard Toolbar

A bar of icons that you click to carry out some of the more common PSP 'housekeeping' actions, as follows:

Button   *Function*

 New - Create a new image.

 Open - Open an existing image from disc.

 Browse - Opens the Browser to view disc-based images.

 Twain Acquire - Opens a channel to your scanner to allow images to be imported into PSP.

 File Save - Saves the current image to disc with the same name.

 Print - Prints the current image.

 Undo Last Command

 Redo the Last Command

 Cut - Cut the selection to the Windows clipboard.

 Copy - Copy the selection to the Windows clipboard.

The Tools Toolbar

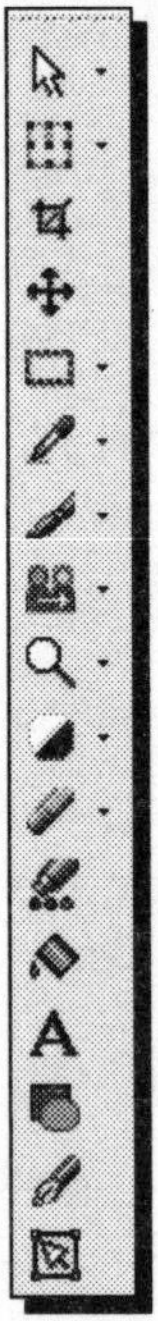

The tools on this bar, shown in Fig. 3.8, are used to perform image editing tasks such as painting, drawing, cropping an image's size, selecting an area and adding text, etc.

You select a tool by clicking its icon, or button, on the toolbar. If a tool button has a small arrow to its right you can click this arrow to display a flyout

Fig. 3.9 A Tools Flyout Menu

menu from which you can choose more tools. In Fig. 3.9 we show the flyout menu that opens when the Paint Brush tool is clicked. In fact, the Tools Toolbar has been completely redesigned in PSP 8 and tools are now organised by their function. It is however easy to 'lose' a tool as the last tool used on a flyout menu is the one whose button shows on the toolbar. This can take a little getting used to. When a tool is activated it is displayed and

Fig. 3.8 The PSP Tools Toolbar

highlighted with a lighter background colour and a blue line around it, as shown here on the right. If you look at Fig. 3.8 again you will see that none of the tools on it appears to be active. That is because of the way we constructed the image, in fact the Pan tool is active when an image is first loaded into the program.

Once you have found and selected the tool you want, you use the settings on the Tool Options palette (see later in the chapter) to control how the tool works.

In Fig. 3.10 we show all the Tools toolbar flyout menus in their default configuration. This may help you find your way around the tools and make it easier to locate that elusive one that maybe you can't seem to find! All the default buttons on the toolbar are then described in a little more detail.

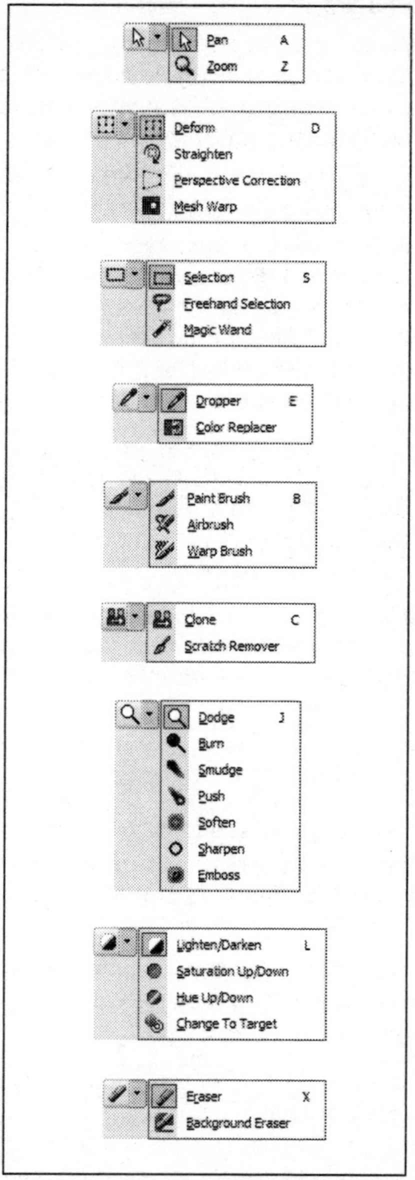

Fig. 3.10 The Tools Toolbar Flyout Menus

Button   Function

Pan - Used to move, re-size or otherwise manipulate the window that surrounds open images. It is also used to move an image around in a window smaller than the actual image, the pointer then changes to a hand 🖐. This is the only tool that does not edit the image itself in any way.

Zoom - Used to focus in or out on areas in an image. The left mouse button zooms in on the area being clicked, while the right mouse button zooms out. As with the Arrow tool, zooming in on an image does not affect the physical size of the image in any way, just the display size.

Deform - Used to rotate, re-size, skew, and distort layers, floating selections, and images. When active, a 'box' with 'handles' will appear and by dragging the handles, the selected part of the image will be modified.

Straighten - Used to straighten a layer or the whole image that may be out of alignment. Very useful for correcting scanned images.

Perspective Correction - Used to correct perspective distortion, where objects in a photograph seem to be leaning or angled.

Mesh Warp - Used to deform images, layers, and selections. A grid (mesh) is placed on the image and deformations are made by dragging grid intersections points, or nodes.

Crop - Used for the cropping, or cutting, of an image down to a reduced size.

Move - Used to reposition a selection or layer. Click on the tool, then left-click and drag on a floating selection, or on the area of a layer that contains image data. To move a non-floating selection right-click and drag in the selection.

Selection - Used to create selections on an image of a set shape , such as a rectangle, circle, or star. You click on the tool, set your Selection Type in the Tool Options palette and drag your cursor over the image to select the area required.

Freehand Selection - Used to make a selection of an irregular shape or around the edges of an object, such as a person, flower or animal. On the Tool Options palette, choose from the following four Selection Types:

> *Edge Seeker*. Lets PSP find the edges between areas with subtle colour or light changes.

> *Freehand*. Lets you very quickly click and drag the mouse pointer to select an area.

> *Point to Point*. Used to make a selection with straight edges, by clicking from point to point. PSP draws straight selection lines between the points.

> *Smart Edge*. Best used for selecting between two areas of highly contrasting colour or light. You click along irregularly shaped edges and let PSP find the edges itself.

Magic Wand - Used to make a selection based on the colour of similar pixels throughout an image. The Tolerance setting in the Tool Options palette is crucial. A selection is formed based on the colour of the pixel clicked on, and the amount of Tolerance indicated in the palette.

Dropper - Allows quick selection of a new colour in the active layer or whole image. Left-clicking on a colour in an open image sets the Materials palette foreground colour, right-clicking sets the background colour.

Color Replacer - Used to replace one colour in an image with another. It works best on images that have solid areas of colour and do not contain gradients, or anti-aliasing.

 Paint Brush - Used to create strokes of solid colour that simulate an artist's paint brush, or to paint with patterns and textures. There is a large range of Presets and brush tips in the Tool Options palette. The brush will paint the foreground (dragging the left mouse button) or background (dragging the right button) material currently selected in the Material palette. To paint a straight line, click once at the beginning point, then press Shift and click the end point.

 Airbrush - Similar properties to the paint brush but used to apply colour with a 'spraycan' effect instead of a brush effect. It is time-dependent, the longer you hold the brush over an area, the more paint will build up on the image.

 Warp Brush - Used to create strokes that produce a warping effect on the pixels of an image. You can push pixels in the direction of the brush stroke, expand pixels away from the brush, contract them into the centre of the brush, twirl pixels clockwise or anti-clockwise and cause random movements of pixels under the brush.

 Clone - Used to take an area from one image and paint it within the same image, or another one. To start a clone you right-click on the source area you wish to clone, then move to the target area, click and hold down the left mouse button and drag to paint the clone.

 Scratch Remover - Used for removing scratches and lines from photographs. Select a size and shape for the tool in the Tool Options palette, then drag your cursor over a scratched area on a photo. PSP will then remove any scratches in the selected area.

Retouch Brushes - The next 11 tools are all brushes for retouching images. You drag the brush in the image to apply the tool. If the tool has two functions (such as Lighten/Darken), drag with the left mouse button to apply the first function and the right button to apply the second function.

 Dodge - Lightens and brings out the details in areas that are in shadow by mimicking the photographic darkroom technique of holding back some of the light when printing photographs to produce lighter areas.

 Burn - This is the opposite of the Dodge tool. It darkens areas of the image that are too light.

 Smudge - Similar to smearing paint it spreads colour and image details from the starting point and picks up new colour and image details as it moves.

 Push - Spreads colour and image details from the starting point but does not pick up any new colour or image details.

 Soften - Smooths edges and reduces contrast.

 Sharpen - Heightens edges and accentuates contrasts.

 Emboss - Causes the foreground to appear raised from the background by suppressing colour and tracing edges in black.

 Lighten/Darken - Lightening increases brightness; darkening decreases brightness. Choose to affect the RGB or Lightness value of pixels.

 Saturation Up/Down - Increases or decreases the saturation (affects the HSL value of pixels).

Hue Up/Down - Increases or decreases the hue (affects the HSL value of pixels).

Change-to-Target - Changes pixels based on a characteristic of the current foreground colour on the Materials palette. This can be colour, hue, saturation, or lightness.

Eraser - Used to remove pixels from your image. When used on a background layer, the erased area will be filled with the current background colour if the left mouse button is used and the current foreground colour if the right button is used. If the tool is used with the left mouse button on a raster layer then the erased area will be transparent. When the right button is used the tool unerases and replaces any previously erased pixels.

Background Eraser - A new tool which is used to selectively erase pixels from the background of an image by reading the colour information of the pixels underneath the 'eraser icon' in the centre of the cursor, as shown here. As you drag the brush across an image, any pixels inside the circle (indicating the brush size) that are the same colour or within a selected tolerance of the pixels beneath the eraser icon are selectively made transparent. You use this tool to erase background you don't want that lies around an object you want to keep. Place the centre of the brush on the background you want to remove and overlap the edge of the brush onto the object you want to keep, then trace around your object.

Picture Tubes - A unique tool to PSP which lets you 'paint' using pre-made objects, known as tubes. PSP comes with built-in tubes, but it is possible to make custom tubes, and to download them from the Internet.

Flood Fill - Lets you fill a complete image, or a selected area in an image, with the colour, gradient, pattern or texture that is currently set in the Materials palette, or with another image.

 Text - offers the ability to make either raster (pixels based) or vector (line based) text, depending on the type of layer the text is added to. The text can have a solid fill, or any combination of textures and styles can be used to make either filled text, or stroked and filled text. One of the largest advantages to vector text is the ability to stretch, shrink, warp, and otherwise edit the text without losing any image quality.

 Pre-set Shapes - Used to draw both raster and vector objects such as rectangles, ellipses, etc., with line (foreground) and fill (background) colours and materials. To draw shapes with no line or no fill, set the colour to transparent on the Materials palette. On the Tool Options palette choose a shape from the Preset shapes drop-down window and mark the Create as vector check box to draw a vector object. Clear it to draw a raster object. Click and drag to draw the shape. When the shape outline is the size you want, release the mouse button. Raster objects become part of the current raster layer. Each vector Preset shape you draw is a separate vector object.

 Pen - Use this tool to draw and edit single lines, freehand lines, Bezier curves, and point-to-point lines, as raster objects on raster layers, or vector objects on vector layers. When you use the Pen tool in vector mode, the objects can be moved, deformed, and edited after they are created, without affecting the rest of the image.

 Object Selection - Used to select vector text and vector objects that you want to move, place in a group, align, distribute or arrange on the canvas.

Other Toolbars

The other PSP toolbars are not as critical to the successful running of the program and are described in more detail as and where they fit into the rest of the book. They consist of:

Photo toolbar - Contains icons used for very rapidly enhancing digital photographs.

Browser toolbar - Displays commands for using the Paint Shop Pro browser to view, open, and manage your image files.

Effects toolbar - Displays commands for applying effects or filters to your images.

Script toolbar - Displays command icons, or buttons, used for creating and running PSP scripts, or macros.

Web toolbar - Displays commands for creating and saving images for the Web.

Don't forget that if the toolbar you want is not showing when a window is opened, you simply open the **View** menu, select the **Toolbars** option and choose which bars you want to show from the menu shown in Fig. 3.7. Selecting them again in the future, will toggle the options off.

The Palettes

In PSP you use palettes mainly to choose tool options, select colours and other materials for the tool to work with, to find your way around a large image and to manage its layers. There are however eight palettes as follows:

- **Tool Options palette** - Used to control and change options for the currently selected tool.

- **Materials palette** - Used to select colours and materials (gradients, patterns and textures) for painting, drawing, filling, and retouching.

- **Overview palette** - Gives a thumbnail view of the active image, and information about the image.

- **Layers palette** - Used to control, organise, view, and edit image layers.

- **Learning Center palette** - Displays quick-help guides and tutorials for common tasks (see page 30).

- **Histogram palette** - Displays a graph of the distribution of red, green, blue, greyscale, hue, saturation, and lightness values in an image. This lets you analyse the distribution of detail in the shadows, midtones, and highlights to decide how to make image corrections.

- **Script Output palette** - Shows the actions you take and the results of running PSP scripts (macros).

- **Brush Variance palette** - Sets additional brush options. This palette is mainly for users of graphics tablets.

Of these the last three are probably too advanced for this book, the Learning Center palette has been looked at already, and the Layers palette is covered in a later chapter. The other palettes are fundamental to the use of PSP 8 and are described in the next few pages.

To open a palette use the **View**, **Palettes** menu command and choose the palette, type the shortcut key (listed to the right of the name), or right-click any palette and choose the palette to open from the context menu.

The Tool Options Palette

Once you have selected a PSP tool to work with from the Tools toolbar, you set how the tool will operate on the Tool Options palette. This includes such things as selecting and modifying options like brush shape and size for a painting tool, or line width for a drawing tool.

Although there is only one Tool Options palette it has different content for every tool on the Tools toolbar, and at the last count there were 37 of them! We obviously can't describe all of these, we haven't the space and you would almost certainly fall asleep. So we will look at several examples only. In general the default settings work well, but if not you use trial and error.

By default, the palette is underneath the Standard toolbar as we saw in Fig. 2.5. If your monitor screen is big enough we recommend that you leave it there permanently open.

Fig. 3.11 Changing the Size of a Floating Palette

Otherwise you can 'float' the palette by dragging it by its ▦ handle as described on page 40. We have done this in Fig. 3.11 above and are in the process of re-sizing the palette by dragging its right-hand corner. For our examples the above configuration of several bands of options one above the other is easier for us to show than one long thin 'ribbon'.

Fig. 3.12
Roll-up

When a palette is floating as in Fig. 3.11 you can drag it to wherever you want on the screen. To get more free screen space you can click the ▲ button to allow the palette to automatically roll-up, and the ◄ button to lock the palette open, as shown in Fig. 3.12.

When a palette is set to roll-up, it will shrink in size whenever you move the mouse pointer off it. To see it again simply move the pointer over the minimised palette. This can be a little disconcerting to start with, but you soon get used to it.

A good way to see the different tool options is to select the buttons on the Tools toolbar one at a time and watch the Tool Options palette change each time.

Fig. 3.13 The Tool Options for the Paint Brush

A rather daunting array of controls, to say the least. The PSP Help system can usually come to the rescue though. In Fig. 3.13 we show the Paint Brush options with the Context Help pointer activated by pressing the **Shift+F1** keys. When this pointer is clicked in the palette the Help system opens to the correct place as shown in Fig. 3.14.

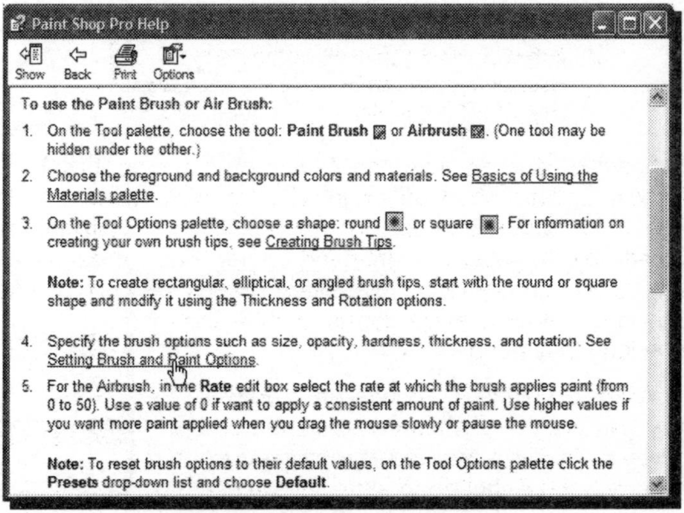

Fig. 3.14 Part of a Context Help Page

With PSP as long as you know where to go there is usually lots of Help available. To go one step further, if you click the **Setting Brush and Paint Options** link pointed to in Fig. 3.14, you can get really detailed help on more of the palette options, as shown in Fig. 3.15.

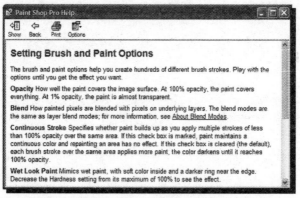

Fig. 3.15 Part of the Help on Brush and Paint Options

One thing to remember is that you must set the options before you use the tool. You can't edit Tool Options for brush strokes or objects you have already created in an image.

As we saw, the items in the Tool Options palette depend upon the active tool, but the Presets option is common to most. **Presets** are scripts provided with PSP that save specific settings for a tool. You can also create your own. In Fig. 3.16 we show a composite of a Preset being chosen and used at the same time.

Fig. 3.16 Using the 'Bar code' Preset Paint Brush

The Materials Palette

Fig. 3.17 The
Materials Palette

This is perhaps the most daunting of the palettes, but it is essential to get to know it, as this is where you select colours, gradients, patterns and textures. In PSP 8 a **style** is the colour, gradient, or pattern and a **material** is the style plus the optional texture.

When the Colors tab is active, as in Fig. 3.17, the Available Colors panel is displayed. If you run your mouse over this the pointer changes to the dropper and you can select either a foreground colour, by clicking the left mouse button, or a background colour (by clicking the right mouse button). A new feature is the greyscale strip below the colours that lets you quickly select black, white and three shades of grey.

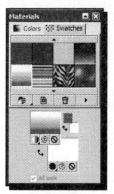

Fig. 3.18 The
Swatches Panel

When the Swatches tab is active, as in Fig. 3.18, a panel of saved 'Swatches' is displayed, where a swatch is a saved style or material that you can use again in the future. Running the pointer over a swatch will show its name and characteristics. You just left-click on a swatch to set the foreground material or right-click to set the background. The four buttons below the Swatches panel give you control of your swatches. With the **View** button you choose which type of swatches are displayed. The **Create New Swatch** button lets you create and name your own swatches. The **Delete Swatch** button deletes the currently selected swatch, and the **More Options** button opens the menu in Fig. 3.19. We will let you have fun exploring here!

New Swatch...
Edit Swatch...
Rename Swatch...
Delete Swatch

View   ▶
Sort   ▶

Small Thumbnails
✓ Large Thumbnails

Fig. 3.19
Swatch
Options

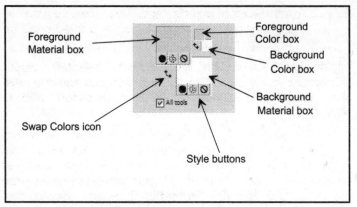

Fig. 3.20 The Material and Color Boxes

The smaller Color boxes shown in Fig. 3.20 above just display the current foreground and background colours, whereas the larger Materials boxes display the current foreground and background materials. If the current material is a solid colour (rather than a colour gradient) the Color and Materials boxes will have the same content. Clicking in any of the boxes opens the JASC Color Picker, shown in Fig. 3.21. Clicking on either of the **Swap Colors** icons swaps the contents of the respective foreground and background boxes.

When the **All tools** check box is ticked the Materials palette settings will apply to any PSP tool used, otherwise they will only apply to the currently selected tool.

The **Style buttons** ●⊛⊘ for each Material box let you select which style to use in that box, as follows:

 Color button - Allows you to set a Solid Color ●, a Gradient ▮, or a Pattern ⊕.

Texture button - Turns the current texture on or off. To choose a new texture, click one of the Material boxes.

 Transparency button - This sets the foreground or background material as transparent (no style or texture). You use a transparent material primarily with vector objects and text. This button is unavailable for tools that require a foreground or background colour.

To change between the most recently selected colour, gradient, or pattern, click the **Style** button and select a new style. To define a new colour, gradient, or pattern, click a Material box.

In PSP you usually use foreground materials for brush strokes and background materials for fills, but when you paint with a brush, right-clicking the brush paints with the background material, and for fill tools, left-clicking fills with the foreground material. For text and Preset shapes, the foreground colour is the stroke (or outline) of the text or shape and the background colour is the fill.

Picking Colours

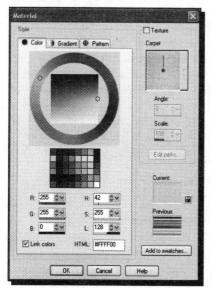

Fig. 3.21 The Material Dialogue Box

As we saw above, to select a new colour you click one of the Material boxes in the Materials palette. This opens the Material dialogue box shown in Fig. 3.21 and with the Color tab selected this shows the JASC Colour Picker. There are several ways you can pick a colour here.

On the colour wheel, click the approximate colour or drag the selection ring around the colour wheel to select the colour. The colour wheel shows the hue of the colour. Notice that the **H** edit box updates with a value between 0 and 255 as you go around the wheel.

You can click on the Saturation/Lightness box, inside the Colour Wheel, to choose a colour variation or drag the selection ring. In this box if you move from left to right you increase the colour saturation, and if you move from top to bottom you increase the lightness.

You can move the cursor over the Basic Colors panel, below the Color Wheel. A ToolTip displays the colour value. When you click the colour you want the RGB and HSL values update with the current colour values and the selection rings on the Color Wheel and the Saturation/Lightness box move to the selected colour.

If you know the RGB or HSL value of the colour you want to select you can enter the values into the individual boxes. When you are ready click the **OK** button to close the Material dialogue box.

Setting Gradients

Fig. 3.22 Gradients

A gradient is a gradual blend between two or more colours. To select a gradient, instead of a solid colour, click the ▶ Gradient tab in the Material dialogue box, as shown in Fig. 3.22. If you click in the example box (over the **Edit** button) you have access to the 56 standard gradients built into PSP 8. Some very impressive ones there are too.

If you want to go deeper into creating and editing your own gradients we suggest you take a look at the Choosing Gradients section in PSP Help.

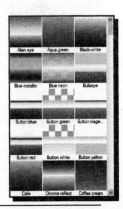

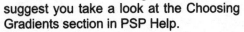

Fig. 3.23 Some Available Gradients

Patterns and Textures

On the Materials palette you can select both a pattern and a texture as part of a material. In PSP a pattern is an opaque, repeated image with specific colours and details, and is as much a style as solid colour or gradient. When you select a pattern as your material each brush stroke will paint the pattern onto the image canvas.

A texture on the other hand uses the current style (such as a solid colour or pattern) and gives a textured effect to the image canvas.

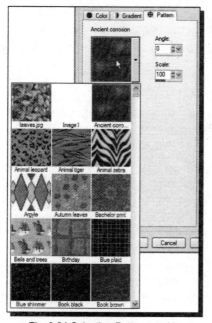

Fig. 3.24 Selecting Patterns to Use

To select a pattern, click the ⊕ Pattern tab in the Material dialogue box, shown in Fig. 3.24. As with gradients, if you click in the example box you have access to the many patterns built into PSP 8.

You can set the **Angle** of the pattern, from 0 to 359 degrees, and the **Scale** from 10 to 250 percent of the image's actual size. At smaller values, the image is repeated more often throughout the pattern. At larger values, it may lose some detail.

If you look carefully at Fig. 3.24 you will see that the first two patterns offered in the drop-down list are actually files that were open in PSP at the time the Material dialogue box was opened. If you select an open image as your current pattern, you can actually paint with it onto another image canvas! We are in the process of doing just that in Fig. 3.25. We have selected leaves.jpg (one of PSP's sample images) as a pattern and are using the Paint Brush tool.

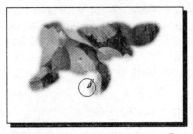

Fig. 3.25 Painting using an Image as a Pattern

Choosing a new Texture to use simply involves ticking the **Texture** check box at the top of the Material dialogue box, as

Fig. 3.26
Textures

shown here in Fig. 3.26, and clicking the Texture Type sample to open the drop-down list of about 50 textures to use.

You can set the **Angle** of the texture, from 0 to 359 degrees, and the **Scale** from 10 to 250 percent.

In Fig. 3.26 we selected 'Bricks 02' as the texture to use and as an example we are dragging the control needle in the sample image to change the angle. While the options are modified, the **Current** box displays the resulting material (the style plus the texture).

The small swatches icon ▦, next to the **Current** box, opens the Swatches panel so you can quickly select a saved Swatch.

As we said, the Materials palette is quite a handful, but I hope we have made it a little easier to get to grips with. At the end of the day you would probably be best just trying everything out several times. That's one good thing about a computer, you can always delete whatever you don't want to keep. With PSP the **Undo** ↺ button really is a great tool.

The Overview Palette

Shows a thumbnail of the active image as well as information about it, which is very useful when you are working with large images, or large magnifications. If you can't see this palette in your PSP window press the **F9** key to toggle it on and off.

Fig. 3.27 The Overview Palette Floating over a Magnified Image

We have this palette docked on the right side of the PSP window under the Materials palette, but in Fig. 3.27 we have dragged it to the middle of the working area. When the Preview tab is active the whole of the current image is displayed in the palette, with the screen area showing as a highlighted rectangle. You can drag this rectangle to move the screen area around the image, or simply click the mouse pointer anywhere in the palette image to do the same. You can also control the zoom magnification with the buttons at the bottom of the palette, as described on the next page.

The Info tab displays image status information, as shown in Fig. 3.28, including width and height, colour depth, memory used, rotation, and the current cursor position in the image.

Fig. 3.28 Image Information

The three **Zoom** buttons on the Preview tab window are actually the same as those shown on the Pan Tool Options palette. They give quick control over the magnification of the image on the screen. They do not change the actual image.

    Zoom out by one step

    Zoom in by one step

Normal viewing - Zoom to actual size.

Numeric Edit Controls

PSP uses standard numeric edit controls throughout the program to provide an easy way to edit numbers and change settings.

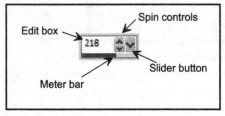

Fig. 3.29 The Numeric Edit Controls

To enter a specific value in the Edit box, double-click the number to highlight it, and then type a new value. If you type a value that is out of range for the control, the box turns red.

To increase or decrease the number by one, click the up or down arrow of the spin controls. To choose an approximate value, click on the meter bar and drag it left or right.

To choose within the range of possible settings (0 to 5,000 in this case), click on the slider button and, holding the mouse button down, drag the slider to select the desired setting, then release the mouse.

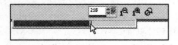

Fig. 3.30 Using the Slider

Dialogue Boxes

Like most Windows programs PSP uses dialogue boxes (called Dialogs in PSP speak) to let you enter information needed for a command procedure. A sample one is shown in Fig. 3.31 which contains some features standard to most dialogue boxes that need some explanation.

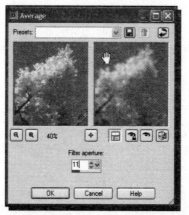

Fig. 3.31 The **Adjust**, **Blur**, **Average** Dialogue Box

If you want to open the same dialogue box, load an image into PSP and use the **Adjust**, **Blur**, **Average** command. The top of the box is devoted to Presets, which are scripts that define the behaviour, properties, or settings for a dialogue box or tool. Many Presets are pre-defined by PSP, but you can save your own as well. Most boxes have two default Presets; **Last Used** - which hold the settings when the box was last used; and **Default** - the out-of-the-box settings, also obtained by clicking the **Reset to default** button 🔁. To choose a Preset simply select it in the drop-down list. At any time you can restore the last settings used in the dialogue box by holding down the **Shift** key and clicking the **Reset to default** button 🔁.

You save a box's current settings by clicking the **Save Preset** button 🔲, entering a name for the new Preset and clicking **OK**. To edit a Preset, select it, modify the settings and save it again with the same name. When you are prompted to replace the current Preset, choose **Yes**. To delete a Preset, select it, click the **Delete Preset** button ⬛, and confirm the deletion by clicking **Yes**.

Below the Presets are two Preview Panes which can be toggled on and off with the **Show/Hide Previews** button ▣. The left pane shows the image as it was when the dialogue box was opened. The right pane shows the result of the current settings in the box.

You can **Zoom Out** ▣ or **Zoom In** ▣ the preview panes or click the **Navigate** button ⊞ to centre different parts of the image in the panes. To see more detail in the panes you can resize the dialogue box by dragging its bottom-right corner, or you can even make the box appear full screen by clicking its **Maximise** button ▣.

If you click the **Auto Proof** button ▣ any changes you make in the dialogue box will be shown in the image straight away. Clicking the **Proof** button ▣ toggles between showing the image unchanged and with the current box settings active. When the **Proof** or **Auto Proof** buttons are selected, clicking the spacebar will turn the selected button on or off.

Last, and probably of least importance, is the **Randomize Parameters** button ▣. This does just what it says and changes the dialogue box settings randomly every time it is clicked. As many of PSP's settings depend heavily on trial and error, randomised settings may be as good a place to start as any other!

4

Selections in Paint Shop Pro

Knowing how to make selections in PSP is essential if you want to use the program to advantage. When you select part of an image you isolate that part temporarily so that you can carry out some sort of operation in it without affecting the rest of the image. This may include cutting or copying, moving, flipping or rotating, editing colours, applying effects or generally painting or drawing inside the selection.

As the way in which you carry out a selection depends upon whether you are working on a raster or a vector layer we had better explain the difference between them.

Raster and Vector Graphics

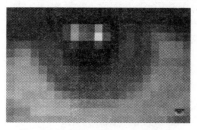

Fig. 4.1 Individual Pixels in a Raster Image

Basically there are two types of computer graphics, raster (or bit-map) and vector. Raster image files (such as **.jpg** or **.gif**) contain information on each and every individual pixel in the image. Fig. 4.1 shows a raster image of a human eye enlarged to show the individual pixels. A vector file however is object orientated and contains mathematical information on the shape, position, colour, etc., of all the objects making up the image.

Vectors produce much smaller file sizes for most graphics, except photographs. They are also very easy to edit, reshape and change colour, since each object can be treated separately. In Paint Shop Pro you can work with either raster or vector images. In fact you can even create images with both raster and vector layers in them. So when do you use raster and when vector?

If you are working with mainly solid colour objects, manipulated text, or many small objects, using vectors will save you time. Once you have mastered the technique of course. If you are working with photographs, complicated drop shadows or other 3D effects, or texture, then raster is the correct choice.

Vector Selections

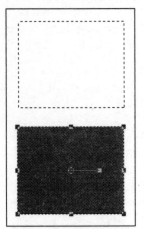

Fig. 4.2 shows a raster selection at the top with a vector selection of a similar rectangular shape below it. The raster selection will restrict whatever operation you wish to perform on the image to within the selection boundary. As you can see though the vector selection is very different, it signifies an object, which is why you see handles around it instead of the dashed line (or marquee) of the raster selection.

Fig. 4.2 A Raster Selection and a Vector Selection

You use the **Object Selection** tool to make vector selections. Simply by clicking this tool on a vector will select it. You can then reduce or enlarge, change the shape and colour of this selected vector object as you like. But to use any of PSP's other tools you have to convert your vector layer to a raster layer. Once a vector layer is converted to a raster layer, it is exactly the same as any raster layer, but it cannot be converted back to vector.

We will refer to raster selections for the rest of this chapter, since the vector selection can be wrapped up fairly simply. Select the **Object Selection** tool and click on the object.

The Selection Tools

As we saw in the last chapter, the tools used for making selections on raster layers are grouped on the Tools toolbar flyout menu shown here in Fig. 4.3.

Selection   S
Freehand Selection
Magic Wand

Fig. 4.3 Selections
Flyout Menu

Selection Tool

The **Selection** tool lets you make selections of the following shapes: rectangle, square, rounded rectangle, rounded square, ellipse, circle, triangle, pentagon, hexagon, octagon, star, or arrow. You choose the shape in the Selection Type drop-down list on the Tool Options palette shown in Fig. 4.4.

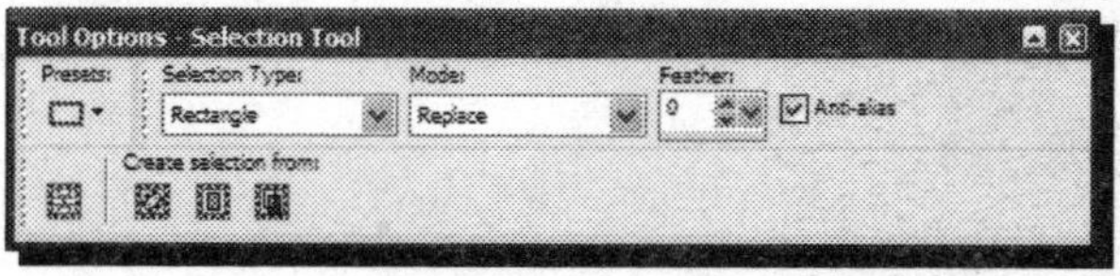

Tool Options - Selection Tool

Presets: Selection Type: Mode: Feather:
Rectangle   Replace   0   Anti-alias
Create selection from:

Fig. 4.4 The Selection Tool Options Palette

The **Feather** option specifies a width in pixels, from 0 to 200, that the selection can be faded along the edges. Feathering

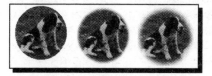

Fig. 4.5 A Selection Pasted with Feather
Values of 0, 5 and 10 (L to R)

helps blend a pasted selection into the surrounding area and makes it appear more natural. The higher the Feather value, the softer the edges, as shown in Fig. 4.5.

Fig. 4.6 An Anti-
Aliased Edge

Select the **Anti-alias** check box to use anti-aliasing, which produces a smooth-edged selection by partially filling in pixels along the edge, making them semi-transparent. Clear the check box to keep the original edges.

The last option to worry about is the **Mode** setting. This defaults to **Replace**, which means that the next selection you make will replace any existing one in the image. You can change this to **Add** or **Remove** new selections to an existing one.

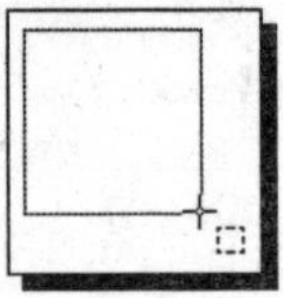

Fig. 4.7

We recommend you play around with an open image and try different options. Once you have chosen your selection settings, move the pointer over the image and holding the left mouse button down drag a selection area in the image, as shown in Fig. 4.7. This shows the selection pointer which is being dragged down and to the right. For all the selection shapes, except circle and ellipse, the point on the image where you

Fig. 4.8

start the selection becomes a corner of the selection area. Circles and ellipses though, use the start point as the centre of the selection. Releasing the mouse button 'fixes' the selection.

When you release the mouse button the pointer changes to a **Move** tool shape when over the active selection. But be careful, if you right-click this the selection disappears and if you drag it you don't move the selection over the image, you drag the selected area of the image, as shown in Fig. 4.8. If this is not what you want,

Fig. 4.9

click the **Undo** button (on the Standard toolbar) to cancel the action. To move the selection marquee itself you must actually select the **Move** tool from the Tools toolbar (or just press the **m** key), then right-click it in the selection and drag the marquee to wherever you want it on the image (Fig. 4.9).

Freehand Selection Tool

 This tool gives you access to four ways of selecting things with irregular borders. Which one is active depends on the setting in the **Selection type** box of the Tool Options palette, shown open in Fig. 4.10.

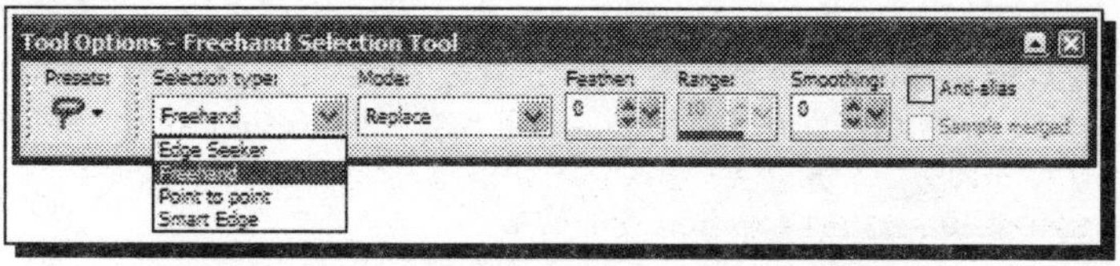

Fig. 4.10 The Freehand Selection Tool Options Palette

Edge Seeker. Lets PSP find the edges between areas with subtle colour or light changes. This is new to PSP 8.

Freehand. Lets you very quickly click and drag the mouse pointer to select an area.

Point to Point. Used to make a selection with straight line edges, by clicking from point to point. PSP draws straight selection lines between the points.

Smart Edge. Best used for selecting between two areas of highly contrasting colour or light. You click along irregularly shaped edges and let PSP find the edges itself.

The **Feather** and **Anti-alias** options are the same as before. **Range** lets you control how far PSP will look for an edge in pixels (0 to 15) from a point you click. In Fig. 4.10 above this option is greyed out as it only applies to the Edge Seeker. The **Smoothing** option lets you smooth the selected border from 0 to 40 to remove uneven 'jaggies'.

The method of using these four tools differs slightly. With the **Freehand** tool you position the pointer on the edge of the area and drag it around to make your selection, as shown here. When you release the button the selection will be closed to the starting point.

Fig. 4.11 Making a Freehand Selection

Fig. 4.12 A Selection with the Edge Seeker Tool

With the **Edge Seeker** and the **Smart Edge** tools you click on points along the edge you want to select and PSP does its best to follow the edge between the points. You usually need to zoom the image to make it easier to follow the edge. Also keep your finger near the **Delete** key as you can press it to go back a stage and delete part of the selection that didn't go quite right. With both tools, to close a selection you right-click (or double left-click) the mouse at a point very near the start and closure is made with a straight line.

Fig. 4.13 A Smart Edge Selection

With Point to Point selection you click at points along your selection border and PSP joins these points with straight lines. As before, you can press the **Delete** key to remove the previous point, and you close a selection by right-clicking or double left-clicking the mouse. This method is only of use if you are selecting a shape bounded with straight lines, such as a triangle or parallelogram.

Magic Wand Tool

The last selection method available in PSP is very different from the others. It is the **Magic Wand** tool which is used to make selections based on the colour, hue, brightness or opacity of similar pixels throughout an image. With this tool you usually select the background behind an object (often in stages) and once this is fully selected you use the **Selections**, **Invert** main menu command to invert the selection. This puts the selection marquee around the parts of the image that were originally unselected. It may sound a little complicated, but it is often the easiest way to select a complex object.

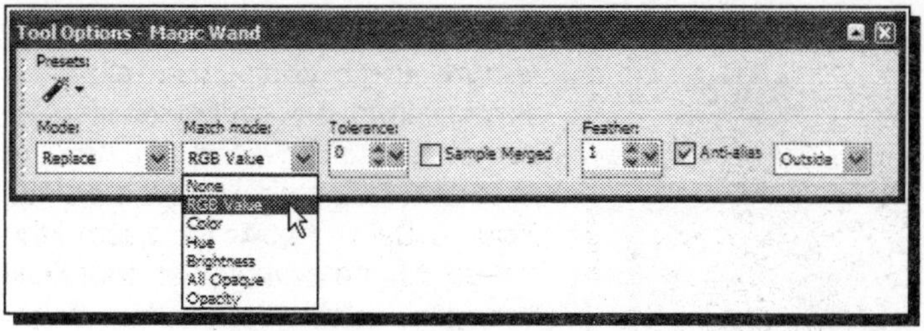

Fig. 4.14 The Magic Wand Selection Tool Options Palette

The selection is mainly controlled by the settings in the **Match mode** and **Tolerance** boxes. In **Match mode**:

None chooses all pixels.
RGB Value chooses pixels that match the red, green, and blue value of the colour that you select in the image.
Color chooses pixels of the same colour.
Hue chooses pixels based on the position in the Color Wheel of the hues you select within the image.
Brightness chooses pixels based on the brightness of the colour you select within the image.
All Opaque chooses only areas containing pixels. No transparent areas are selected.
Opacity chooses pixels based on their opacity.

The Tolerance setting in the Tool Options palette is crucial. A selection is formed based on the property of the pixel clicked on, and the amount of Tolerance indicated in the palette. At a setting of 0 the match must be exact. Our example in Fig. 4.15 has a very detailed guitar on a very plain white background. This is perfect for the Magic Wand. Using the above settings we clicked the pointer in the background and selected everything but the guitar as shown here. You may have to look closely though!

Fig. 4.15 Using the Magic Wand Selection Tool

Fig. 4.16 A Very
Detailed Selection

It was then just a case of using the **Selections**, **Invert** main menu command to invert the selection. This left the guitar selected for us to manipulate however we wanted, as shown in Fig. 4.16. As you can see, this would have been quite a difficult selection to make with the other tools.

In most situations you are not likely to be this lucky though. The background is usually more complex and you would then need to change the **Mode** option to 'Add' and keep raising the **Tolerance** setting after every time you click in the image, to select more and more of it until you were left with the selection you want. Trial and error, and much of it, is the order of the day. That way you will get proficient and be able to select anything that is 'thrown' at you.

Manipulating Selections

Selections	
Select All	Ctrl+A
Select None	Ctrl+D
From Mask	Ctrl+Shift+B
From Vector Object	Ctrl+Shift+B
Invert	Ctrl+Shift+I
Matting	▸
Modify	▸
Hide Marquee	Ctrl+Shift+M
Load / Save Selection	▸
Edit Selection	
Promote Selection to Layer	Ctrl+Shift+P
Float	Ctrl+F
Defloat	Ctrl+Shift+F

Fig. 4.17 The Selections
Menu Options

PSP has a whole range of actions that can be taken to manipulate an active selection in an image. As one might expect, these are found in the **Selections** menu, as shown in Fig. 4.17.

The **Select All** command selects all the pixels on the current layer. You can deselect a selection which removes the marquee and integrates the selection back into the image with the **Select None** command, or by pressing the **Ctrl+D** keys.

Cleaning Selection Edges

When you copy a feathered or anti-aliased selection some of the pixels surrounding the border are also included, which can look 'ugly'. The **Selections**, **Matting** command has three options for removing these border pixels and thus cleaning up the selection edges:

 Remove Black Matte - used when the selection is from an image with a black background and removes the black pixels at the selection edges.

 Remove White Matte - used when the selection is from an image with a white background and removes the white pixels at the selection edges.

 Defringe - used when the selection is from an image with a coloured background and bleeds non-feathered pixels in the selection edges outward and over the 'jaggies' in the feathered part of the selection.

If the selection is not already a 'floating' one (see next section) the Auto Actions box of Fig. 4.18 is opened. You must select **OK** to float the selection.

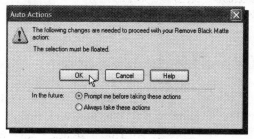

Fig. 4.18 A PSP Auto Actions Box

Auto Actions boxes show short warning messages when PSP needs to carry out a specific step before it can carry on with an action. The Actions can be toggled on and off, as shown in Fig. 4.18 above, or can be controlled with the **File**, **Preferences**, **General Program Preferences** command by selecting the Auto Actions tab, as shown in Fig. 4.19.

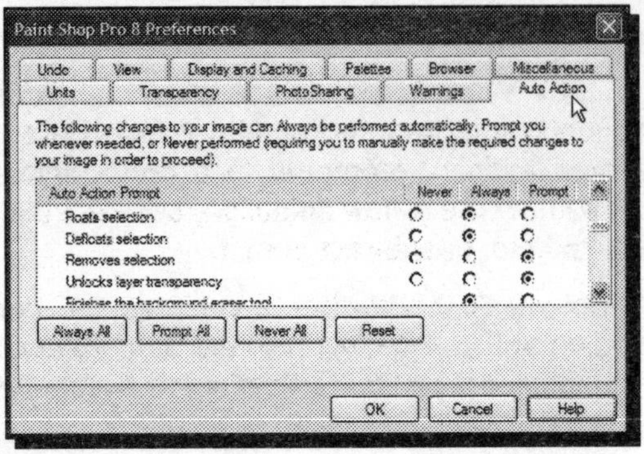

Fig. 4.19 Setting Auto Action Preferences

From here you can set how PSP handles all of the Auto Action procedures - individually in the scrolling list, or globally by using the four buttons below the list.

You may want some Auto Actions to be **Always** carried out (like **Floats selection** in our case above, or promoting an image to 16 million colours) without bothering with a prompt. Others (perhaps converting a vector layer to a raster layer) you might consider dangerous enough that you **Never** want them to happen automatically. Finally, some of them you may wish to be asked about with a **Prompt**. These can all be set in the Preferences box shown above.

Standard and Floating Selections

As we saw in the previous section, selections can be either standard or floating. A standard selection, as created with the **Selection**, **Freehand**, and **Magic Wand** tools, is actually part of the image or layer and when you edit it you modify the image itself.

A floating selection, however, temporarily hovers above the image or layer. Changes made to a floating selection do not change the original image or layer until the selection is defloated.

Selections are automatically floated when you: move a selection with one of the selection tools, paste a selection with the **Edit**, **Paste As New Selection** menu command, or when you select the Floating option when creating text.

Floating selections are automatically defloated to the nearest raster layer, or promoted to a raster layer of their own, when you: create a new selection, deselect the existing selection, or add to, or subtract from it.

The upshot of all this is that if you use the preference settings shown in Fig. 4.19, most of the time you won't need to worry whether a selection is floating or standard as PSP will take care of it for you. Big sigh of relief?

You will still be able to float a selection manually using the **Selections**, **Float** command, which creates a copy of the selection that you can move or modify without changing the original image. When you finish editing the floating selection, you would then use the **Selections**, **Defloat** command.

Editing Selections

In version 8 of PSP, selections are fully editable. Once you have made your selection, you can change its shape or location, or alter the selection in many ways. To edit a selection, choose the **Selections**, **Edit Selection** command, when a ruby coloured overlay appears on a special selection layer, in the Layers palette. You can then use the **Move** tool to move the selection, the **Deform** tool to change its size or shape, or apply any of the filters and effects that work on greyscale images to obtain exciting and different effects. While **Edit Selection** is active you can also:

Paint with white to add to a selection

Paint with black to remove areas from a selection

Erase with black to add to a selection

Erase with white to remove areas from a selection

Add tubes to a selection

Warp the selection with the Mesh Warp and Warp Brush tools

Seamlessly tile the selection.

Some of these actions may not mean much to you until later sections of the book! When you have finished editing a selection, toggle the **Selections**, **Edit Selection** command to re-display the selection marquee.

Modifying Selections

Fig. 4.20 Modify
Menu Options

You can use the **Expand** command to increase a selection by a specific number (1 to 100) of pixels. The marquee expands while keeping its original shape.

The **Contract** command contracts the selection by a specific number of pixels. The marquee contracts while keeping its original shape.

To add to selections based on pixel colour values you can use the **Select Similar** command, which opens the dialogue box shown here in Fig. 4.21.

In this box, **Tolerance** sets how closely pixels must match the colours of the initial selection. At low settings, the values must be close, with higher settings more pixels will match. If the **Sample merged** check box is marked, PSP selects matching pixels in the merged image. If it is not checked, pixels in the

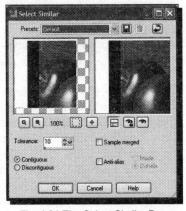

Fig. 4.21 The Select Similar Box

active layer only will be selected. Tick the **Anti-alias** check box to use anti-aliasing and produce a smooth-edged selection by partially filling in pixels along the edge, making them semi-transparent. Mark whether you want the areas

Inside or **Outside** the selection marquee to be anti-aliased. The **Contiguous** option selects all adjacent pixels of a similar colour, whereas **Discontiguous** selects all pixels of a similar colour anywhere within the image. When you click the **OK** button the selection changes to include matching pixels.

The **Select Colour Range** command is used to add or remove a colour from a selection. The command opens the Select Color Range box shown on the right in Fig. 4.22.

Fig. 4.22 Selecting a Colour to add to the Selected Range

Select either the **Add color range** or **Subtract color range** option. Moving the cursor over the image displays the colour dropper, as shown on the right above. When you click a colour in the image, the **Reference color** box displays the selected colour. In the **Tolerance** box, specify a colour tolerance from the range 0 to 200. If the value is 0, no colours are added or removed from the selection area. If you specify a higher value, shades of the colour or related colours are added or removed. In the **Softness** edit box, specify the amount of softness for the referenced colour. When you click the **OK** button the selection borders will change to add or exclude the colour you specified.

Feathering, as we saw on page 67, specifies a width in pixels (0 to 200) that the selection is faded along the edges. When you move or paste the selection, feathering helps blend the selection into the surrounding area and makes it appear more natural. The higher the Feather value, the softer the edges. You would usually use the Tool Options palette to set the feathering before creating a selection. But if you forget all is not lost, you can modify the feathering amount and the feathering position (inside or outside the selection border) using three commands from the **S̲elections**, **M̲odify** menu.

You use the **F̲eather** command to change the feathering amount both inside and outside of the selection.

The **I̲nside/Outside Feather** command lets you adjust the position and amount of feathering.

The **U̲nfeather** command is used to unfeather a selection, after you choose a threshold value. The higher the value chosen the more feathering will be removed from the selection.

Use the **Shape Based Anti-alias** command to anti-alias (see page 68) a selection based on its shape. You can anti-alias inside or outside the selection marquee.

Use the **R̲ecover Anti-alias** command when you want to restore the original anti-aliasing of an object that was pasted into an image. This command is useful if you made the selection without anti-aliasing, and now want the edges of the selection to be smooth.

With some selection methods, especially the Magic Wand, you often get holes in the selection. If you were selecting a girl's face for instance you would probably get holes for the eyes, eyebrows, nostrils and mouth. This is where the **Remo̲ve Specks and Holes** command comes in. Choosing **Remove Holes** and the size of hole to remove, will fill in all holes up to that size. Specks are those isolated 'blobs' of selected stuff outside your main selection. You can get rid of those too, by choosing the **Remove Specks** option to remove only specks from the selection.

To smooth the boundary of a selection use the **Selections**, **Modify**, **Smooth** command. This opens the dialogue box shown in Fig. 4.23.

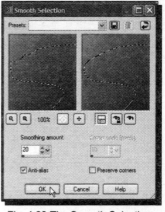

In the **Smoothing amount** box enter a number for the level of smoothing that you need. In our example here, 20 gave a very smooth outline to the selection. For **Corner scale** enter the number of pixels at the corners of the selection to smooth. Mark the **Anti-alias** check box to smooth the

Fig. 4.23 The Smooth Selection Box

edges of the selection and the **Preserve corners** check box if you want the corners preserved. Clear this check box if you want the corners to be smoothed. When you click the **OK** button the corners of the selection will be smoothed.

You use the **Select Selection Borders** command to add a border around the selection. This command is useful when you want to add a border around the selection, and then fill that border using the **Flood Fill** tool.

Hiding the Selection Marquee

To hide the selection marquee (often known as the 'marching ants') when it becomes too much of a distraction, you can use the **Selections**, **Hide Marquee** menu command, or press the **Ctrl+Shift+M** quick key combination. You also toggle the marquee back on with the same command.

Note that the selection remains active even when the marquee is hidden.

Saving and Loading Selections

Some selections are quite intricate
and take a long time to carry out,
such as our jigsaw piece shown in
Fig. 4.24. If there is any chance that
you may need a similar selection in
the future, you might want to save it
while it is still active. There are two
ways of doing this. You can save
the selection as a file with a
.PspSelection extension on your
hard disc or on a removable disc, or
you can save it as an alpha channel
within the image you are working

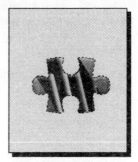

Fig. 4.24 A Selection
Worth Saving

on. The selection is then stored as part of the image.

An alpha channel is a data storage area in an image that
holds selections and masks. Alpha channels are like secret
compartments in which you can store things you may need
later. Selections and masks stored in alpha channels have
no effect on the look of an image. To use the stored
selections or masks later on, you just load them into the
same image or even into another image.

One thing to remember though is that when you save the
image to a file format other than **.PspImage** format, say to
.jpg or **.gif**, alpha channels are not saved. So it is a good
practice to always keep a master copy of your image in
.PspImage format.

To save a selection to an alpha channel, choose
Selections, **Load/Save Selection**, **Save Selection to
Alpha Channel** to open the Save Selection to Alpha
dialogue box shown in Fig. 4.25. The **Add to Document**
panel contains the image name in a drop-down list. Below
the image name is a drop-down list of all alpha channels in
the document, if there are any. The **Name** panel contains a
default name for the alpha channel, you type a new name
here if you want to change this name. The Preview panel
shows a preview of the selection being saved. Clicking the
Save button will save the selection to the alpha channel.

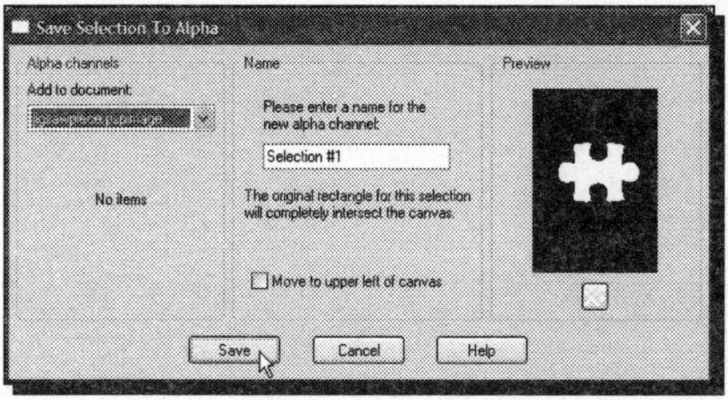

Fig. 4.25 Saving a Selection to an Image Alpha Channel

There are only 24 alpha channels available within a PSP image, if you try to save more, the **Save Selection to Alpha Channel** option is greyed out. You will then have to delete an existing alpha channel, or save the selection to disc.

To load a selection from an alpha channel, open the image or layer on which you want to place the selection, and then choose **Selections**, **Load / Save Selection**, **Load Selection from Alpha Channel** to open the Load From Alpha dialogue box shown in Fig. 4.26 below.

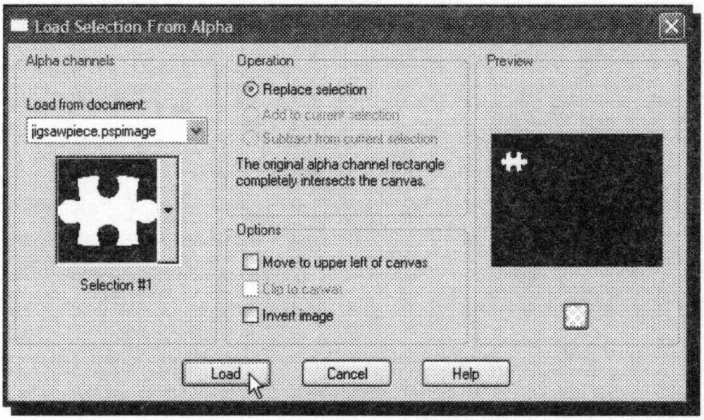

Fig. 4.26 Loading a Selection from an Alpha Channel

To load a selection from the active image, leave the current image name in the **Load from document** box. To load a selection from another image, use the Load from document drop-down list to find the image, and highlight its file name.

Then, in the drop-down list below the document name, choose the alpha channel that contains the selection you want to load. When you have chosen your selection and set the other options, click the **Load** button and the selection should display on the current layer of your image, as shown below in Fig. 4.27.

Fig. 4.27 The Jigsaw Selection loaded in a New Image

You can then treat the selection as if it had been made in the image itself. To move it around the image, click on the **Move** tool in the Tools toolbar, and with the pointer in the selection hold the right mouse button down and drag the selection to where you want it in the image, as shown in Fig. 4.27. You can then copy the selection to the clipboard with the **Edit**, **Copy** command, or more easily by clicking the **Copy** button on the Standard toolbar. Then if you want to you can paste it into a new or existing image or layer with one of the paste commands covered in the next chapter.

We actually built a Web page for a client like this using jigsaw pieces, but each one having a part of a different photograph on it.

The **Save Selection To Disk** and **Load Selection From Disk** commands work in the same way except that the selection is saved as an independent file with a **.PspSelection** extension to it. In some ways this is a safer option to use.

Converting a Selection into a Layer

We have not covered PSP layers yet, so you may want to come back to this section later. When you promote a selection to a layer the original selection contents are unchanged and a copy of the selection is added to the image as a new layer with the automatic name of Promoted Selection. You can then modify the detail inside the new layer selection without changing the original image data.

To do this, first make your selection in the image and then action the **Selections**, **Promote Selection to Layer** menu command. The new layer is placed above the original selection's layer in the image. This command works on 16 million colour and greyscale images only.

Adding to a Selection

You can add to an existing selection using the **Selection** and **Freehand Selection** tools by holding down the **Shift** key while you outline the area you want to add. With the **Magic Wand** tool you hold down the **Shift** key while clicking the area to add. In PSP 8, you can add to a selection using the **Add Mode** on the Tool Options palette, see page 68. In this mode, there is no need to hold down the **Shift** key as every new selection you make is added to the previous one.

Subtracting from a Selection

You can subtract from an existing selection using the **Selection** and **Freehand Selection** tools by holding down the **Ctrl** key while you outline the area you want to take away. With the **Magic Wand** tool you hold down the **Ctrl** key while clicking the area to remove. In PSP 8, you can subtract from a selection using the **Remove Mode** on the Tool Options palette, see page 68. In this mode, there is no need to hold down the **Ctrl** key as every new selection you make is removed from the previous one.

Selecting Using Co-ordinates

If you know the co-ordinates of the image area you want to select, left-click on the **Selection** tool to bring up the Selection Tool Options palette, click on the **Custom selection** button shown here, and enter the co-ordinates into the dialogue box that is opened, as shown in Fig. 4.28 below.

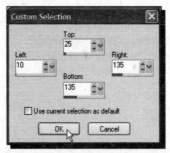

Fig. 4.28 Entering Specific Selection Coordinates

This method can be very useful if you have a batch of similar selections to make. Carry out the first selection manually, then while the selection is active click the **Custom selection** button to open the above box and check the **Use current selection as default** box. The current selection co-ordinates will be placed in the **Top**, **Bottom**, **Left** and **Right** boxes.

Now you can place new selections of the same size and in exactly the same place in the current or other loaded images simply by clicking the **Custom selection** button and pressing **OK**.

5

Working with Images

Before we get too involved with the general procedures of editing and manipulating graphic images in Paint Shop Pro we will look at how and where images are saved on your computer and the types of files used.

Saving Images

In PSP the procedure for saving files is the same as most other Windows programs. You use the **File**, **Save** command **Ctrl+S**, or click the **File Save** button shown here, to save existing files when you want the file format to be preserved, and the **File**, **Save As** command **F12** to save new files or when you want to save in a different format, as shown in Fig. 5.1.

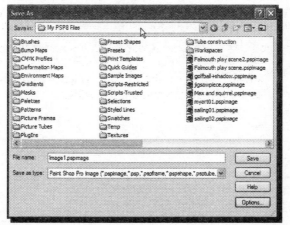

Fig. 5.1 The Save As Dialogue Box Showing Default PSP File Set Up

The Save As box shown in Fig. 5.1 also opens when you use the **Save** command for the first time with a new file. Most of the features in this box are similar to the Open box shown previously in Fig. 3.4, so we will only look at the differences.

The **Save in** box lets you select the folder in which you want to save your image. By default this will be 'My PSP8 Files' a folder set up by PSP 8 when it was first installed (inside My Documents). You can accept this, or click the down-arrow to the right of the box and select any folder on your PC.

Fig. 5.1 shows the complete folder structure that PSP sets up for you. All of the sub folders shown are initially empty but are there for you to store any files as you work with PSP. For example any selection files saved, as covered in the last chapter, would by default be placed in the Selections folder. For your information Appendix B lists the folders, their use and the file types that are stored in them.

The **File name** text box initially contains a highlighted PSP suggested name for the file, in our case this was **Image1.Pspimage**. You will want to type a new and relevant name here for your file, but don't worry about the second part of the name in this box. The default **Save as type** is Paint Shop Pro Image (*.Pspimage......). If you are happy with that, fine. If you want to save in a different format, click the down-arrow on the right of the **Save as type** box and select a file type from the enormous list of file formats that PSP can handle, then click the **Save** button to complete the operation. Appendix C lists the file formats that are supported by PSP 8.

To fine-tune the saving operation for the file type selected, you can click the **Options** button. Options are different for every file type. In Fig. 5.2 we show those for **.Pspimage** files. As you can see, there are options for compressing the saved file and for saving in past versions of PSP.

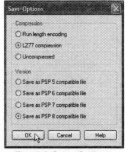

Fig. 5.2 Save Options

PSP's Image File Format

Paint Shop Pro 8 has a new native **.PspImage** file format (or **.pspimage**) that supports all of the program's powerful features, such as layers, alpha channels, grid and guide settings, etc. We strongly recommend that you save your images in this format while you are working on them and then, if necessary, copy them to a different format when they are complete. You can then use the **Save Copy As** or **Export** commands from the **File** menu to save a copy of the file in the desired output format. This will leave your original image intact in case you need to make changes to it later. Keeping your **.PspImage** files intact is especially important when you start using Layers and Alpha Channels.

Viewing Images

In PSP every open image is contained in its own window which can be manipulated, minimised, maximised, moved and re-sized in the usual Windows ways. Many of these operations are handled by the commands in the **Window** menu, as described earlier on page 27.

Zooming In and Out

When you zoom in on an image in a window the image detail gets larger but you see less of the image in the window. When you zoom out the image detail gets smaller and you see more, or all of, of the image in the window. In both cases, though, the image is not actually changed, only the way you see it on the screen.

There are several ways of zooming your images in PSP, depending on your set-up. If you have a wheel on your mouse, rolling it forward will quickly zoom in and rolling it backwards will zoom out. This is the way we nearly always use. Another way is to click the **Zoom** tool on the Tools toolbar and then left-click the area you want to magnify. The view magnifies to the next preset percentage with each click, up to the maximum magnification of 5,000%.

Yet another way is to choose either the **Zoom** or the **Pan** tool, and then in the Tool Options palette select a **Zoom (%)**, or click the + or – **Zoom by 1 Step** or **Zoom by 5 Steps** buttons, as shown in Fig. 5.3 below.

Fig. 5.3 Zooming from the Pan and Zoom Tool Options Palette

There are also some predefined setting options in the **Presets** drop-down list. As shown above, the title bar of the image window displays the zoom percentage, so you can always tell what size the image is.

You can also control image magnification and where you are in a large image in the Overview palette, as described on page 61. If necessary this is opened with the **F9** key.

 A quick way to return an image to its normal size (where the zoom factor is 100%) is to click the **Normal Viewing** button, **Ctrl+Alt+N**, on the Pan and Zoom Tools palettes. We find this button so useful that we have added it to our Standard toolbar.

Viewing Full Screen

It is often necessary to look at an image full screen with a plain black background, to make sure the edges are clean. To preview an image full screen at its current magnification use the **View**, **Full Screen Preview** menu command, or the **Ctrl+Shift+A** keyboard shortcut, or more easily click the **Full Screen Preview** button shown here, but you will have to add it to your Toolbar first. When you have finished just press any key to return to the normal PSP workspace.

A command we don't seem to use very much is the **View**, **Full Screen Edit** command, or **Shift+A**, which expands the entire workspace, giving you the largest possible space for editing images. The palettes and toolbars remain visible but the menus, title, and status bars are hidden. In this mode, if you left-click the cursor on the top of the screen the menus will appear as you move the mouse along the top. Press **Shift+A** to return to the previous window size.

Image Information

There are several places in PSP where you can see information about the image you are working on.

Status Bar Information

First look at the Status bar (at the bottom right of the PSP main application window), as shown in Fig. 5.4 below.

(x:817 y:452) -- Image: 1024 x 768 x 16 million

Fig. 5.4 Image Information on the Status Bar

This shows the cursor position as x: and y: co-ordinates, the image height and width in pixels, and the colour depth. In the above example the cursor (or pointer) was located 817 pixels to the right of the top left corner of the image and 452 pixels down.

This information is expanded while you are making a selection or using the **Crop** tool, as shown in Fig. 5.5.

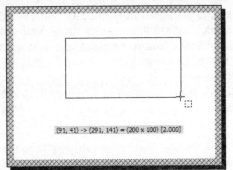

(91, 41) -> (291, 141) = (200 x 100) [2.000]

Fig. 5.5 Status Bar Information for Making a Selection

Here we have a rectangular selection being made in an image but with the status bar information about the selection superimposed to show them both together.

This shows the x: and y: co-ordinates of the top left corner of the selection as (91, 41), and of the bottom right corner as (291, 141). The selection size is 200 pixels wide by 100 pixels high and the Aspect Ratio of width/height is 2.000. With a little practice it is very easy to use this information to very accurately make selections and crops in your images.

The Overview Palette

As we saw on page 61 you can also use the Overview palette to view information about the image. Choose **View**, **Palettes**, **Overview**, or use the **F9** key, and then click the **Info** tab. The information displayed depends on what tool is selected as shown in Fig. 5.6.

Overview	
Preview	Info
Image Width:	1024
Image Height:	768
Upper Left:	181.192
Lower Right:	488.395
Size:	307 x 203
Aspect Ratio:	1.512315

Fig. 5.6 Overview Palette Information

The Image Information Command

To view all the information that PSP has on an image choose the **Image**, **Image Information** menu command, press the **Shift+I** keyboard shortcut, or click the **Image Information** icon if it is on your toolbar.

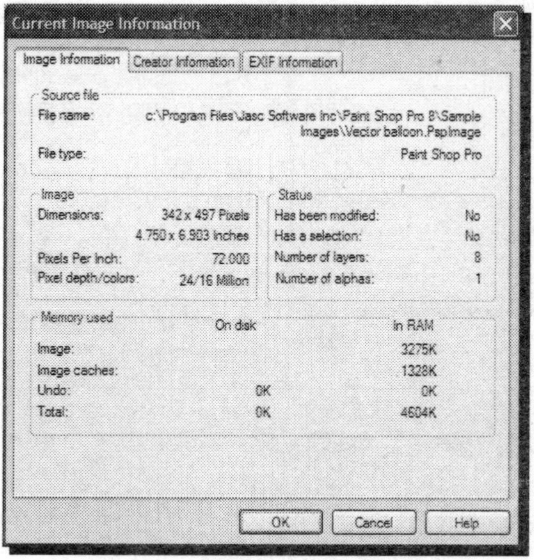

Fig. 5.7 Viewing Current Image Information

If necessary click the Image Information tab, shown in Fig. 5.7, to view the file name and format, the image dimensions, its resolution and colour depth, its modification status, the number of layers and alpha channels it has, and the amount of RAM and disc space used for the image and its selections, masks, alpha channels, and undo storage.

The Creator Information tab lets you view and edit the image title, the artist's name, copyright, description, date created, and the date it was last modified.

The EXIF Information tab shows information for images that were taken with some of the latest digital cameras.

Editing Images

It will not be long when you are using PSP before you will need to edit an image you have opened or created. This could be to remove unwanted features or to copy or move an image feature to another part of the same image or to another image. All these operations are very easy to carry out using the cut, copy, and paste operations. The data to be edited must first be 'selected' before the operation can be carried out using the methods and tools described in the previous chapter. As you might expect, the editing functions are found on the **Edit** sub-menu shown in Fig. 5.8.

Edit	
↶ Undo Selection	Ctrl+Z
↷ Redo Paste New Selection	Ctrl+Alt+Z
☞ Repeat Paste New Selection	Ctrl+Y
↶ Command History...	Ctrl+Shift+Z
✕ Cut	Ctrl+X
📋 Copy	Ctrl+C
📋 Copy Merged	Ctrl+Shift+C
Paste	▸
✕ Clear	Delete
📋 Empty Clipboard	

Fig. 5.8 The Edit Menu Options

The Windows Clipboard

Many of the editing commands make use of the Windows clipboard, which is simply an area of computer memory used for temporary storage. Data that is cut or copied (either text or image data) is stored here. The basic Windows clipboard only holds the last data that was cut or copied to it, anything that was on it previously is just discarded. There are clipboards around that will hold the data from multiple editing operations, but we will not mention these again.

Emptying the Clipboard

 PSP is a graphics program and some of the files you work with can be very large indeed. Placing large amounts of data on the clipboard can seriously slow your computer's performance, especially if it is getting a little long in the tooth. Sometimes it is necessary to empty the clipboard with the **Edit**, **Empty Clipboard** command which erases all of the clipboard contents.

Cutting and Clearing

The **Edit**, **Cut** command, the **Cut** Standard toolbar button, or pressing **Ctrl+X**, removes either a selection, or if no selection is made, the entire current layer of the active image to the clipboard and replaces it with the selected background colour or with transparency. So if you are deleting part of an image you no longer want it is best to select the background colour in the Materials palette before you start, (have a look back at page 55 if necessary!).

If you don't want to use the data that you are deleting from an image you can use the **Edit**, **Clear** command, the **Clear** button if you have it on your toolbar, or just press the **Delete** key. This will clear the data from inside any selection you have made, or will clear the whole active layer if there are no selections.

Whereas the **Cut** command places your data in the Windows clipboard so that you can paste it later on, the Clear command throws away the data. Otherwise their actions are the same.

Copying Data

Once a selection has been made it can be copied to the clipboard without altering the original image data. As with most of the editing operations there are several ways of doing this. The **Edit**, **Copy** command, the **Copy** Standard toolbar button, or the **Ctrl+C** keyboard shortcut all copy a selection, or if no selection is made, the entire current layer, to the clipboard.

To copy all the layers of the selected area, use the **Edit**, **Copy Merged** command, the **Copy merged** toolbar button, or press **Ctrl+Shift+C**. The **Copy Merged** command copies a flattened (or merged) version of all the layers in a selection to the clipboard without altering the original. If there is no selection in the image all the layers of the image will be merged and copied to the clipboard.

The Paste Commands

Paste As New Image	Ctrl+V
Paste As New Layer	Ctrl+L
Paste As New Selection	Ctrl+E
Paste As Transparent Selection	Ctrl+Shift+E
Paste Into Selection	Ctrl+Shift+L
Paste As New Vector Selection	Ctrl+G

Fig. 5.9 The Paste Menu Options

Once you have data on the clipboard you can place it just where you like in an image with one of the paste commands shown in Fig. 5.9. This menu is opened with the **Edit**, **Paste** command. This operation is called 'pasting' because it is similar to that carried out in older times with scissors and a glue pot! There are so many command options here because in PSP 8 you can paste data just about anywhere you like, as long as you know how! We will go through the options.

Use the **Edit**, **Paste**, **Paste As New Image** command, the **Paste as new image** toolbar button, or press **Ctrl+V**, to paste a cut or copied selection from the clipboard as a new image in PSP.

Use the **Edit**, **Paste**, **Paste As New Layer** command, the **Paste as new layer** button if you have placed it on your toolbar, or press **Ctrl+L**, to paste a cut or copied selection from the clipboard as a new layer in the currently active PSP image.

Use the **Edit**, **Paste**, **Paste As New Selection** command, the **Paste as new selection** button if you have placed it on your toolbar, or press **Ctrl+E**, to paste the contents of the clipboard as a new floating selection above the current layer. If the image already contains a floating selection, it is defloated first.

Use the **Edit**, **Paste**, **Paste As Transparent Selection** command, the **Paste as transparent selection** button if you have placed it on your toolbar, or press **Ctrl+Shift+E**, to paste the contents of the clipboard as a new floating selection above the current layer, but with a transparent background. If the image already contains a floating selection, it is defloated first. The command makes transparent any pixels in the clipboard data that exactly match the current background colour in the Materials palette. When you use this command you should select the background colour before you paste.

 Use the **Edit**, **Paste**, **Paste Into Selection** command, the **Paste into selection** button if you have placed it on your toolbar, or press **Ctrl+Shift+L**, to paste a cut or copied selection from the clipboard into the current selection in another image. The clipboard contents are resized to fit the current selection. If you are not very careful this option can produce some ugly results when the selection proportions are not matched.

What we suggest you do right now is open one or two files from the Sample Images folder we looked at on page 37. Then use the **Window**, **Duplicate** command from each file and close the original. You can now safely practice making selections with the different selection tools and using the edit commands to cut, copy and paste in the different ways described here. The only way to learn PSP is to use it, so have fun.

In the examples below we have used some photographs taken earlier at St Ives, that 'Centre of Cornish Art'.

Fig. 5.10 An Edge Seeker Selection

Here, in Fig. 5.10, we have quickly used the **Edge Seeker** tool to first select the outside of the pot and handle, and then in **Remove** Mode have selected the area inside the handle.

We then used the **Edit**, **Copy** command to place the selection on the clipboard.

We first used the **Edit**, **Paste**, **Paste As New Image** command, which opened a new image with the selection from the clipboard pasted in it on a transparent background, as shown in Fig. 5.11. The chequer- board pattern indicates the transparent area.

Fig. 5.11 The Selection
Pasted as a New Image

You can tell that the original selection was done quickly as it is very irregular in places. Much more care would be needed in real life.

In the next example we had the original image active and used the **Edit**, **Paste**, **Paste As New Selection** command to paste the clipboard contents as a new floating selection above the image, as shown in Fig. 5.12 below.

Fig. 5.12 Pasting a Selection into an Image

When the selection first appears in the image you can move it to wherever you want by dragging the pointer. When you right-click the mouse, the selection will be placed with the marquee active, so if necessary you can modify it with any of the **Selections** menu commands. To move the selection further you then need to use the Move Tool and drag it with the right mouse button depressed. When you are ready you fix the selection in place by right-clicking, if a selection tool is active, or with the **Selections**, **Select None** command, or **Ctrl+D** shortcut, with any tool active.

Fig. 5.13 Pasting a Selection as a New Layer

As a last example of pasting, Fig. 5.13 shows the result of using the **Edit**, **Paste**, **Paste As New Layer** command to paste our selection from the clipboard as a new layer in another image. To get the above affect we opened the Layers palette, selected the newly added layer and changed it to an Opacity of 40%. This lets the background image show through. Just a small example of the effects you can easily achieve with PSP. Play on.

We haven't covered layers yet, so if you need help have a look in Chapter 7.

Using Undo and Redo

If you do make a mistake while working with PSP (and believe us you will make many) all is not lost as you can click the **Undo Last Command** Standard toolbar button, or use the **Edit**, **Undo..** command, or the **Ctrl+Z** shortcut. This reverses your most recent editing command. In fact you can undo 100s of actions this way, heaven forbid! The Undo process is controlled from the Undo tabbed sheet in the Preferences dialogue box opened with the **File**, **Preferences**, **General Program Preferences** command, as shown in Fig. 5.14.

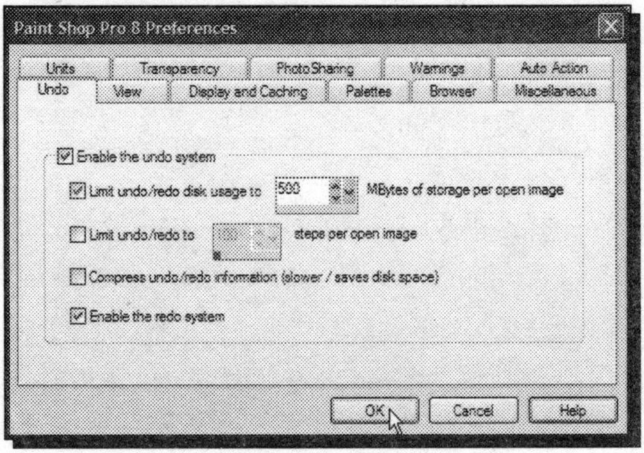

Fig. 5.14 PSP's Undo Preferences

After you undo a command or action, the **Edit**, **Redo..** menu command and the **Redo Last Command** button, shown here, become active, so you can step backwards and forwards through your actions.

With PSP you can undo most actions as you edit an image except; renaming, opening, closing and saving files and changes that are not specific to the current image (such as changes to preferences). Try using the dialogue box opened with **Edit**, **Command History** to view which actions you have performed on an image and to jump back to a previous state of the image. You can also open the last saved version of an image with the **File**, **Revert** command. All in all a lot of tools to get you out of trouble.

Changing the Size of Images

In PSP an image's size, or its physical dimensions of height and width are expressed in pixels, inches, or centimetres. For printed images you should use inches or centimetres and for images to be displayed on screen, use pixels.

 You can adjust an image's size using the **Image**, **Resize** command, or the **Shift+S** shortcut. This opens the Resize dialogue box shown in Fig. 5.15. This is new to PSP 8 and to say the least is somewhat confusing. In this box you can do two main things, depending on the setting of the **Resample using:** check box. With it checked, as shown in Fig. 5.15, you change the physical dimensions of the current image. When it is not checked you change the **Resolution** or **Print Size** of the image (see next section).

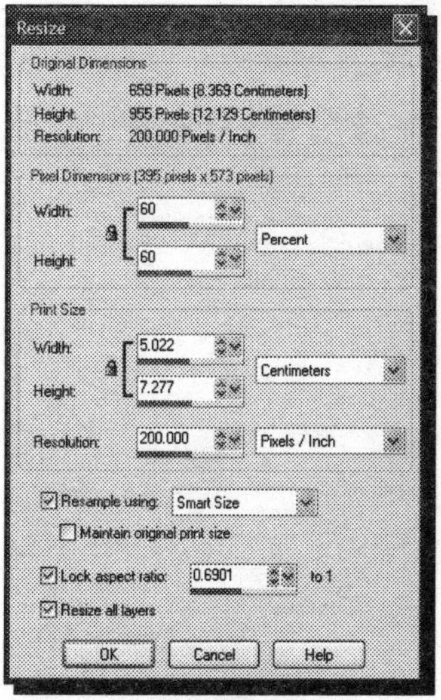

In our example, in the **Pixel Dimensions** section we have set the **Width:** and

Fig. 5.15 Changing Image Pixel Dimensions

Height: to 60 Percent. In the drop-down list you can choose whether to enter values in pixels or as a percent of the original size. As shown at the top of the box this will reduce the image size from 659 x 955 pixels to 395 x 573. For the resampling type it is best to use the **Smart Size** option, which lets PSP choose the best resampling algorithm for the job in hand in the drop-down list. If you need more information on these we suggest you click the **Help** button. To keep the image's current proportions, mark the **Lock Aspect Ratio** check box, where, as we have seen before, aspect ratio is the width-to-height ratio. When you are ready the **OK** button will reduce the image size.

As increasing the size of an image causes a loss of detail and sharpness, PSP recommend that for best results you do not increase an image's size by more than 25 percent. Also you should only resize an image once. If you are not happy with the first result, **Undo** it and try again.

Changing Image Resolution

The resolution, or print size, of an image is the number of pixels printed per inch. When you increase the resolution, more pixels per inch (ppi), will create smaller printed pixels and a smaller printed image. When you decrease the resolution, fewer ppi, will create larger printed pixels and a larger printed image.

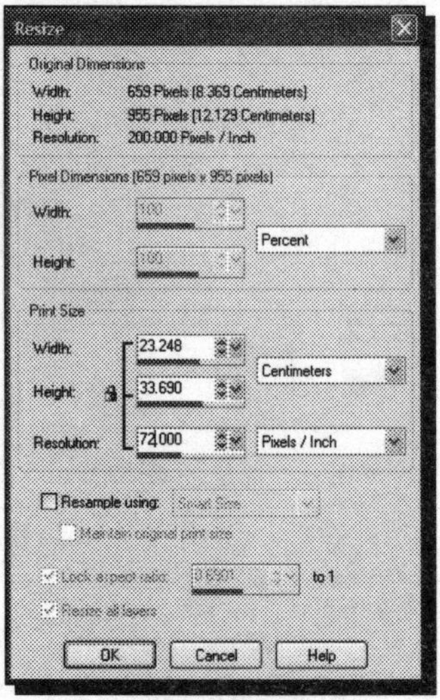

Fig. 5.16 Changing Image Resolution

Too low a resolution causes pixelation where large pixels produce a coarse output, and too high a resolution increases the image memory requirements without producing a proportional increase in its quality. Simplistically we use a resolution of 72 ppi for screen images and 200 ppi for those we want to print.

Fig. 5.16 shows the Resize dialogue box, which as before is opened with the **Image**, **Resize** command, set up to reduce the resolution of our example image from its scanned value of 200 ppi to 72 ppi. This will minimise the memory requirements (file size) of the image and make it suitable for screen use and for Web pages. We have cleared the **Resample using** check box and chosen 72 as the new **Resolution** value. All the other options on the box are greyed out, which means they are not available when the **Resample using** check box is cleared. Then just click the **OK** button.

Changing Canvas Size

In PSP the image canvas is the work area of the image and defines the image's dimensions, for example, 200 by 300 pixels. Often you will need more canvas to add elements to an image. In Fig. 5.17 below, we show a small image that needs more canvas added on all sides. To do this we used the **Image**, **Canvas Size** command to open the Canvas Size dialogue box shown on the right of Fig. 5.17.

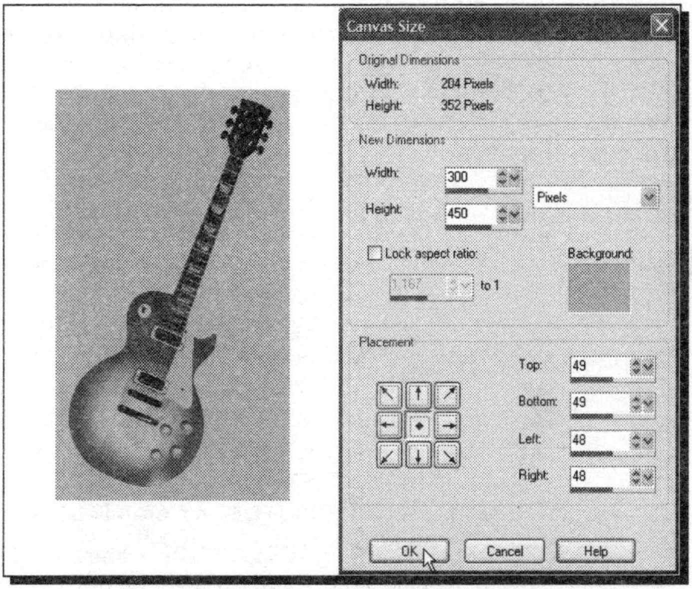

Fig. 5.17 Changing the Size of an Image's Canvas

In the **New Dimensions** group box you enter **Width** and **Height** values for the new canvas size. When you move the pointer from the dialogue box to the image it very cleverly

changes to the **Dropper** tool, as shown here, so you can just click this on the background of the image to set the **Background** colour in the dialogue box for any added canvas.

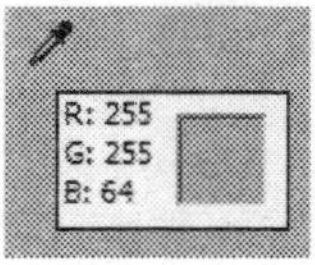

In the **Placement** group box you click a placement button. The fields to the right of the placement buttons will show the amount of canvas added or subtracted from each edge. In our example we clicked the central button to add equal canvas to every side. Clicking the **OK** button makes the selected changes.

Cropping Images

Cropping an image is a way of trimming it, by first selecting a crop area and then permanently removing the parts of the image outside of that area. The easiest way to do this is to use the **Crop** tool to select the crop area which shows as a rectangle (with edge and corner handles). You then size and drag the crop area rectangle over the image as shown in Fig. 5.18 below.

Fig. 5.18 Cropping an Image Showing the Tool Options Palette

Fig. 5.19 Cropped Image

You can use the Tool Options palette to crop to a specific size by entering values for the **Height** and **Width** of the crop area. You can also enter positions for the **Top**, **Bottom**, **Left**, and **Right** sides of the crop area. To remove the crop area and start again just right-click anywhere in the image. To crop the image, double-click inside it or click the **Apply** button (shown here) on the Tool Options palette.

Fig. 5.20 Cropping a Selection

In PSP, you can make a selection of any shape and then crop the image using that selection. A crop area rectangle is placed around irregularly shaped selections, such as the star selection in Fig. 5.20. You then either use the **Image**, **Crop to Selection** command, or click the **Crop** tool, and click **Current selection** in the **Snap crop rectangle to** group box on the Tool Options palette, as shown in Fig. 5.20.

Fig. 5.21 Opaque Cropping

To crop to the opaque (non transparent) area of a layer or image with the **Crop** tool, select either **Layer Opaque** or **Merged Opaque** from the **Snap crop rectangle to** group box on the Tool Options palette, as shown in Fig. 5.21.

Rulers, Grids and Guides

In PSP you can use rulers, grids, and guides to help you align and arrange artwork and elements within an image.

Using Rulers

To display or hide rulers use **View**, **Rulers** command or the **Ctrl+Alt+R** shortcut. By default, rulers are hidden. When the cursor is on the image, a thin line appears on each ruler to show the cursor's position, as shown in Fig. 5.22.

Fig. 5.22 An Image with Rulers Active

You can display rulers in pixels, as above, inches, or centimetres and change the colour of the ruler. These are controlled from the Units tabbed sheet in the Preferences dialogue box opened with the **File**, **Preferences**, **General Program Preferences** command.

Using Grids

Grids are horizontal and vertical lines that help you position items. To display or hide the grid use the **View**, **Grid** command or press **Ctrl+Alt+G**. When you have display grids active, they appear in all open image windows.

Using Guides

Guides are horizontal or vertical lines that you drag onto your image to use for positioning items or aligning brush stokes. While grids place a series of horizontal and vertical lines at certain intervals, you place guides at the locations you want, as shown in Fig. 5.23.

Fig. 5.23 An Image with Rulers Active and Guides Set

Before you place guides, you must display the rulers with the **View**, **Rulers** command. Then use the **View**, **Guides** command. To place a horizontal guide, click the top ruler and drag a guide to the desired position. To place a vertical guide, click the left ruler and drag a guide to where you want it. As you drag, the Status Bar displays the guide's position in pixels.

To move a guide, click the guide handle on the ruler and drag it to a new position, as shown for the top horizontal guide above. You can also double-click or right-click the guide handle to display the Guide Properties dialogue box,

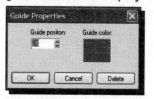

Fig. 5.24 Guide Properties

as shown in Fig. 5.24. You can enter a new **Guide position** value, change the colour by clicking in the **Guide color** box and selecting a colour from the **Color** box that opens, and finally click the **OK** button.

Printing Images

As long as your printers are properly set up in Windows you should have no problems printing your images from PSP. The program is very strong in this department, but as usual there are several ways of going about the process.

Printing Single Images

Single images are best printed straight from the PSP working area, even if you want to print multiple copies of the image on the same sheet of paper.

 With the image you want to print open, use the **File**, **Print** command, click the **Print** Standard toolbar button shown here, or use the **Ctrl+P** shortcut. All of these open the Print dialogue box shown in Fig. 5.25.

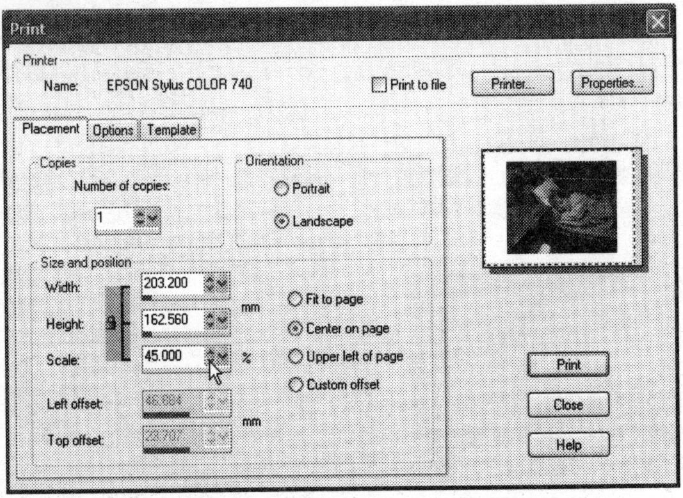

Fig. 5.25 Placement Controls for Printing an Image

This shows the currently selected printer at the top. To change this you click the **Printer** button and choose from the other printers (if any) that are available to you. Next you click the **Properties** button to set up the chosen printer.

Depending on the printer this may involve choosing paper type, size and location. Every printer has its own set of properties and we obviously cannot cover them here!

On the Placement tab, choose the **Number of copies** to print, the page orientation (either **Portrait** or **Landscape),** and the **Size and position** of the image. In our example in Fig. 5.25 we selected to **Center on page** and then used the **Scale** control to size the image. The pane on the right shows how the result will look with the current selections.

Clicking the Options tab opens the page of choices shown here in Fig. 5.26.

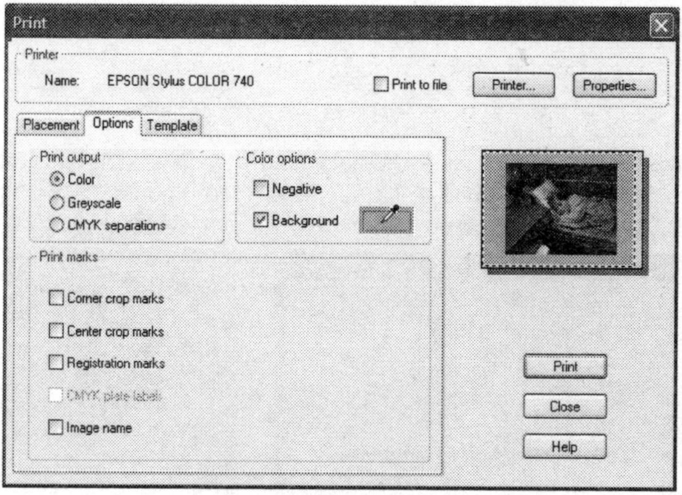

Fig. 5.26 Option Choices for Printing an Image

Most of these options are pretty self explanatory and if you select one you can see the result in the sample image. The **Background** option lets you choose a colour for the background of the page to be printed in, as shown above. For special purposes you can choose to print crop marks at the corners of the image or at the centre of the image edges, to print registration marks at the corners of the image, or to print the image file name below the image. Clicking the **Close** button at any time will apply the settings and close the dialogue box.

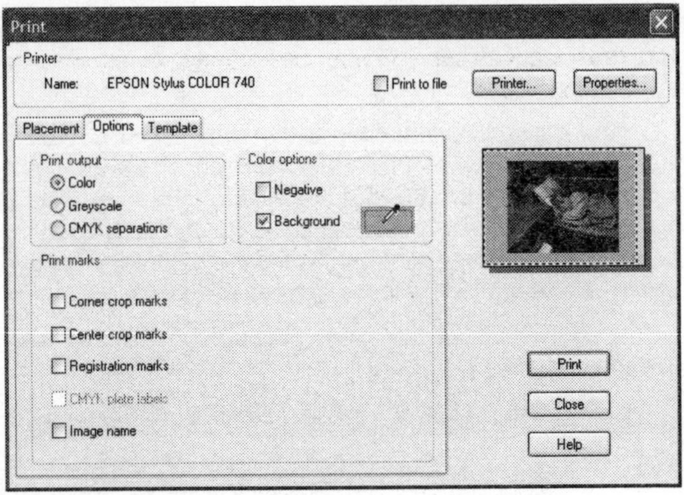

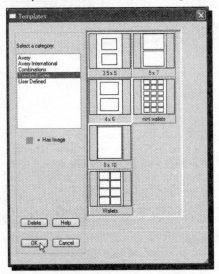

Fig. 5.27 Using Templates for Printing an Image

When you want to print an image in a particular size, or print multiple copies on the same sheet you should click the Template tab, as shown in Fig. 5.27. This allows you to fill templates with the current image. Once you have clicked the **Print to template** check box you will be able to action the **Select template** button command which opens the Templates box. In this box you can choose from a range of over 30 standard designs. In our example we chose the 4 x 6 option as shown in Fig. 5.28, to print two 4-inch by 6-inch copies of the image.

Fig. 5.28 Selecting Print Templates

Click **OK,** check that the sample image in the Print dialogue box is what you want, and then click the **Print** button to start the printing action.

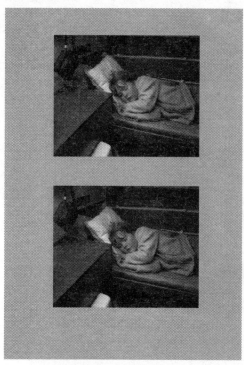

Fig. 5.29 The Final Print Output

Our print results from the example are shown above in Fig. 5.29. With a little care it is very easy in PSP to print out all your images or photographs to exactly the sizes you want.

One thing to remember though is that the quality of the paper you use will affect the quality of the prints. This is especially true if you are using an inkjet printer. With these the paper is critical to the results.

Printing Multiple Images

You can also use the Print Layout feature to print multiple images in a variety of ways, such as printing wallet-size copies of the same or various images, printing two different images on the same page, or arranging an image to print on labels.

 With the images you want to print open in the PSP workspace use the **File, Print Layout** command, or click the **Print Layout** toolbar button if it is on one of your toolbars. These both open the Print Layout window shown in Fig. 5.30 below.

Fig. 5.30 The Print Layout Window with an Empty Template Open

Thumbnails of all the images open in PSP display on the left side, and the page layout to be printed is shown in the centre of a grey print layout workspace. The window has its own menu bar and toolbar. In our example (Fig. 5.30) we used the **File, Open Template** command to open the Templates box we saw in Fig. 5.28 and chose from the Combinations list. It is then just a case of dragging pictures from the thumbnails on the left to their template frames in the layout window.

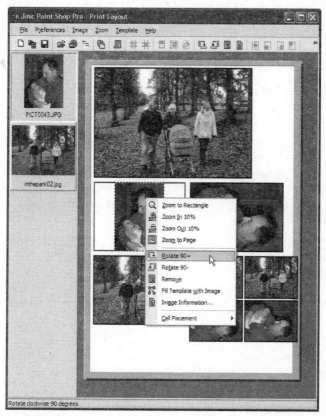

Fig. 5.31 Using a Template in the Print Layout Window

You can then use the menu commands, toolbar buttons or the right-click context menu options (as shown in Fig. 5.31) to re-size and re-orientate the images as you require.

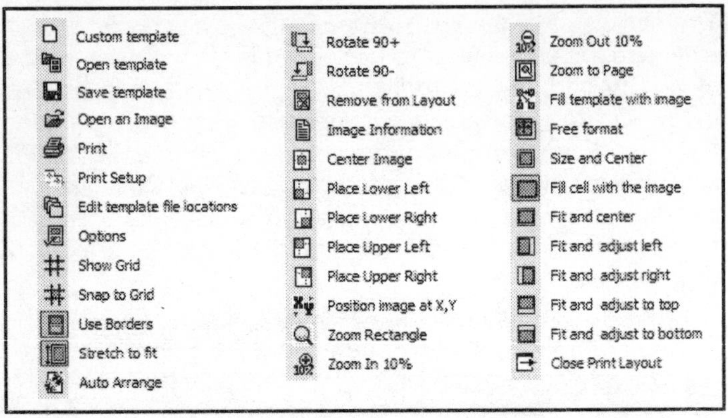

☐	Custom template		Rotate 90+		Zoom Out 10%
	Open template		Rotate 90-		Zoom to Page
	Save template		Remove from Layout		Fill template with image
	Open an Image		Image Information		Free format
	Print		Center Image		Size and Center
	Print Setup		Place Lower Left		Fill cell with the image
	Edit template file locations		Place Lower Right		Fit and center
	Options		Place Upper Left		Fit and adjust left
#	Show Grid		Place Upper Right		Fit and adjust right
#	Snap to Grid		Position image at X,Y		Fit and adjust to top
	Use Borders		Zoom Rectangle		Fit and adjust to bottom
	Stretch to fit		Zoom In 10%		Close Print Layout
	Auto Arrange				

Fig. 5.32 The Print Layout Toolbar Buttons

All the toolbar buttons available are shown in Fig. 5.32 above, if you need more information on any of them we suggest you use the PSP Help system.

When you are ready to print, use the **File, Print Setup** command to open a dialogue box similar to that of Fig. 5.25, or the **File, Print** command or **Print** toolbar button to print the page with the current settings. When you have finished you must close the Print Layout window before you can return to Paint Shop Pro.

We have used a template here, but you do not need to. You can arrange your images any way you want in the print layout workspace. You can even save a layout you particularly like as a new template, either with its images or without, for you to place new ones the next time you use it.

6

Electronic Painting

With Paint Shop Pro you can draw and paint on the screen in the same manner as an artist works on paper or canvas. The tools used are actually very similar, brushes, airbrushes and erasers. The techniques though are a little different and for the first timer it takes a little getting used to.

The Paint Brush Tool

The **Paint Brush** tool is used to create strokes of colour, with hard or soft edges, that simulate an artist's paint brush, or to paint with patterns and textures. The brush will paint the foreground (dragging the left mouse button) or background (dragging the right mouse button) material currently selected in the Material palette. To paint a straight line, click once at the beginning point, then press **Shift** and click the end point. To continue the straight line, move to the next point and press **Shift** and click again.

 To use the Paint Brush, click the **Paint Brush** button on the Tools toolbar, as shown here. Set the foreground and background colours and materials in the Materials palette (look back to page 55 if necessary) and make what selections you need on the Tool Options palette, such as size, opacity, hardness, thickness, and rotation, as shown in Fig. 6.1 on the next page.

In PSP 8 there are only two **Shape** options, round, or square, but to create rectangular, elliptical, or angled brush tips, start with the round or square shape and modify it using the **Thickness** and **Rotation** options. As you make changes here you can see the brush head pointer change.

Fig. 6.1 Using the Paint Brush showing Tool Options and Materials

There are a large range of both Presets and brush tips available in the Tool Options palette, where a tool **Preset** contains all the settings saved for a particular tool and is available only when you select that particular tool. Brush tip settings, on the other hand, can be applied to any tool that

has a brush tip control in the Tool Options palette. Clicking the **Brush Tip** drop-down window displays the brushes that are available, as shown in Fig. 6.2. Brush tip settings include the brush **Size**, **Hardness**, **Step**, **Density**, **Thickness**, **Shape** and **Rotation**.

Figures 6.1 and 6.2 both show the default Tool Options palette settings for the **Paint Brush** tool, as described in the next section.

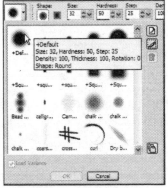

Fig. 6.2 The Brush Tip Drop-down Window

Fig. 6.3 The Presets
Window

Clicking the **Presets** button opens the drop-down window shown in Fig. 6.3. This lists the Presets available for the **Paint Brush** tool.

To set the Brush to its Default values click on the **Reset to default** icon pointed to here. You can save the current brush settings by clicking the **Save Preset** button 🖫, entering a name for the new Preset and clicking **OK**. To delete a Preset, select it, click the **Delete Preset** button 🗑, and confirm the deletion by clicking **Yes**.

Basic Brush Options

The following options are available on the Tool Options palette for all the painting tools.

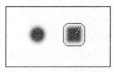

Shape - Controls the shape of the brush tip. Round 🔘 and Square 🔲 are the standard brush tips. You use Round to create curved strokes that look more smooth, or Square to create brush strokes with corners. Other shapes in the Brush Tip drop-down window can be used to create interesting effects.

Size - The size of the brush, from 1 to 500 pixels.

Hardness - Sets the sharpness of the brush edges. The harder the brush, the more defined the edges of paint are. At 100%, the brush stroke has sharply defined edges. As the hardness decreases, the brush edge softens.

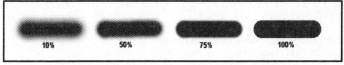

Fig. 6.4 The Effect of Hardness Brush Tip Settings

Step - Controls how frequently the brush touches the image during a stroke. The step value is a percentage of the brush size. As the step decreases, as shown in Fig. 6.5, the brush makes more impress-

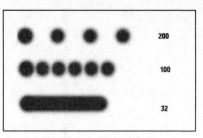

Fig. 6.5 The Step Settings

ions, its shape becomes less noticeable, and its strokes appear smoother and more dense.

Density - Sets the amount of paint applied with each stroke. At 100%, paint covers the surface completely. As the density decreases, the amount of paint applied with each stroke decreases. At 1%, only a few pixels of paint appear, as shown here in Fig. 6.6.

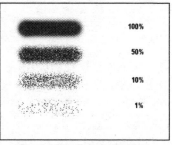

Fig. 6.6 The Density Settings

Thickness - The width of the brush in relation to the brush height as a percentage. At 100% thickness, the brush width is the same as the brush height. At 50% thickness, the brush width is half the brush height.

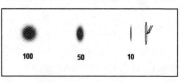

Fig. 6.7 Thickness Settings with the Pointer for the 10 Setting

Rotation - The degrees of rotation of the brush tip, from 0 to 359. Fig. 6.8 demonstrates some of these at a brush **Thickness** of 24.

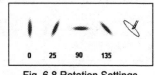

Fig. 6.8 Rotation Settings

Opacity - How well the paint covers the image surface. At 100% opacity, the paint covers everything. At 1% opacity, the paint is almost transparent.

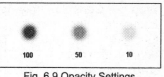

Fig. 6.9 Opacity Settings

Blend - How painted pixels are blended with pixels on underlying layers. The blend modes are the same as layer blend modes. These are detailed in Appendix E.

Specific Brush Options

The following options are specific to the **Paint Brush** tool:

Continuous Stroke - Specifies whether paint builds up as you apply multiple strokes of less than 100% opacity over the same area. If this check box is marked, paint maintains a continuous colour and repainting an area has no effect. If it is cleared (the default), each brush stroke over the same area applies more paint; the colour darkens until it reaches 100% opacity.

New Stroke - Click this button to cancel the effect for all previous brush strokes. Only new brush strokes will darken if you paint over them.

Wet Look Paint - This option copies wet paint in real life, and gives soft colour inside and a darker ring near the edge. You need to decrease the Hardness setting from its maximum to see the effect.

Using Previous Brushes in PSP 8

To use custom brushes created in previous versions of PSP, they must be converted to the PSP 8 format. Use the **File**, **Import**, **Custom Brush** command, click **Open** in the Import Custom Brush dialogue box, and browse to the folder that contains the custom brush. This will open the brush file with all the brushes in that file in the left pane. Click the **Add All** button and all the brushes will move to the right pane. When you click the **OK** button the brushes will be added to the folder set in your **File**, **Preferences**, **File Locations**.

The Brush Variance Palette

The basic controls covered so far are just the beginning. If you want to really explore the limits of PSP 8 brushes, press **F11** and take a look at the Brush Variance palette.

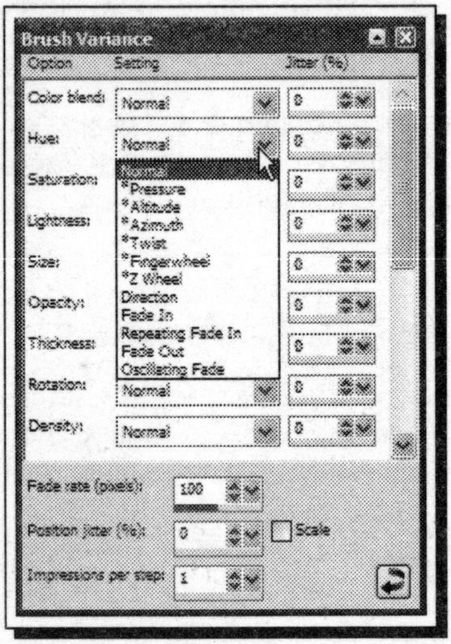

Fig. 6.10 The Brush Variance Palette showing Settings

Figure 6.10 shows the Brush Variance palette for the Paint Brush and Airbrush. There are multiple options, and you set the variance for each option by selecting a Setting and adjusting the **Jitter (%)** (a control of randomness). Each option has the same group of setting options. The first (and default) setting is Normal. Then there are six settings (marked by an asterisk) that can be used with a pressure sensitive graphics tablet. Next are five settings that can also be used with a mouse or other standard input device: Direction, Fade In, Repeating Fade In, Fade Out, and Oscillating Fade.

Increasing the **Jitter(%)** setting increases the degree of randomness in the variation for a particular option. For example, if you set Rotation to Normal and set Jitter to a high value, the rotation of your brush will vary randomly between the Rotation setting specified in the Tool Options palette and that amount increased by the percentage specified by the Jitter.

The Brush Variance palette is available for all of the painting tools, and with it you can create all sorts of cool effects by using different brush variance settings. If you are really interested, try combining various settings using different options and see what effects you can produce.

Some Examples

It is not possible in a book like this to provide a tutorial on painting with PSP. We have really only explained the principles behind the **Paint Brush** tool, but to whet your appetite on what can be achieved here are a couple of examples.

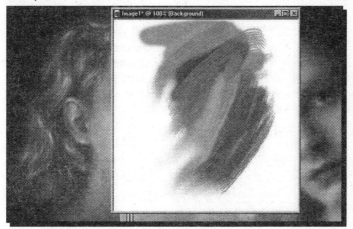

Fig. 6.11 PSP Portrait Work showing Brushwork Buildup

These examples were both placed on the Jasc User Forum (http://forums.jasc.com) by PSP artists who wanted to show off their work. The one below is a copy of an impressionist painting by Berthe Morisot but done completely with PSP. There is scope here for us all!

Fig. 6.12 A Berthe Morisot PSP Original!

The Airbrush

You use the **Airbrush** tool in a similar way to the Paint Brush but it simulates the actions of an airbrush or spray can. It is time-dependent, so the longer you hold the Airbrush over an area of your canvas, the more the brush produces the effect.

 To use the **Airbrush**, click the **Airbrush** button on the Tools toolbar, as shown here. Set the foreground and background colours and materials in the Materials palette (look back to page 55 if necessary) and make what selections you need on the Tool Options palette, such as size, opacity, hardness, thickness, and rotation, as described earlier.

In the **Rate** edit box select the rate at which the brush applies paint (from 0 to 50). Use a value of 0 if you want to apply a consistent amount of paint. Use higher values if you want more paint applied when you drag the mouse slowly or pause the mouse. To build up colour in one area click and hold the mouse at one position.

We will leave it to you to play with the Airbrush. With practice it can be a useful tool, but the strokes produced by it tend to look a little less refined than those from the standard Paint brush.

Painting with an Image

As we have seen, with all the PSP painting tools you can paint with whatever material is set in the Foreground and Background Material boxes of the Materials palette. The left mouse button uses the foreground material and the right button the background. An interesting feature is that you can thus paint with an existing image as the brush.

To do this, open the image you want to make the brush and click on the Background Material box of the Materials palette. This will open the Material box shown in Fig. 3.21, click the Pattern tab and click inside the example box in the top left of the tabbed sheet. This opens the drop-down pane of patterns available as shown in Fig. 6.13.

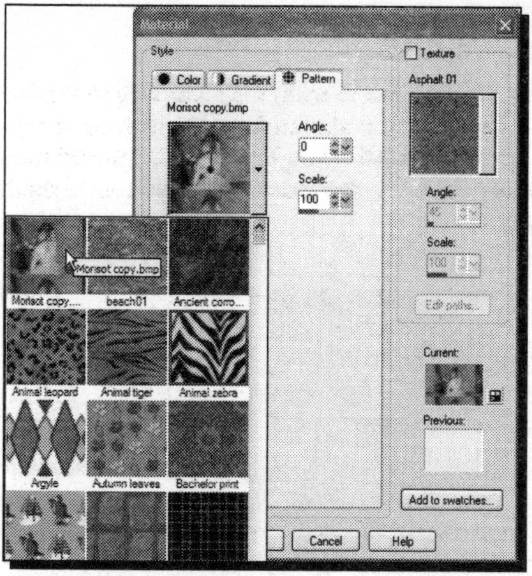

Fig. 6.13 Setting an Open Image as the Current Pattern

The first available pattern, as shown above, is the image open in PSP. In our case the painting copy of Morisot. Clicking this will make it the current pattern, as above.

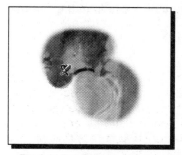

If necessary, open a new canvas and select the **Airbrush** tool. To paint with the new image brush, hold the right mouse button down and stroke the pointer where you want on the empty canvas. The image will be placed for you as you work, as shown in Fig. 6.14.

Fig. 6.14 Painting with an Image as a Brush

Don't forget that if you do something wrong while painting, or you don't like what you have done, all you have to do is click the **Undo...** button. Probably our most used button!

Using the Eraser

To use the Eraser, click the **Eraser** button on the Tools toolbar, as shown here, or use the **X** shortcut key. The **Eraser** tool replaces colours in an image either with the background colour or with transparency. When you drag the Eraser across a raster layer, all the pixels in its path become transparent, as shown

in Fig. 6.15. When you use it on a background (or an image with no layers), the Eraser produces a different effect, acting like a paintbrush in reverse. With the right mouse button depressed, it 'paints' with the foreground colour, and when you use the left mouse button, it 'paints' with the background colour.

Fig. 6.15 Using the Eraser to remove the Background

The **Eraser** tool retains the information it has removed from a layer and you can restore the erased image by dragging the Eraser over the transparent areas with the right button depressed. This comes in handy when you're cleaning up an image and your mouse slips. No need to hit the undo button and lose everything you've just done - just unerase those pixels back in with the right mouse button! This works even after you close an image and then re-open that image file, as long as the image is saved in PSP format!

If you right-drag the Eraser on a layer, the paint you re-apply might look somewhat different than it looked originally. The Eraser's settings for Opacity, Density, or Hardness, and the Textures mode setting can produce different effects from the original.

Many of the **Eraser** tool options help erase smoothly. We especially like the effect produced when reducing the Hardness option to near 0. This allows you to erase around the edges of an object, leaving very soft edges, almost like antialiasing! In Fig. 6.15 we reduced the Thickness tool option to 18 and Rotation to 25. This produced a thinner sloping eraser shape.

Background Eraser

The **Background Eraser** tool is one of the most fascinating of the PSP 8 innovations. It allows you to selectively erase pixels from the background while leaving an image intact. Its purpose is to erase background you don't want that lies around an object you want to keep. Place the centre of the brush on the background you want to remove and overlap the edge of the brush onto the object you want to keep. Now trace around your object.

The Background Eraser performs its magic by erasing pixels similar to those under the brush, while leaving the other pixels unchanged. It constantly samples the pixels under its centre, and uses complex algorithms to erase similar pixels in the surrounding area defined by the brush. The key is to keep the centre of the brush away from the graphic you are trying to isolate, as shown in Fig. 6.16 on the next page. The edges of the brush should overlap the graphic as you erase, but the centre of the brush should always remain outside the graphic.

While you are in the **Background Eraser** tool, using the left mouse button will erase, based on the definition of the background, and the right mouse button will unerase based on that same definition, but not completely. Holding down the Spacebar and using the left button will erase unconditionally, just as the regular Eraser does. Additionally, holding down the Spacebar and using the right mouse button unconditionally unerases. For the lifetime of the tool the original image colours are remembered in the transparent areas, even though actual colours in these areas are changing. So, you should really stay with the **Background Eraser** tool until you are finished.

Fig. 6.16 Using the Background Eraser on Max

Here we are removing the background from a photo of our Westie, called Max. We will use the result in the next section on 'Tubes'. We used the Background Eraser to carefully

outline the edge and then with the spacebar depressed we removed all the 'debris' that was left. After this we broke our own rule and used the **Eraser** tool with Hardness set to 1 to finish the final edge. The result is shown in Fig. 6.17. You can see the Eraser pointer just under Max's collar.

Fig. 6.17 The Background Removed

In the next section we repeat some specific Background Eraser tips that were bandied around the Internet when PSP 8 was first being developed.

Some General Tips

- Most of the time you can use the default settings for the brush - these seldom need to be changed.

- You will find it very helpful to enable **Show brush outlines** on the Display and Caching tab of the **General Program Preferences**, (see page 235). We have done this throughout the book.

- When you have an image with internal holes containing background, use Discontiguous **Limits** rather than Contiguous. If you have trouble preserving edges use Find Edges for **Limits**.

- If the brush seems to consistently bite into your object, increase the **Sharpness** setting slightly to 80 or maybe 90.

- For preserving subtle edges, setting **Limits** to Contiguous is better than Discontiguous, and setting Find Edges is even better than Contiguous.

- You can get a better differentiation of object and background by increasing the **Sharpness** setting, in a restricted fashion since it is a very sensitive control.

- When either your object is vividly coloured but your background is unsaturated, or when you have a rather unsaturated object on a brilliantly coloured background, consider checking **Ignore Lightness**.

- For very careful detail work, switch off **Auto Tolerance** and manually set the Tolerance, but it is difficult to do this better than the tool itself.

The real secret to getting great results with the Background Eraser is practice, as with PSP's other features. We suggest you pick out some of your favourite digital images and when you have the time, play with it. It won't take long to really get the hang of using it, and then you will never look back. Go on, try it!

Using Picture Tubes

Tubes, unique to Paint Shop Pro, are a way of storing and applying your favourite images. You can use a picture tube for either adding a picture to an image, or you can paint with a tube image without having to draw it. PSP comes with built-in tubes, but you can make your own custom tubes, or download tube sets from the Internet. When you are working seriously, and not just playing which is easy with tubes, it is best to place tubes on separate image layers. You can then easily move them around without disturbing other components of the image.

 Let's play. First open a new raster image with a white background and a **Color depth** of 16 Million . Click the **Picture Tube** button on the Tools toolbar, and make sure the Tool Options palette is open, as shown in Fig. 6.18 below.

Fig. 6.18 The Picture Tubes Tool Options Palette

Clicking the **Picture Tube** drop-down button, pointed to in Fig. 6.18, opens the window of available tubes, shown in Fig. 6.19. Any tubes that you have created will be listed first,

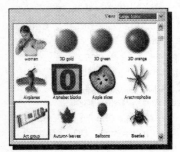

Fig. 6.19 The Available Picture Tubes Window

such as the 'woman' shown here. You now have the option for viewing your tubes in this window as large icons, as shown, or as small icons.

Select the Art group option, which should have been installed by PSP, and click the mouse on your empty new image. Every click makes a new image.

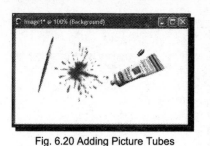

Fig. 6.20 Adding Picture Tubes

The **Tubes** tool does not have many settings, so it is easy to use. The main setting, **Scale**, controls how large or small the tube will paint. The other main setting is **Step** which determines how far apart tubes will be placed on the image. The Step setting is based on a percentage of the Scale setting.

If you open a Picture Tube file in PSP you can see the structure of a Tube. In our case **Art group.PspTube** was located in the folder:

C:\Program Files\Jasc Software Inc\Paint Shop Pro 8\Picture Tubes

Fig. 6.21 The Structure of a Picture Tubes File

As shown in Fig. 6.21 a Picture Tube is an image with a transparent background and a series of objects laid out in a grid. The Tube brush will use the grid to spray each object in turn onto your image when you paint with it.

You can also check and see how many items are in the group by clicking on the **Settings** button ✎ of the Tool Options palette, which opens the box shown in Fig. 6.22. As you can see there are 16 items in our file. The group is set for incremental placement, which means it will place items from the top left to the bottom right. But unless

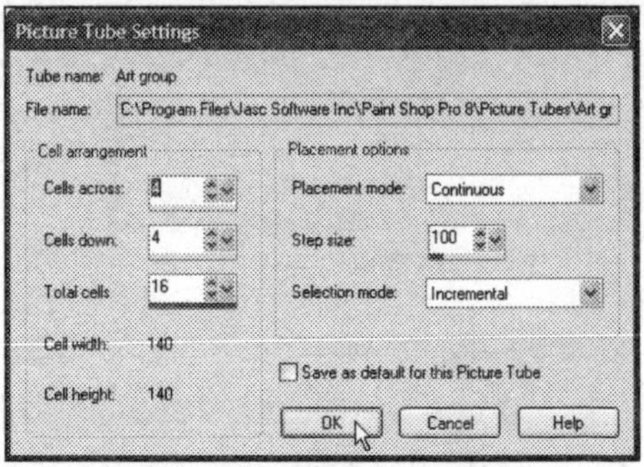

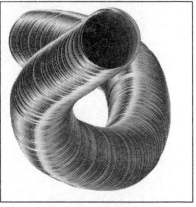

Fig. 6.22 Picture Tube Settings

you have the tube image open or memorised, you won't know which object is going to appear when you next click your tube. You have to use the **Undo** button to remove the ones you don't want.

You can get some amazing effects with some of the Picture Tubes provided with PSP8. There is a metal hose, which you can single-click and have just a single piece of hose, or you can paint it by dragging with the mouse button held down. This produces the instant 'pipe' image shown in Fig. 6.23. Well worth a look.

Fig. 6.23 Dragging a Picture Tube

Creating Picture Tubes

To create your own Picture Tube from an image, the image must be 24-bit, and must have only one raster layer with a transparency. Our image created in Fig. 6.17 just fits this bill. First you should trim off any excess around the image. This is best done with the **Crop** tool using the **Layer Opaque** option described on page 103.

When you are ready use the **File**, **Export**, **Picture Tube** command, and type in the name you want for your tube in the **Tube name** text box of the Export Picture Tube box. PSP will add a **.PSPTube** extension to the name. Accept

the settings offered and press **OK**. A new tube should now be available in the Picture Tube drop-down window, as shown here. We used this to create the image of Fig. 6.24 with just four mouse clicks. It's that easy.

To place multiple images in your own tube you have to place each tube element carefully, as shown in Fig. 6.21. Using a suitably dimensioned grid helps here (page 104). Then in the Export

Fig. 6.24 A Pack of Westies

Picture Tube box (similar to that in Fig. 6.22) set the file options as follows:

In the **Cell arrangement** panel, enter the number of **Cells across** and **Cells down**. In the **Placement mode** box, choose a placement mode, usually Random. In the **Selection mode**, choose a selection mode, probably Random again. You can use the **Help** button for an explanation of selection modes.

Picture tubes really are quite exciting to play with. Some PSP users seem to get quite obsessed with them!

Cloning Parts of Images

The Clone brush allows you to pick an area of an image that you want to duplicate, called the source area, and place the image from that source area in another location, known as the target area. This can be in the same image or in another one. As an

Fig. 6.25 A Scanned Image

example, we will clone out the unwanted text in the scanned image of Fig. 6.25 and give the old Cornish engine house a new window.

To remove the text we will replace it with small sections of the surrounding image. Fig. 6.26 shows the Clone brush positioned in the sky next to the unwanted text and the Tool Options that were selected.

The procedure is to right-click the mouse (to select the source area), move the brush over the text and then 'dab' it over the text by left-clicking it and moving it to another section. The **Aligned mode** option, shown active here, controls the position of the source area each time you release the left mouse button and then press it again to resume cloning.

Fig. 6.26 The Clone Brush with Tool Options

The source area moves with the brush each time you release the left mouse button. This can be seen in Fig. 6.27, where the new

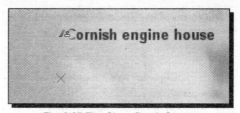

Fig. 6.27 The Clone Brush Source

source area is shown by the 'X' which maintains the same position relative to the brush. As the brush is moved to the right and clicked, the source is also moved to the right.

When the **Aligned mode** option is unchecked it remains on the original source area at all times.

To add a window we used a slightly different technique. We set the source area by right-clicking the Clone brush near the centre of the existing window and then moved the brush point to a position below. We then pressed and held the left mouse button while carefully dragging in small circular strokes until the window was duplicated, as shown in Fig. 6.28. We let go of the

Fig. 6.28 Cloning a New Feature

left mouse button when it was completed. The resulting engine house is shown in all its glory in Fig. 6.29. If only it was so easy to carry out structural changes in real life!

If **Sample merged** is enabled you can clone all visible pixels even if those pixels are on underlying layers. With Sample merged disabled only pixels on the active layer can be cloned.

Fig. 6.29 The Changed Image

Some Clone Brush Tips

Below we list some tips that you might find helpful when you are using the Clone Brush.

- If the Clone brush refuses to work, you may have a selection active in the image. Try the **Selections**, **Select None** command to cancel it. If this doesn't work, make sure you are not working on a different layer with nothing on it.

- Unless you want the current Foreground texture to be merged with the cloned image, you should click the **Transparency** button ◎ in the Foreground Material box of the Materials palette, see page 56. This sets the foreground material as transparent with no style or texture.

- To clone texture or rough areas in an image, it is often wise to dab with the clone brush, rather than stroke. This often produces a better result.

- You should leave the **Hardness** and **Opacity** at full when there is a lot of sharp detail that needs to be cloned. Reducing the **Hardness** may cause the sharp details in the clone to become soft or blurred.

- You will often want to set the source area as close to the target area as possible to ensure the pixels surrounding the target area match well, making signs of editing harder to detect.

- Try to clone in the direction of existing lines and shadows in the image. It is often not necessary to set new source areas if you are working with the **Aligned mode** option enabled, and your clone work is moving horizontally or vertically on the image. If the target area path is curved or on a diagonal, or scattered throughout the image, it is better to set a new source area near the new target area.

Retouching Images

When you have carried out cloning or other selection editing processes, you might want to tidy up the areas that you have worked on and help them seamlessly 'marry in' to the rest of the image. This is where the retouch brushes come in. There are 11 brushes on the Tools toolbar arranged in two sections which are all brushes for retouching images. These brushes have many uses in graphics design and photo restoration. They allow for editing existing pixels within an image. They are not used to apply new paint, but rather to change the pixels that already exist in an image. You drag the brush in the image to apply its effect. If the brush has two functions (such as Lighten/Darken), you drag with the left mouse button to apply the first function and with the right button to apply the second function.

 Dodge - Lightens and brings out the details in areas that are in shadow by mimicking the photographic darkroom technique of holding back some of the light when printing photographs to produce lighter areas.

 Burn - This is the opposite of the **Dodge** tool. It darkens areas of the image that are too light.

 Smudge - Similar to smearing paint it spreads colour and image details from the starting point and picks up new colour and image details as it moves. This is the retouch brush we use most often for removing blemishes from pictures.

 Push - Spreads colour and image details from the starting point but does not pick up any new colour or image details.

Soften - Smoothes edges and reduces contrast. You can blend 'rough' or aliased edges of a pasted-in figure into a background to approximate an antialiased effect by using the Soften Brush. This also works when trying to blend elements from different layers.

Sharpen - Heightens edges and accentuates contrasts.

 Emboss - Causes the foreground to appear raised from the background by suppressing colour and tracing edges in black.

 Lighten/Darken - Lightening increases brightness; darkening decreases brightness. Choose to affect the RGB or Lightness value of pixels.

 Saturation Up/Down - Increases or decreases the saturation (affects the HSL value of pixels).

 Hue Up/Down - Increases or decreases the hue (affects the HSL value of pixels).

 Change-to-Target - Changes pixels based on a characteristic of the current foreground colour on the Materials palette. This can be colour, hue, saturation, or lightness.

To get used to these tools we suggest you open a copy of an image and experiment with each one in turn, using different option settings as you go. Don't forget the **Undo** button.

Some of the retouch brushes can be quite harsh when applied, especially Dodge and Burn. To get more control it is a good procedure to duplicate the image as a new layer, with the **Layers, Duplicate** command, and apply the Retouch to the new layer. Once complete, it is easy to use the new layer's Opacity slider to lessen the effect if necessary.

When large brush sizes are being used, some of these brushes are very resource-intensive especially Smudge and Push. If you notice your PC slowing down, it is a good idea to clear the Command History with the **Edit, Command History, Clear** command. You may also want to empty the clipboard using the **Edit, Empty Clipboard** command. Before doing these, though, you should make sure you don't need the data that will be destroyed.

Warping Images

Another tool you may find a use for is the **Warp Brush**. Its starting button is probably hiding under your **Paint Brush** on the Tools toolbar.

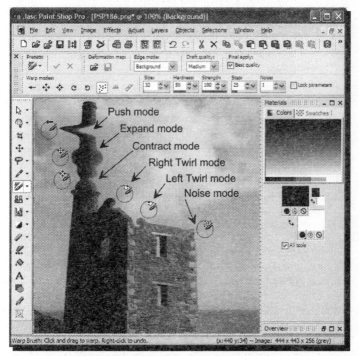

Fig. 6.30 Warping Mode Pointers and Actions

The Warp brush is used to create strokes that produce a warping effect on the pixels of an image. Depending on the Mode chosen, you can push pixels in the direction of the brush stroke, expand pixels away from the brush, contract them into the centre of the brush, twirl pixels clockwise or anticlockwise and cause random movements of pixels under the brush. Our example in Fig. 6.30 shows each of these effects, alongside the mode pointer, applied to a small section of our engine house. We haven't yet found a real use for this tool though!

Replacing Colours

There are two main ways of quickly replacing colours in PSP images. Although these are similar they have quite marked differences.

Color Replacer Tool

 The **Color Replacer** tool uses the foreground and background colours from the Materials palette to replace one colour in an image with a new colour. It makes its replacement based on the RGB values of the colours. You can use brush strokes to replace only those pixels that the brush touches or you can replace all pixels of a certain colour in a selection or a layer. You can also set a **Tolerance** value so that the Color Replacer replaces colours that are similar, not just identical, to the original. As the tolerance value is increased, more colours are replaced. If you set Tolerance to 0, the pixels to be replaced must match the specified colour exactly. With a setting of 200, all the pixels are changed.

It is easiest to use the **Dropper** tool to select the colours from your image that you want replacing. Activate this by clicking the **Dropper** button on the Tools toolbar, shown here, or if another brush is active, by holding the **Ctrl** key down for as long as you need the Dropper. Left-clicking on a colour in an open image sets the Materials palette foreground colour, right-clicking sets the background colour.

To replace the background colour of a whole selection or layer with the foreground colour, double-click the left mouse button anywhere in it. To replace the background colour under the brush tip with the foreground colour, use the left mouse button.

To replace the foreground colour of a whole selection or layer with the background colour, double-click the right mouse button anywhere in it. To replace the foreground colour under the brush tip with the background colour, use the right mouse button.

Flood Filling

When the **Match mode** is set to 'None', as in Fig. 6.31 below, the **Flood Fill** tool lets you fill a complete layer, image, or a selected area in an image, with the colour, gradient, pattern or texture that is currently set in the Materials palette, or with another image.

Fig. 6.31 The Flood Fill Tool Options Palette

The other **Match mode** settings are the same as those for the **Magic Wand** tool, described previously on page 71. With all of these modes the **Flood Fill** tool fills matching pixels that are contiguous (or adjacent to) the initial pixel that is clicked on by the tool. The **Tolerance** setting determines how much of the selected area will be filled. It is unavailable with a **Match Mode** of None, as above. Higher Tolerance allows more of an area to be filled, whereas a lower setting constrains the fill to areas that are similar in colour or exactly the same colour as the pixel you initially clicked.

When using the **Flood Fill** tool to fill several selected areas at the same time, be sure the **Match Mode** on the Tool Options palette is set to None. Then, when you click in one of the areas with your **Flood Fill** tool, all the areas will be filled. The value entered into the **Opacity** field determines how opaque the fill will be, with higher numbers making the fill more opaque, and lower making it more transparent.

As you should expect by now, to fill with the foreground material click the left mouse button, and to fill with the background material click the right mouse button.

Using Recent Materials

For a quick change of colours, or materials, you can use the Recent Mater... (or Materials) dialogue box, which opens when you right-click on either the Foreground or Background Material boxes of the Materials palette.

Fig. 6.32
The Recent
Materials Box

The top section contains the ten materials you have used most recently. The middle section of the Recent Materials box always displays the same basic 10 colours or greys, they are red, green, blue, dark grey, light grey, cyan, magenta, yellow, black, and white. For greyscale images, the greys are evenly spaced from black to white. After you have used more than ten materials, each new one replaces the earliest one selected.

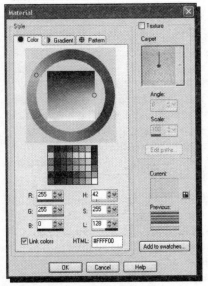

Fig. 6.33 The Material Dialogue Box

Just click any of the last 20 choices to make it the current selection.

The bottom section displays the current Foreground and Background materials and the **Other** button. Click this button to open the Material dialogue box shown in Fig. 6.33 and described on page 57.

In this box you can select whatever colour and material you want, including Gradients, Patterns and Textures.

7

Layers and Masks

Using layers in PSP allows you to work separately on different parts of your image without affecting the other parts. In a simplistic way, layers are like sheets of glass or acetate. You draw or paint or place photos on them, shift them around and change their order in the stack. And when you look down on the stack, you can see the composite image, as shown on the left of Fig. 7.1 below.

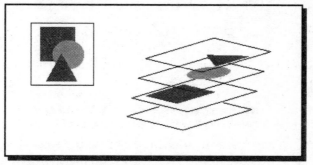

Fig. 7.1 An Image with Three Layers and a Background

Once you know your way around PSP layers, it is best to place every new element, or addition to an element, on its own layer. You can always merge or combine layers, and it is much safer and faster to build each element a layer at a time. Once you are satisfied with the look, you can then combine the elements that make up that object. Our example in Fig. 7.1 above shows a simple image with three shapes, each on its own layer. As long as the layers are separate, it is easy to make changes to each of the separate shapes, such as changing their colour or position.

The Layer palette, shown for the above image in Fig. 7.2, is where you control the layout and properties of your layers.

The Layer Palette

To open the Layer palette use the **View**, **Palettes**, **Layers** menu command, press the **F8** function key, or right-click any palette and choose it from the **Palettes** option on the drop-down context menu.

Like the other PSP palettes you can place this where you want in your working space. To get more free screen space click the ▲ button to allow the palette to automatically roll-up, and the ◀ button to lock the palette open.

The Layer palette contains an enormous amount of power and information. When you finally master it, you'll wonder how you ever worked without it.

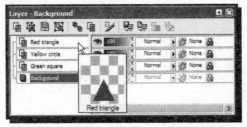

Fig. 7.2 The Layer Palette, showing the Contents of a Layer

This palette uses mouseover thumbnails to identify the contents of each layer. Simply hold your mouse over a layer name in the Layer palette and a thumbnail image will pop-up, as shown in Fig. 7.2 above. Clicking on the name will select a layer and make it the active layer in the image.

The left panel of the Layer palette displays the names of layers and layer groups. The icon to the left of each name indicates the type of layer (background ■, raster 🖫, vector 🖫, mask ♥, adjustment ▲, group 🖫, or floating selection 🖫). If there are more layers than the palette can display, use the scroll bars on the right side to move through the list.

The right panel displays options for the layer, including a **Visibility** toggle ●, an **Opacity (0 - 100%)** bar ▦, a **Blend Mode** drop-down menu ▭, a **Layer Link** toggle ▭, and a **Lock Transparency** button ▦.

The Layer Palette Toolbar

The default Layer palette toolbar includes buttons for the following command tasks:

 Add a new raster layer to the image

 Add a new vector layer to the image

 Make a new mask that shows the entire area

 Create a new layer group with the current layer

 Duplicate the current layer

 Delete the current layer

 Edit the selection as if it were an image

 Load a mask from disc

 Load a layer mask from an alpha channel

 Save the mask image to disc

 Save the current layer mask to an alpha channel

The last four buttons for loading and saving masks from and to disc and alpha channels carry out operations similar to loading and saving selections that we described on page 80.

Types of Layers

As we saw earlier there are five basic types of layers supported by PSP 8. These are Background layers, Raster layers, Vector layers, Mask layers, and Adjustment layers. We describe the first three here and the others later on.

Background Layers

When you create a new document in Paint Shop Pro, it is automatically created as a background layer ▓. This is a special raster layer that always sits below any other layers. But you can easily convert the background layer to a regular raster layer. Right-click on the background layer and choose **Promote to Layer** from the pop-up menu. The layer name will change from 'Background' to 'Layer plus a number'. You can double-click on the layer listing to open the Layer Properties window and rename the layer. Your layer is now a regular raster layer. It is best to keep a background layer though as usually, when you are working with layered images, you want the layers to have transparent backgrounds. Without an image background, you would be working with the chequered background that signifies transparency, and that is not easy.

Background layers cannot be renamed, display transparency, be moved up or down in the stack, or be moved with the mover tool. You cannot use the Background Eraser on a background layer as this type of layer does not support transparency. The two things that you can only do on a background layer are adding borders and using the scratch removal tool.

When you try to use a tool, adjustment or an effect that can only be used on a background layer, you'll either see the tool greyed out or you will get a prompt to flatten your image into a single layer.

In our example of Fig. 7.1 we first clicked the ▣ **New** Standard toolbar button, and accepted a raster background, 16 Million Colors (necessary for layers) and a white background. This opened the empty Background level.

Raster Layers

Raster layers ▣ are used to hold raster images. As we saw on page 65, photographs are raster images, as are many kinds of drawings and paintings. Raster graphics are the preferred format for photo-realistic images or images containing thousands, or millions, of colours. Since raster images are composed of pixels, it is more difficult to stretch or re-size them without experiencing blurring or distortion. You should use raster layers for displaying subtle changes in tones and colours and for objects on which you want to apply raster-only commands and tools. The effects commands, the painting tools, and many other tools apply only to raster layers.

Until recently, graphics programs either used raster data (pixels) or vector data (lines, nodes, and fills), not both at the same time. PSP is one of the few programs that can generate both true raster and true vector images. However, because of the very different technology used to create these different types of objects, PSP uses layers to keep the data types separate.

Vector Layers

Vector Layers ▣ are the next type of layer used in PSP. As we shall see in Chapter 10, Vector objects are made up of a series of nodes (points) joined by lines. These lines can be combined to form closed shapes, and those shapes can have coloured, patterned, or gradient fills. Graphical elements in a vector file are called objects. PSP calls its pre-defined objects Preset Shapes. Vector objects must be on vector layers. If you create a vector object while a raster layer is selected, Paint Shop Pro creates a vector layer just above the current layer. In addition, you cannot move a vector object to a non-vector layer.

Since each vector object is defined by geometric co-ordinates rather than dots of colour, you can move and change its properties over and over again while maintaining its original clarity and crispness. You can easily re-size vector images from a thumbnail sketch to a billboard-sized graphic, and you can print in any resolution. Vector images don't become grainy when re-sized or lose detail and proportion. Smooth curves are easy to define in vector-based programs and they retain their smoothness and continuity even when enlarged. You can change vector-based images into raster formats when needed, but it is not so easy to change rasters to vectors. So you use vector layers to create objects or text that you can easily edit.

To display the names of each of the vector objects on a vector layer, click the plus sign in front of the layer name on the Layer palette.

Working with Layers

Adding New Layers to Images

To add a layer, right-click on the name of any layer in the Layer palette and choose **New Raster Layer** or **New Vector Layer**, depending on what the layer will hold. As a shortcut you can click on the **New Raster Layer** 📲 or **New Vector Layer** 📲 buttons of the Layer palette toolbar.

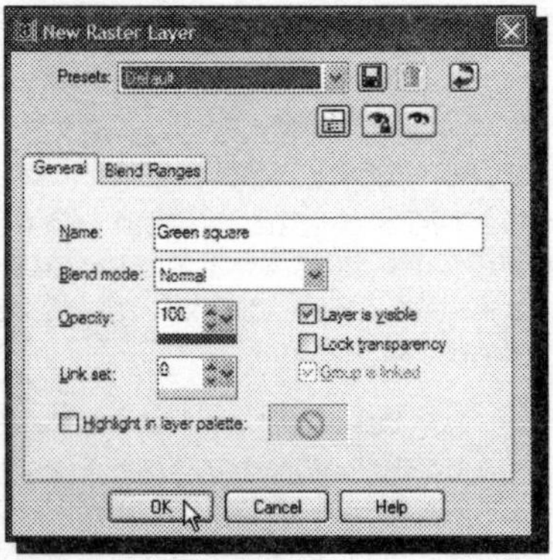

Fig. 7.3 New Raster Layer Properties

Continuing our example of Fig. 7.1 we added three raster layers in turn, by opening the Layer palette and clicking the **New Raster Layer** button 📲. Each time, this opened the New Raster Layer box shown here in Fig. 7.3. We typed useful names in the **Name** text box as shown, accepted the other options, and clicked on **OK**.

With a raster layer active, you can also add a vector layer automatically by simply choosing either the **Preset Shape** or **Pen** tool, and creating a new object. A vector layer will be created to hold the new object. However, if a vector layer is active, the new vector object will be placed on that active layer, not on a new one.

Duplicating a Layer

Fig. 7.4 The Layer Name
Right-Click Menu

Often you will find that you wish to repeat elements in different places in your image. You can easily make a duplicate of any layer by right-clicking on its name in the Layer palette to open the pop-up menu shown in Fig. 7.4. If you choose **Duplicate** a new layer will be created. Paint Shop Pro will name the layer as 'Copy of' the original layer name. It is a good idea to double-click on the new layer and give it a name that identifies the contents of the layer for more efficient work.

Changing Layer Order

To change the order of your layers, simply click on a layer name in the Layer palette and drag the layer up or down to a new position. Layers that are higher in the order will appear on top of layers that are below.

Deleting a Layer

To delete a layer, simply right-click on the layer name in the Layer palette and choose **Delete** from the pop-up window. Another way, when the layer is active, is just to click the **Delete Layer** button in the Layer palette toolbar.

Merging Layers

With a big detailed image you can easily end up with a huge number of layers, which can be a little cumbersome, so you might want to merge some of the layers. Sometimes, you will want to merge all of your layers together, or flatten your image. You have to do this when you save the image in any other file format except **.PSPImage**. Be cautious though, once layers are merged, you cannot get them back. You may wish to make a change in the future, and you will regret not having your layered image file. Much better to merge a copy of the file and keep the original intact.

To merge the entire image, simply right-click on any layer name in the Layer palette and choose **Merge**, **Merge All (Flatten)**. You will be left with exactly the same result visually, but all your layers will have merged into one. If you didn't really want to do this, use the **Undo** command, but don't leave it too long!

You can also merge only the layers that are visible in the document. To make a layer invisible, click on its Visibility toggle 👁 on Layer Palette. A red 'X' will appear through the icon 👁 and the contents of that layer will disappear from the document screen. (Clicking again will make it visible.)

To merge several layers, but not all, simply turn off the visibility for any layers you do not wish to merge. Right-click on any layer and choose **Merge**, **Merge Visible**.

Version 8 of PSP has the **Merge**, **Merge Down** command, which merges the active layer with the one below it in the layer stack. So to merge two layers, arrange them so that they are adjacent, make the upper one active, right-click on its name in the Layer palette and choose **Merge**, **Merge Down** in the menu that opens.

Linking Layers

A much less intrusive way to combine layers for the purposes of moving objects together, is to link them. You do this from the **Layer Link** toggle buttons 👁 Name in the right panel of the Layers palette. Initially each layer will have a

'None' on the **Layer Link** buttons indicating that they are not linked, as shown in Fig. 7.2. Links are arranged by assigning numbers and you link layers together by clicking their **Layer Link** buttons until they show the same number. A left-click increases the number and a right-click reduces it.

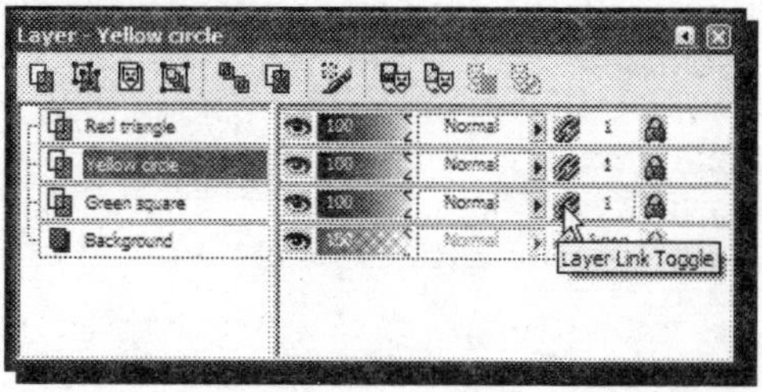

Fig. 7.5 The Layer Palette, with Three Layers Linked

Here in Fig. 7.5 we show the three raster layers of our example linked with a common number '1'. Now if we move any of the layers by selecting the **Move** tool on the Tools toolbar and dragging it over a layer, all of the layers will move together, as shown in Fig. 7.6.

Fig. 7.6 Moving Linked Layers

This also shows that you can drag layer data outside the image area. It is not lost as you can just drag it right back again.

Layer Palette Effects

Opacity - To make the contents of a layer partially or completely opaque (or transparent), and allow the objects on

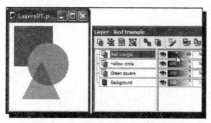

the layers below to show through, you can adjust its **Opacity** slider in the Layers palette. In Fig. 7.7, the Red triangle layer has been set to 40% opaque. At 0% it would be transparent.

Fig. 7.7 Changing Level Opacity

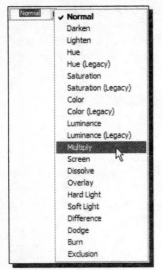

Fig. 7.8 Layer Blend Modes

Blend Mode - As a variation, you can also set the way that the pixels of a layer blend with those of all the layers below. To bring up a long list of blend mode choices, as shown in Fig. 7.8, click in the **Blend Mode** button and select the desired effect. The image will show the effect but the layers will not actually be changed.

With the default mode of 'Normal', pixels are blended based on the opacity of the layer. It is well worth experimenting with the other modes. For a listing of the effects of the Blend Modes see Appendix E.

Lock Transparency - This button allows you to restrict the results of any editing to the opaque sections of the layer. If transparency is not locked (the default) the lock icon 🔒 on the button is grey. Any changes to the layer, including painting, pasting of selections, applying effects, etc., will affect the whole layer including the transparent area.

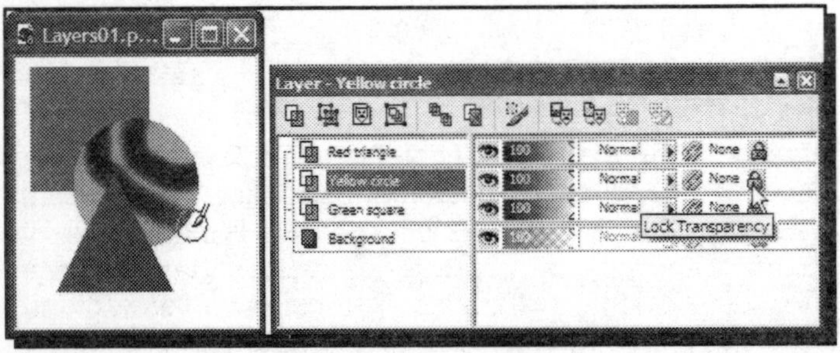

Fig. 7.9 The Lock Transparency Effect on a Layer

When transparency is locked by clicking the button, the lock icon becomes blue 🔒 and further changes to the layer do not affect the transparent area of the layer. This is shown in Fig. 7.9 where the Yellow circle layer is locked.

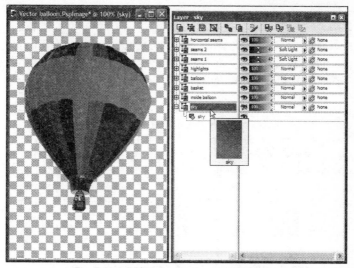

Fig. 7.10 A PSP 8 Sample Image with Layers

If you want to have a look at an image made up with lots of layers, take a look at **Vector balloon.PSPImage** which should be in the Sample Images folder created by the installation program of PSP 8 (discussed earlier on page 37).

We suggest you place it in your workspace alongside the open Layers palette, as shown in our Fig. 7.10. This way you can easily check the contents and settings of each layer. The best way to learn something in PSP is often to play around with an example. Try changing settings in turn and see what happens to the image.

We made the Sky layer above invisible, which meant the balloon and its basket has a completely transparent background. Even though this is made up of multiple layers it would be very easy to copy it to the clipboard and paste it onto another image background. You could do this with the **Edit**, **Copy Merged** menu command, or **Ctrl+Shift+C**, which merges all the layers as it copies the image.

Are you happy working with layers yet?

Mask Layers

Masks are greyscale images that are added as a layer and are used to hide all or some of the information on the layer or layers below it. Wherever the mask is pure black, it hides all the information on the layer below. Wherever it is pure white, it will be completely transparent and not hide any information on the layers below. Where the mask has grey values between black and white, the image will be shown at varying degrees of opacity. In other words, a mask is a layer composed of 256 shades of grey from white to black. When placed on another image with a 24-bit colour depth the mask can be used to hide, show, and adjust the opacity of the underlying image. You use masks to fade between layers or to create special effects with precision.

Loading a Mask

Perhaps the above will make more sense after a small example. Fig. 7.11 here shows a photograph of our favourite boat. The image is a **.jpg** file taken with a digital camera. When opened in PSP it was placed as a Background layer, as shown on the Layer palette and in the image title bar.

Fig. 7.11 Image with Layer Palette

We then clicked the **Load Mask from Disk** button in the Layer palette to open the mask loading dialogue box shown in Fig. 7.12. We could also have used the **Layers**, **Load/Save Mask, Load Mask from Disk** menu command.

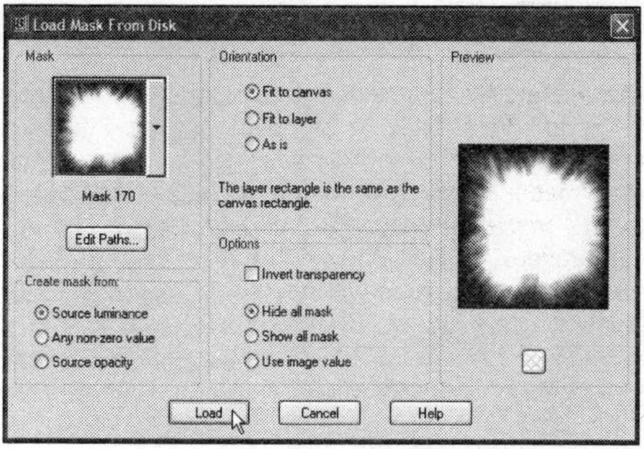

Fig. 7.12 The Load Mask from Disk Dialogue Box

Before this dialogue opened we accepted an Auto Action 'to promote the target to a full layer', as a mask can't be placed on a Background level.

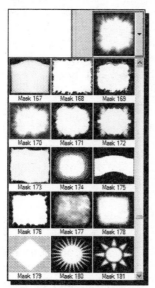

Fig. 7.13 The Mask Group Box Drop-down Window

Clicking in the **Mask** group box (top left corner of the above dialogue box) opens a drop-down window showing all the masks that are available on your PC, as shown in Fig. 7.13. For us there were well over 200 masks available.

Paint Shop Pro 8 comes supplied with a fine collection of premade masks. They are also available for download on many Web sites. If you can find what you want, these premade masks work well for adding special effects to images.

We used the drop-down window to browse for a mask and selected **Mask 170** for our example. We left the other settings as shown in Fig. 7.12 and then clicked the **Load** button to apply the mask.

Fig. 7.14 Image with Mask Placed showing Layer Palette

The mask was applied to a new Layer group with the mask placed above the image, as shown in the Layer palette of Fig. 7.14. In PSP 8, when you add a mask to an image, PSP automatically creates a Layer group. This is new to version 8. Layer groups don't only apply to mask layers, they can be used with all types of layers.

Fig. 7.14 shows the mask applied to the image, but the Raster 1 layer (the promoted Background layer) has a transparent background, so the image does not look very clear.

That's no problem. We selected the Raster 1 layer in the palette and clicked the **New Raster Layer** button. This opened the New Raster Layer box of Fig. 7.15. We typed a suitable name in the **Name** field, and could have changed any of the new layer's properties here, but as we were happy with the defaults, we just pressed **OK**.

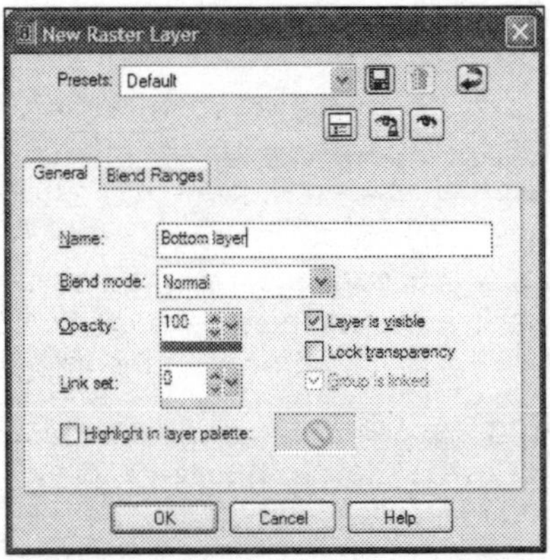

Fig. 7.15 New Raster Layer Properties

Layer - Bottom layer

Group - Grace

Mask - Grace

Grace

Bottom Layer

Fig. 7.16 Image with Mask Placed
showing Layer Palette

We dragged the new layer to the bottom of the stack and filled it with white using the **Flood Fill** tool. The result of using this simple mask on an image is shown in all its glory in Fig. 7.16.

While we were at it, we also renamed three of the levels by right-clicking their name and selecting **Rename** from the context menu, and typing the new name. The name of the boat is Grace by the way!

Mask layers function the same as other types of layers. You can turn the visibility of the mask layer on or off, change the overall opacity of the mask layer, or link the mask layer to other layers as described earlier.

Editing Masks

As long as the mask is the active layer (the one selected in the Layers palette) you can edit it any way you like. You can easily tell when a mask is the active layer by looking at the image title bar, as shown in Fig. 7.14. PSP 8 adds the active layer's title from the Layers palette and this will start with 'Mask', as a reminder that any editing operations will now affect the mask rather than the image or other layers.

The available colours in the Materials palette change to black, white, and shades of grey. The tools available for editing masks are the same ones as for editing any greyscale image, such as **Paint Brush**, **Airbrush**, **Flood Fill**, and **Eraser** - even the **Text** tool works.

Fig. 7.17 Image with Mask Overlay

If you want to edit the mask it is best to view it in Overlay mode by clicking the **Mask Overlay** Toggle button 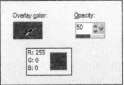 pointed to here in Fig. 7.17. The mask then turns a 50% opaque red which lets you see the results of any editing operations you carry out on the mask.

You can adjust the colour and opacity of the overlay by right mouse clicking its layer in the Layer palette and choosing the **Properties** option from the context menu. This opens a dialogue box similar to that of Fig. 7.15, but with an Overlay tab sheet, part of which is shown here in Fig. 7.18.

Changing a mask's properties does not affect the function of the mask, only the way it is viewed.

Also remember that the layers to which a mask is applied do not really change, they just look like they do when the mask is active. To

Fig. 7.18 The Mask Overlay Properties

deactivate a mask you make it invisible by clicking its Visibility toggle ◎ on the Layer Palette. A red 'X' will appear through the icon ✖ and the masked layers will return to their true state. (Clicking again will reactivate the mask.)

It is a good idea while editing a mask to display the Overview palette (opened with the **F9** key) so that you can see the image as it will actually display or print.

Creating Masks

A mask is like a stencil, enabling you to protect part of the image before you apply an effect such as a filter or transformation. The level of protection can vary, so you can moderate the effect as well as turning it on and off.

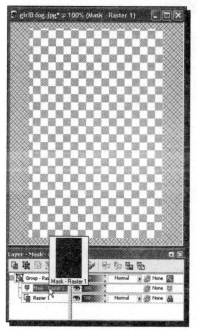

Fig. 7.19 New Mask Layer Options

As well as using the masks that come with PSP you can create your own in one of three main ways; from scratch, from an existing image, or from a selection. All these options are available on the menu shown in Fig. 7.19 opened with **L**ayers, N**e**w **Mask Layer**.

To create a mask from scratch, click the layer you want to mask on the Layer palette, select **L**ayers, **N**ew **Mask Layer** from the main menu and then choose the type of mask you want. Where, **S**how All creates a pure white mask which shows all of the underlying layer, and **H**ide All creates a pure black mask which hides all of the underlying layer, as shown here in Fig. 7.20.

Fig. 7.20 A Hide All Mask

You can then paint the mask with white or greys to show portions of the underlying layers as we do next. Remember that black areas are protected, grey areas partly protected and white areas are exposed.

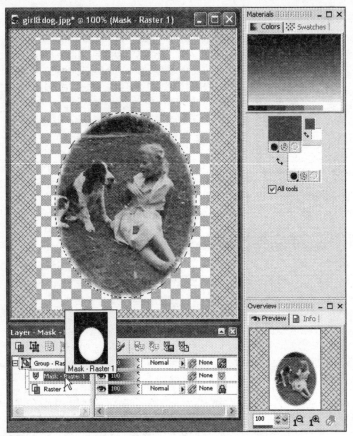

Fig. 7.21 A Simple Mask also Showing an Overview

In Fig. 7.21 above, with the mask layer active, we used the **Selection** tool to create an elliptical selection with Feather set at 5. We then used the **Flood Fill** tool to fill the selection with white. The resultant mask can be seen in the pop-up shown above, and the resultant image with the mask active is shown in the Overview palette.

Creating a Mask from an Image

Our next example shows how you can use a PSP mask in exactly the same way as you would use a stencil when

creating artwork on paper. One problem though is that our book is in greyscale (or black and white!) and this technique produces subtle colouring changes which to some extent lose their effect. No problem really, please just use your imagination when reading and follow the example to see the complete result.

Fig. 7.22 The Image to be Masked

To create a mask from an image, you should first open the image that you want to create the mask from. In our example we use a picture of our dog shown here in Fig. 7.22. For your own mask, any high-contrast image with a simple background will do.

Next open a new 16 million colour (24-bit) raster image of about the same size as your mask source image, choose **Raster Background**, make sure that **Transparent** is unchecked, and pick a background colour by clicking on the **Color** box and choosing a colour in the Material dialogue box that opens. We used a shade of purple.

If necessary, open the Layers palette with the **F8** key and create a new layer in the new image by clicking the **New**

Raster Layer button 🔲 on the Layers palette toolbar. The new layer, named 'Raster 1' by default, will be entirely transparent. With Raster 1 the active layer, use the **Layers**, **New Mask Layer**, **From Image** main menu command. For **Source window** choose the open file that you want to use for your mask. Be sure that the **Source luminance** check box is selected

Fig. 7.23 Adding a Mask from an Image

under **Create mask from**, as shown in Fig. 7.23, and click the **OK** button to create the mask.

At this stage your image will look the same, but a new layer group will have been added in the Layers palette, including the mask layer and Raster 1, as shown in Fig. 7.24 below.

Fig. 7.24 Using the Mask as a Stencil with the Airbrush Tool

With Raster 1 still the active layer, as above, select the **Airbrush** tool, and set the Foreground colour in the Materials palette to whatever colour you'd like to use as your paint - we used white. Now for some visible action. In the image canvas, spray the **Airbrush** tool across the masked areas where you want colour to show. Used this way, a mask is like a stencil or silk screen. Masked areas of the layer will resist paint and unmasked areas will accept it.

Depending on your choice of Background and Foreground colours you can get some very spectacular results with this technique. To get the effect you want you may have to play with the Airbrush settings in the Tool Options palette.

Creating A Mask From A Selection

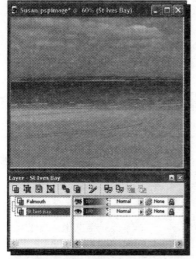

Fig. 7.25 The New Background Layer

Fig. 7.26 The Original Image with the Selection Made

Maybe you have wanted to select a figure in one image and place it on a new background. There are several ways in PSP of doing this, but probably the best way is to use a mask. A mask lets you 'black out' the old background, letting you see another one underneath your figure.

We will work through another example to demonstrate the process. First open the image you want for your new background, and if it has just one Background layer, use the **Layers**, **Promote Background Layer** command to change this to a Raster layer called 'Raster 1'. In ours we renamed this layer to 'St Ives Bay' as shown in Fig. 7.25.

Next open the image which contains the figure (or whatever it is) you want to place on the new background, copy it to the clipboard, and then close the image. Then use the **Edit**, **Paste**, **Paste as New Layer** command to add the image as a new layer above the new background, as in our example of Fig. 7.26.

To make the selection we used the **Freehand Selection** tool, and in the Tool Options palette set Selection type to **Smart Edge**. Then we dragged the selection tool around the edge of the figure, keeping the edge within the tool's bounding box and clicking at points along the edge wherever the angle of the edge changed. The final selection is shown in Fig. 7.26.

Fig. 7.27 The Mask in Place

At this point we could simply copy the selected figure and paste it onto the new background. However, we can refine the selection further by creating a mask from the selection.

To create the mask, make sure the layer with the selection is active (Falmouth in our case), choose **Layers**, **New Mask Layer**, **Show Selection** command, then turn the selection off with **Selections**, **Select None**. The result should be something like ours in Fig. 7.27. The figure is now standing in front of the new background. If you click the mask's **Visibility** toggle ☜, you can turn off the mask and the background will revert to the original. What PSP has done is create a mask that hides everything outside the selection, leaving everything inside the selection showing.

Mask - Falmouth

Fig. 7.28
Our Mask

You can now refine the edges of your figure by editing the mask. You must do this with the mask layer selected and if you want to see the red colour that indicates the mask, choose Overlay mode by clicking the **Mask Overlay Toggle** button 🛡, as described earlier in the chapter.

Saving and Loading Masks

As with selections, you can save your masks to use again or to share with others. To do this, use the sub-menu commands of the **Layers**, **Load/Save Mask** command. These let you save and load masks to and from disc or alpha channels as shown below in Fig. 7.29, and described for selections on page 80. If you need help on this, we suggest you go back to page 80 and read that section, but substituting 'masks' for 'selections'.

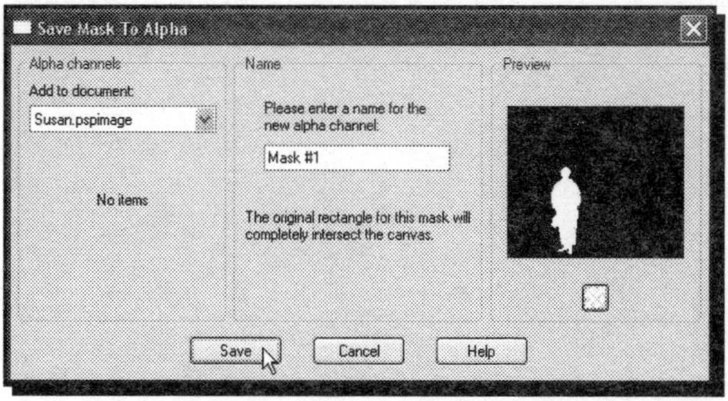

Fig. 7.29 Saving a Mask to a File's Alpha Channel

Adjustment Layers

Adjustment layers are correction layers that adjust the colour or tone of underlying layers. Each adjustment layer makes the same correction as an equivalent command on the **Adjust** menu, but does not change image pixels like the command does. Adjustment layers cannot be the bottom layer, and you will not be able to delete other layers if deleting them causes an adjustment layer to become the bottom layer.

Once you have mastered masks, adjustment layers become a little easier. Like masks, they don't change the image, they just temporarily change the way it looks. Turn off the layer, and you're right back to the original.

There are nine kinds of adjustment layers:

Brightness/Contrast, Channel Mixer, Color Balance, Curves, Hue/Saturation/Lightness, Invert, Levels, Posterize, and Threshold.

Each one works exactly like the PSP menu bar effect with the same name.

Why should we bother with them? Mainly because they make life a little easier. If you don't like the effect they produce, you can change it without changing everything else in the image.

8

Working with Text

As you would expect with a graphics application as powerful as Paint Shop Pro, the ability to add and work with text is well covered. You use the **Text** tool to create text on an image. PSP 8 has a new and improved Text Tool which has been radically changed from the previous version 7. To open the tool you can click the **Text** tool button on the Tools toolbar, or more simply, just press the **T** key on the keyboard.

You select your text colours, textures, gradients, etc., on the Materials palette (see page 55), and text options on the Tool Options palette (see Fig. 8.1 below), then click in the image and enter text in the Text Entry dialogue box.

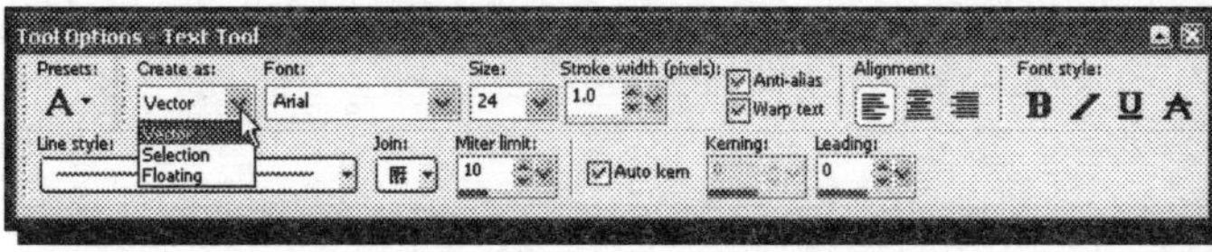

Fig. 8.1 The Tool Options Palette for the Text Tool

Creating Text

There are three types of text that you can create depending on the option selected in the **Create as** drop-down list of the Tool options palette. These are Vector, Selection and Floating. We will describe each of these a little later, but first we will look at the initial settings that are common to all three. With the **Text** tool it is often better to select these settings before actually typing the text to be placed.

On the Materials palette, choose the foreground material as the text outline and the background material as the text fill (the area within characters), as shown in Fig. 8.2 below.

Fig. 8.2 Text Outline and Fill Construction

For standard text with no outline, or stroke (as shown with the first 'P' above), either click the Foreground Material box's **Transparent** button ⊘, or set the **Stroke width** on the Tool Options palette to 0. For hollow text with no fill, as with the 'S' above, click the Background Material box's **Transparent** button ⊘. The **Stroke width** controls the outline thickness.

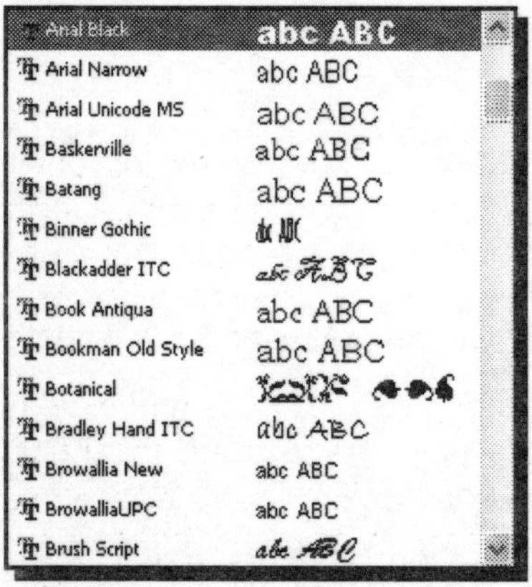

On the Tool Options Palette, pick a font from the **Font** drop-down box, usually any boldish font will do. Notice in Fig. 8.3 the preview of the font on the right side of this box. This should help you choose the type of font you want.

Fig. 8.3 The Font Drop-down Box

Set the font **Size** to a suitable size that fits the text on the page using the size drop-down box.

The three **Alignment** options set how text is aligned in relation to where you clicked the cursor in the image to insert the text. The ▤ button aligns the left edge of each line of text to the initial cursor position, ▤ aligns the centre of each line of text to the initial cursor position, and ▤ aligns the right edge of each text line to the initial cursor position.

The **Font Style** options B͟ ⁄ U͟ A͟ are self explanatory and control the style of the entered text; from left to right they are; bold, italic, underline and strikethrough.

The bottom row of the Tool options palette, as shown in Fig. 8.1, has a series of options to control the look of the text outline, or stroke. These include **Line style** (such as solid, dashed and many other unusual styles), **Join**, and **Miter limit** which set the types of line corners.

The other Tool options control the spacing of the text characters and lines. **Kerning** sets the horizontal space between characters, with 0 using the font's automatic kerning. Positive values increase the spacing and negative values decrease it. This control is only available if you clear the **Auto kern** check box. **Leading** sets the vertical space between lines of text. Use a positive value to increase the spacing or a negative value to decrease it. If you play around with these two settings you can get some unusual results!

Vector Text

This is the usual option to choose as it produces the only type of text you can later edit by changing the words, font type, style, and alignment. You either put this type of text on a vector layer of its own, or if you have a raster layer active, PSP will open a new vector layer when it places the text.

 As usual let's work through an example and play a little bit. First open a new image using the **File**, **New** menu command or by clicking the **New** icon on the Standard toolbar, shown here. In the New Image box (see page 35 if necessary), set the dimensions to 400 x 300 pixels, the **Resolution** to 72 pixels/inch. Set the **Image**

Characteristics to Raster Background, 16 million colors, and make sure the **Transparent** box is not checked.

Click the **Text** tool button on the Tools toolbar to open the tool. When you move the pointer over the image area notice its new $+_A$ shape. Make sure that Vector is selected in the **Create as** drop-down list of the Tool options palette. Clicking the pointer in the image opens the new Text Entry box, which is smaller and less cluttered than in previous versions of PSP. Just type some text in the Text Entry box, maybe the same as ours in Fig. 8.4 below.

Fig. 8.4 Using the Text Entry Box

As you type it in the box, the resulting text also appears in the image, as shown above. This feature is new to version 8, so if your version of PSP is older don't expect it to happen!

In the Text Entry box select all the text with the cursor so it is highlighted in blue. Now, any changes you make on the Tool Options or Materials palettes will immediately be reflected in the text placed in the image. These changes actually only effect any text that is highlighted in the Text Entry box, so you can even change individual characters.

Now is the time to master the **Text** tool. Just make changes to all the settings in the Tool Options palette, and see how these are reflected in the text. Then try playing with the Materials palette, choose different foreground materials for new text outlines and different background materials for the text fill. It's great when things suddenly become clear!

When you have had enough, click the **Apply** button, which closes the Text Entry box and places vector selection handles around the text, as shown in Fig. 8.5 below.

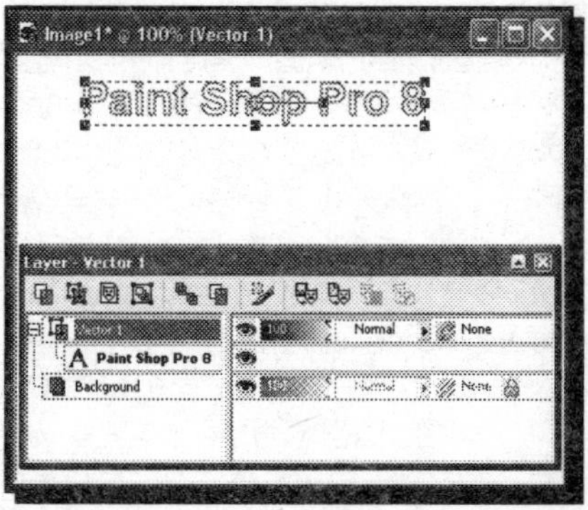

Fig. 8.5 Text Placed on a New Vector Layer

The vector text has been placed as a vector object on its own vector layer, as shown in Fig. 8.5. You use the **Object Selection** tool to make vector selections. Sometimes just clicking this button will select the text on an active layer, if not, simply move the ⁺◲ pointer over the text and when it changes shape to ⊹ click on the text to select it. You can then reduce or enlarge, or change the shape and colour of the text as you like.

Here in Fig. 8.6, we have dragged the bottom right handle to enlarge the text. Notice that

Fig. 8.6 Enlarging Vector Text

the pointer has changed shape yet again. When you enlarge text in this way you can virtually make it whatever shape you want. The beauty of vectors is that the character edges will always be crisp and clear however many enlargements you make. This is certainly not the case with raster text, which pixelates, or goes 'fuzzy' very quickly.

Editing Vector Text

As long as you leave vector text on its vector layer you can fully edit it at any time in the future. This means that if you save the image file containing it, you will have to save it as a **.Pspimage** file (see page 85), otherwise the layers will be merged and the text will then be raster text.

To edit the text you need to have the Text Edit box containing the original text open. There are several ways to do this, one being to pick the **Text** tool, move the mouse pointer over the text you want to edit, then click when the cursor changes to a bracketed [A] ⊤[A] shape. You can also click the **Object Selection** tool (at the bottom of the Tools toolbar) and double-click it on the text you want to edit. A third way to get the Text Entry box back is from the Layer palette, by expanding the vector layer (by clicking the + sign next to it), then double-clicking the sub-layer with the text you want to edit.

With the text selected in the opened Text Entry box you can manipulate individual characters, or words, or the whole text by changing the properties on the Tool Options palette, or the Materials palette.

Fig. 8.7 Editing Previously Placed Text

In Fig. 8.7, we have changed the font size of some characters and the colour of others. The '8' is currently being edited. Pressing the **Apply** button makes the changes permanent.

When the **Remember text** check box is ticked, the current text will be displayed the next time the Text Entry box is opened, wherever on an image that is.

Selection Text

When **Selection** is chosen in the **Create as** drop-down list of the Tool options palette the **Text** tool creates text in an image with a selection marquee surrounding it (remember the marching ants!). You can move, copy, fill, or edit it just like any other selection. This technique is perhaps best used to produce two types of special effects.

Fig. 8.8 Creating a Text Selection

The two stages of creating selection text are shown in Fig. 8.8 above. As usual you click the **Text** tool button and click this in the image where you want the text, then choose the font and size in the Tool Options palette. As you type your text it is shown in the image as in the top of Fig. 8.8.

When you click the **Apply** button the text selection is placed in the image, as shown in the lower part of Fig. 8.8.

Simply pressing the **Delete** key will delete the text selection to create a text cutout effect in the image, as shown in Fig. 8.9 below.

Fig. 8.9 Creating a Text Cutout

Another useful effect can be obtained by copying the selection to the clipboard and then pasting it to a new image. This results in text filled with parts of the original image, as shown in Fig. 8.10.

Fig. 8.10 Creating Text with an Image

Floating Raster Text

When **Floating** is chosen in the **Create as** drop-down list of the Tool options palette the **Text** tool creates raster text that is a floating selection. You cannot edit raster text later on, so you should only use this type when you know that the text and formatting will not change.

We use floating raster text when we want to apply 3D effects to the text. It is best to create raster text on a new raster layer so that you can easily move it around relative to the rest of the image. While the text is floating you can use any of the PSP raster painting tools to change its looks. When the selected text is defloated, such as when you make another selection in the image, it is merged with the underlying raster layer.

The following 3D text effects are examples of using floating raster text. They are all easy to do and well worth the effort.

Drop Shadow Text

An easy effect to achieve with text is to create a drop shadow. To do this, first create a new blank image, maybe 500 x 300 pixels, and create a new transparent raster layer with the **Layers**, **New Raster Layer** command.

Activate the **Text** tool, choose **Floating** in the **Create as** drop-down list of the Tool options palette then type in your text, and click the **Apply** button when the font, size, and other options are set to your satisfaction, as in Fig. 8.11.

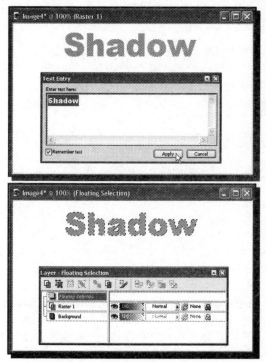

Fig. 8.11 Placing the Shadow Text
Above: Before Clicking the Apply Button   Below: After Clicking It

The next step is to apply the drop shadow effect with the Drop Shadow filter. This is opened with the **Effects**, **3D Effects**, **Drop Shadow** menu command. Once the dialogue box opens you can use the right preview window to see the result of adjusting the various settings. In Fig. 8.12 we used the default settings, but you may want to refine these. For more help just click the **Help** button.

Fig. 8.12 The Drop Shadow Box

Choose **OK** in the Drop Shadow box, and the effect will be applied. Your text will still be selected so use the **Selections**, **Select None** menu command, or **Ctrl+D** to deselect it. That's all there is to it, a simple, attractive, and classic effect, as can be seen below.

Fig. 8.13 The Finished Drop Shadow

Cutout Text

This is another text effect that is easy to do and looks good on most Web pages. As before, create a new blank image, maybe 500 x 300 pixels, and create a new transparent raster layer with the **Layers**, **New Raster Layer** command.

Activate the **Text** tool, choose **Floating** in the **Create as** drop-down list of the Tool options palette and create your text. This effect looks best with a relatively thick, heavy font face, and a relatively medium to light colour. Otherwise it may not show up too well.

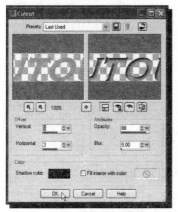

Fig. 8.14 The Cutout Box

Creating a cutout effect is as easy as applying a drop shadow. You use the **Effects**, **3D Effects**, **Cutout**, menu command to open the Cutout dialogue box, shown in Fig. 8.14. Uncheck the **Fill interior with color** option and use your existing text colour, and then adjust the box settings and use the preview window on the right until you achieve the cutout effect that suits you. The settings will depend on the size and shape of your text. When you are happy with the preview, click on **OK** to apply the effect.

Fig. 8.15 An Example of Cutout Text

Your text will still be selected so use the **Selections**, **Select None** menu command, or **Ctrl+D** to deselect it, and then sit back and enjoy your work.

Bevelled Text

There seem to be hundreds of tutorials on the Internet for creating different types of bevelled text in Paint Shop Pro, as this used to be a somewhat involved and time-consuming process. With PSP 8 this is no longer true, as we shall see.

As with the previous examples, start with a new, blank image, create a transparent raster layer, and use the **Text** tool to create your new floating text. Use a medium colour shade for your text.

Fig. 8.16 The Inner Bevel Box

With the text still selected, use the **Effects**, **3D Effects**, **Inner Bevel**, menu command to open the Inner Bevel box, shown in Fig. 8.16. In this example we selected Default in the list of **Presets**. But there were 23 other Presets to choose from, where a Preset is a set of saved properties for the particular dialogue box. In this case they were all provided with the PSP software.

When you are happy with the settings, click on **OK** and your bevel will be rendered, as shown in Fig. 8.17 below.

Fig. 8.17 The Default Inner Bevel Text

As before, your text will still be selected so use the **Selections**, **Select None** menu command, or **Ctrl+D** to deselect it. In Fig. 8.17, on the next page, we show the list of Presets, and what some of them look like in real life. Of course you can make your own as well.

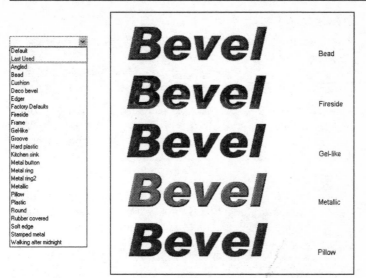

Fig. 8.18 The Inner Bevel Presets, with some Examples

We will leave it to you to explore the other 3D effects that are on offer, but have some coffee first.

Creating Text on Object Paths

Just one more effect to go before we leave the subject of text. This uses vector type text, and shows how easy it is with PSP to type text along any line, curve or shape, as long as it is a vector object. Here we will use a circular path for our text, but you can play with others.

First create a new blank image, maybe 500 x 300 pixels, with any colour background you like. We used white. Boring!

 Click the **Preset Shapes** tool button on the Tools toolbar, or more easily if you can remember it, the **P** key on the keyboard, to activate the **Preset Shapes** tool. On the Tool Options palette, shown in Fig. 8.19 on the next page, select Ellipse from the Shape List and make sure the **Create as vector** option is ticked.

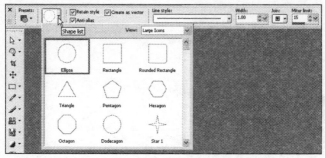

Fig. 8.19 The Tool Options Palette for Preset Shapes

 Create a circular shape by dragging the pointer, shown here, to get the shape you want. Releasing the pointer will fix the shape as a vector object.

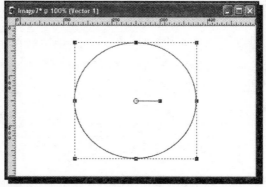

Fig. 8.20 The Vector Circle Drawn and Centred on the Canvas

While the circle is still selected, tidy up the image with the **Objects**, **Align**, **Center in Canvas** command which, as you might expect, moves the circle object to the centre of the open image window, or canvas in PSP speak.

 We have only placed the circle to act as a path for the text, so we don't really want to see it any more (now we know it's there), so we will next make it invisible. This is best done by opening the **Object Selection** tool, clicking on the circle to select it and then setting the Foreground box in the Materials palette to the same colour as the image background. The circle itself should then disappear, just leaving the selection handles.

Open the **Text** tool, select a colour for the text in the Background box of the Materials palette, and move the cursor over the circle vector field. When it crosses over the edge of the circle, the $+_A$ text cursor changes to a $\text{\textipa{}}$ shape, with a vector angle. Clicking then will open the Text Entry box. Any text you type in the box will be placed on the circle starting from the position you clicked. In our example below, we clicked on the 9 o'clock position of the circle (or 270°), so this is where the text started.

Fig. 8.21 Text on a Circular Path

If necessary you can change the type point size and kerning to get the effect that suits you. When you are happy click the **Apply** button to fix the text.

Please, don't just read this, try it in PSP. You will find it is much easier than it sounds. It also works inside squares, triangles and pentagons, to name but a few shapes! With a little practice you can easily design and make that logo you were really keen on.

9

Working with Photographs

The last few years has seen an explosion in the use of digital cameras, which of course produce a digital image which is usually downloaded to a computer. Here it can be manipulated, retouched and improved, before it is printed to become the same as the 'more old fashioned' photograph. Paint Shop Pro is an ideal software package to use for working with your photographic image files, as we shall see. But first some words on how to get the images into PSP itself.

 If they are already on your hard disc or on a CD, you simply use the **File**, **Open**, or **File**, **Browse** commands, or of course click their Standard toolbar buttons shown here, as covered previously starting on page 37.

If the images you want to work with are in your digital camera, on hard copy such as an already printed photograph, or on your screen in another application, such as a Web browser, it is a little more complicated, but don't worry, we will show you how.

Digital Cameras

With PSP you can access images while they are in your digital camera in several ways. The most common ways are with a direct link between your camera and your PC through a USB connection, or using a card reader which itself has a USB connection. Before doing this, you must install the special software drivers that will make this work for your camera, card reader, and computer. Unfortunately you may have to read the documentation that came with the camera or card reader. We don't know what it is, so cannot be more helpful here!

To make matters worse there are three types of connection that can be used:

WIA - The default for the latest computers running Windows XP or ME operating systems. The external device must also support WIA.

To download from a WIA camera with Windows XP or Me, connect the camera or card reader to a computer USB port, and use the **File**, **Import**, **From Scanner or Camera** command to download the images to your computer.

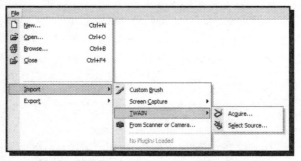

Fig. 9.1 PSP File Open and Import Menu Options

Mounted Drive - This is probably the most common type of connection, where the external device is viewed by your PC as an extra disc drive.

To download from a camera or card reader, that appears as a mounted drive with its own drive letter, use the **File**, **Open**, or **File**, **Browse** commands to locate the images on the mounted drive and open them into Paint Shop Pro.

TWAIN - Many cameras and most scanners can use this type of connection, which is an image capture interface for Windows and Macintosh operating systems. Believe it or not, TWAIN does not actually stand for anything!

To import images using the TWAIN interface, you first use the **File**, **Import**, **TWAIN**, **Select Source** command, as shown in Fig. 9.1, and select your device in the Select Source dialogue box. You only need to do this once. In the future you only need to use the **File**, **Import**, **TWAIN**, **Acquire** command to run the TWAIN software.

For digital cameras, this opens an Import box for you to select the images you want. Clicking the **Download** button will send them to the working area of PSP for you to process and/or save to your hard disc.

Scanning into PSP

As we saw above, Paint Shop Pro is TWAIN compliant, which means you can import any image from virtually any scanner into the program. Once you have gone through the one-off procedure of selecting your scanner in PSP, as described above, turn it on and place the photograph on the scanner bed. Then use the **File**, **Import**, **TWAIN**, **Acquire** command from the PSP menu, or click the **Twain Acquire** toolbar button, shown here.

Once the TWAIN software, provided with the scanner, launches, Paint Shop Pro goes into hibernation in the background. You carry out the scanning operation using the software that came with your scanner. As this software is hardware specific it will vary depending on the type and model of scanner you are using. It is very unlikely to be the same as ours shown in Fig. 9.2 on the next page.

Most scanning software will have the following three settings:

Colour/Image Type - This determines the colour quality of the scan. Scan a colour photograph with your colour settings on 24-bit RGB or higher. A black and white photograph will require the colour setting at 8-bit Greyscale. Text, or black and white line art, requires the Black and White (2 colour) setting.

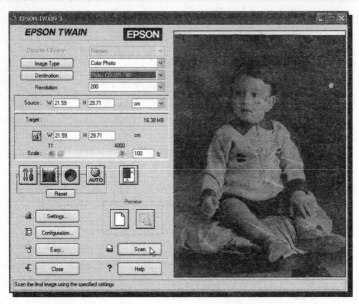

Fig. 9.2 Scanning an Old Photograph with Epson Twain

Resolution - This determines the quality of detail in the scan. The higher the resolution, the more detail you get from the image. If you have a printer capable of 600 dpi (dots per inch), you do NOT need to scan at 600 ppi (pixels per inch) to get the most out of your print. Dpi is actually a much finer measurement than ppi and one pixel can contain many dots. Without getting too involved, a good rule of thumb is to scan all your images at about 200 ppi.

Size/Scale - This determines the size of the scan and can be a percentage measurement, or be in inches or centimetres. You should set these sizes to whatever settings you prefer.

For further help with scanning we suggest you have a look at 'A few scanning tips' by Wayne Fulton. This is available as a book, but is also published on the following Web site.

www.scantips.com/

Capturing from the Screen

There will be times when you have an image visible on the screen, but in another software application. If you can see it on the screen, you can capture it straight into PSP, or save it to your hard disc and open it into PSP.

Via the Clipboard

In most Web sites you can right-click on an image, such as a photograph, and use the **Copy** command to place it on the clipboard. It's simple then to paste this into PSP, with the **Edit**, **Paste**, **Paste as New Image** command. If right-clicking is disabled on a page, maybe because the author doesn't want you to copy his pictures, use the **Print Scrn** key to copy the visible part of the page to the clipboard. Then in PSP use the **Edit**, **Paste**, **Paste as New Image** command and crop the image to what you want.

Using Drag and Drop

It may be quicker to arrange the two program windows alongside each other, left-click on the image and with the mouse button depressed drag it over the PSP working area. When the mouse button is released the picture will be placed in PSP for you to work on.

Saving a Web Image

As long as you can right-click on an image you can save it straight to your hard disc with the **Save Picture As** command.

Using PSP's Screen Capture

PSP has its own screen capture facility built in. You can take a screen capture, of all or part of the computer screen, and then edit and save it in the usual way. In fact, all the images in this book have been produced in this way. Before you capture screens you need to configure the screen capture options by using the **File**, **Import**, **Screen Capture**, **Setup** command to open the Capture Setup dialogue box.

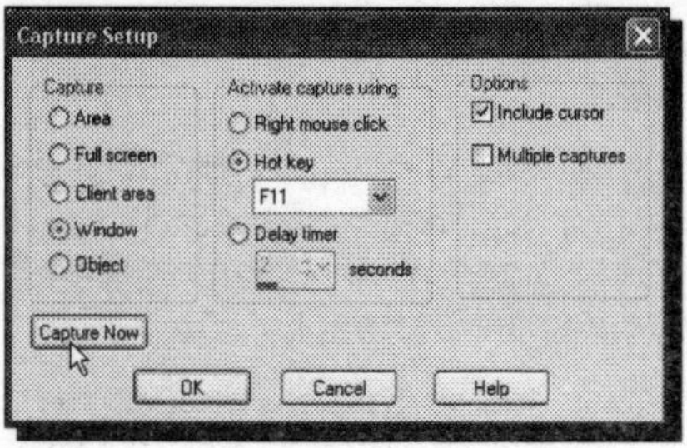

Fig. 9.3 The Capture Setup Box

In the **Capture** group box, select the type of capture, where **Area** captures an area of the screen that you select by clicking once at one corner of the area and again at the opposite corner. The other options should be fairly self explanatory. If not there is always the **Help** button. Once the options are set the actual capture is a two-stage process.

First, if the Capture Setup box is open, click the **Capture Now** button, if not, use the **File**, **Import**, **Screen Capture**, **Start** menu command (or the **Shift+C** shortcut) from PSP. These will all start the process by minimising PSP to the Windows Task bar so that you can find whatever it is you want to capture. When you are ready to capture a screen, or part of a screen, go to the second stage and activate the **Hot key** that you previously set up. In our case above, pressing the **F11** key at this stage would capture the screen or feature and re-open PSP with the captured image placed in it. All that remains is to edit the screen captures and save them to disc.

 If you do a lot of screen capturing, as we do, it is a good idea to add the **Capture Setup** and **Capture** buttons (shown here) to the Standard toolbar. If you need to, have a look at chapter 12. It is very much easier clicking these, than going three levels deep into the menu system!

Calibrating Your Monitor

To get the best results when working with photographs, you should check to see if your monitor needs calibration. This ensures that the monitor's brightness and contrast are optimised and that you are getting the most out of PSP.

This is easy to do, just go to the following page on the jasc.com Web site and follow the on-screen instructions, also given in Fig. 9.4 below.

www.jasc.com/support/customercare/articles/monitor.asp

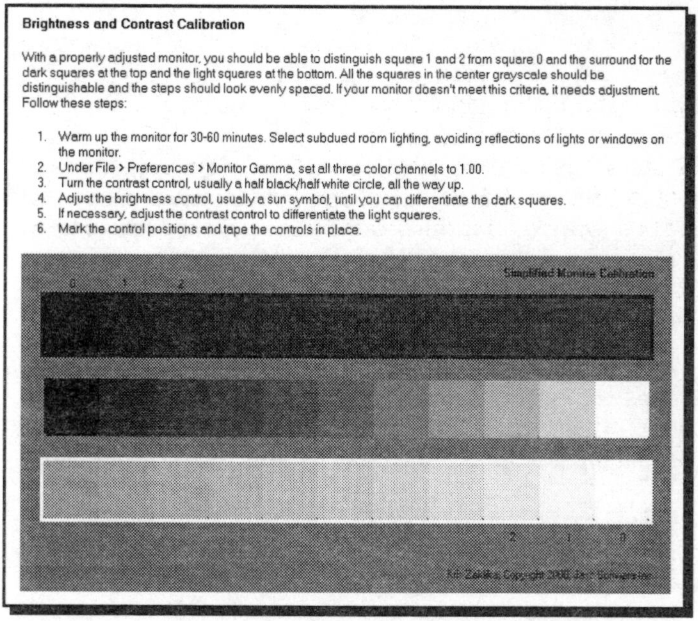

Fig. 9.4 Tool for Monitor Calibration

Basic Steps in Improving Photographs

Paint Shop Pro strongly recommend that whenever you work on improving photographs, you should follow the same set procedure to get the best results. This is because some of the editing procedures remove image data that may be needed in the earlier stages.

1 First improve colours, contrast, and saturation with PSP's automatic adjustment commands, followed if necessary by manual adjustments.

2 Correct defects caused by the image source, including unwanted patterns on scanned images.

3 Correct image defects, such as black or white specks, and image distortions caused by camera lenses.

4 Retouch photos, including removing scratches and red-eye effects on people and animals. During this step you can also remove unwanted highlights and objects from your photos.

5 Clarify and sharpen images.

When you are enhancing your photographs, we suggest you keep this list in mind, and until you can work through it without thinking, keep coming back and referring to it. We have it printed out on a sheet of paper for good measure!

For the rest of the chapter we will very briefly cover the tools built into PSP that you can use, but these will not necessarily be covered in the same order as the list.

Almost all of these tools open a specific PSP dialogue box for you to control the enhancement. If you aren't yet happy with the standard features of PSP dialogue boxes, have a look back at page 63, where they are all explained.

There are a lot of tools and some of them are quite complex, so you may well need to click the **Help** button a few times to get specific information about specific controls.

The Photo Toolbar

Most of your photo enhancement work can be carried out from the Photo toolbar, which is opened with the **View**, **Toolbars**, **Photo** menu command, or by right-clicking on the toolbar area and selecting **Toolbars**, **Photo** from the context menu.

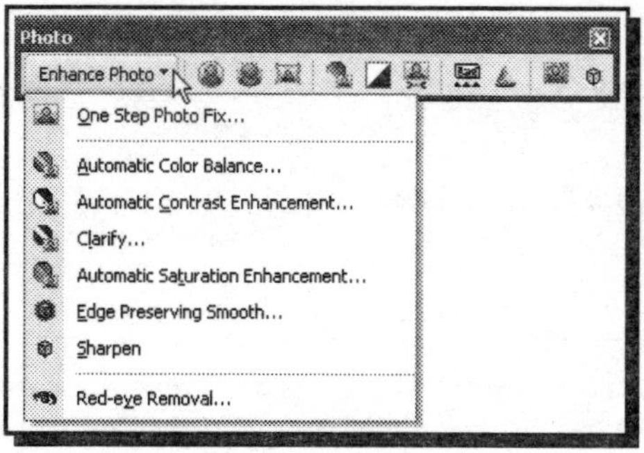

Fig. 9.5 The Photo Toolbar

The **Enhance Photo** button options are shown above in Fig. 9.5. The other Photo toolbar buttons have the following functions:

Button   *Function*

 Barrel distortion correction.

 Fisheye distortion correction.

 Pincushion distortion correction.

 Fade correction. Restores colour and contrast to faded photographic images.

Black and white points. Shifts all colours based on known true black and true white points.

Manual colour correction. Adjusts all colours based on the shift from a manually selected source colour to a selected target colour.

 Histogram adjustment. Uses graphs to adjust the contrast and colour balance of an image.

 Adjust HSL. Uses the Hue, Saturation and Lightness properties to shift all image colours and change their strength and lightness.

 JPEG artifact removal. Attempts to restore a JPEG image to its original appearance.

 Unsharp mask. Sharpens the mid- to high-contrast edges in an image without enhancing noise.

Most of these effects work only on greyscale and 16 million colour (24-bit) images. To increase the colour depth of an image, use the **Image**, **Increase Color Depth**, **16 Million Colors (24-bit)** menu command.

Automatic Photo Enhancement

Clicking the **Enhance Photo** button [Enhance Photo ▾] opens the drop-down menu shown in Fig. 9.5. We will work our way through the options on this menu.

▣ One-step Photo Fix

This is the first place to start if you want to enhance a photograph. Clicking this option starts a PSP script, or macro, that steps automatically through a sequence of enhancements. If you like the result, fine, that's all you need to do. If not, press the **Undo..** Standard toolbar button ⟲ to remove the unwanted enhancements.

You will then need to try the other automatic enhancement options in the Enhance Photo list, until you are happy with the result. If none of these work, you can go to the manual enhancement options on the rest of the Photo toolbar.

🔍 Automatic Color Balance

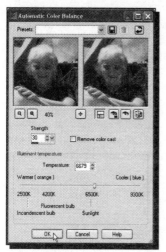

Fig. 9.6 The Automatic Color Balance Dialogue Box

This tool creates more natural colours and can remove any colour cast. As with most of these tools, you can apply the command to a selection or the entire image.

Adjust the **Strength** of correction until the image looks the most natural. The default starts with 30 as shown here.

You can adjust the **Illuminant temperature** for the image, from warmer tones (oranges) to cooler tones (blues). The default setting is 6500K, which gives the effect of a typical daylight photo.

Click the **OK** button to fix the enhancement.

🔍 Automatic Contrast Enhancement

Fig. 9.7 The Automatic Contrast Enhancement Box

Contrast is the variation of dark and light intensities within an image. There should be a good balance of highlights, midtones, and shadows.

To achieve this, adjust the Bias (brightness of the correction), Strength and Appearance options. (Flat is a slight difference between light and dark areas, Natural is an average difference, and Bold is a striking difference). Click **OK** to fix the enhancement.

📎 Clarify

Fig. 9.8 The Clarify Box

The Clarify command adds a sense of depth and clarity to the image, making hazy, foggy, or slightly out of focus images look clearer, as shown here in Fig. 9.8.

For **Strength of effect**, use the smallest value that gives a suitable result. Click the **OK** button to fix the enhancement.

Note. Clarify does not work if the image contains a selection.

📎 Automatic Saturation Enhancement

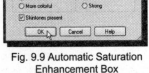

Fig. 9.9 Automatic Saturation Enhancement Box

Saturation is the vividness of colours due to the amount of grey in each colour. Saturated colours appear bright and brilliant, but de-saturated ones, such as pastel shades, appear subdued or washed-out. This command has no effect on greyscale images because they have no colour, but can be used on sepias.

The **Bias** setting adjusts the vividness of the corrected colours, whereas **Strength** adjusts the correction strength.

Check the **Skintones present** box if you have human skintones in the image. This gives people more natural colouring. Clear the check box if the image has few or no skintones.

When you are happy with your selections, click **OK** to fix the enhancement.

● Edge Preserving Smooth

Fig. 9.10 Edge Preserving
Smooth Dialogue Box

This tool removes noise in an image without losing edge details. It finds details such as object edges and preserves them, while smoothing the areas between the edges. You can preserve the edges of facial features while removing a blotchy complexion. You can also use the **Edge Preserving Smooth** tool to minimise film grain on a photograph.

Change the **Amount of smoothing** value until you get the result you want. Choose the smallest amount of smoothing that removes the specks while retaining image detail.

● Sharpen

This is the only tool on the Photo toolbar that does not open a dialogue box. When clicked it sharpens your image by increasing the contrast of adjacent pixels where there are significant colour contrasts.

● Red-eye Removal

Sometimes in a flash picture the eyes of people or animals look red. This is the result of the light from the flash reflecting off the eye's retina. With PSP this is no problem, you can easily use the Red-eye Removal command to return eyes to natural colours, or even to enhance or change eye colours. You always did want blue eyes, didn't you? This tool will not work if the image contains a selection.

To make the correction, click the **Red-eye Removal** button on the Photo toolbar, or use the **Adjust**, **Red-eye Removal** menu command. Both open the dialogue box shown in Fig. 9.11 on the next page.

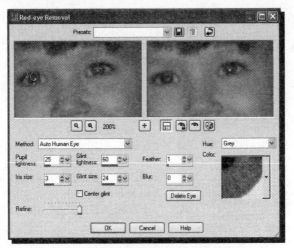

Fig. 9.11 Using the Red-eye Removal Tool

This dialogue box is slightly different from the others we have seen, as you use the right preview pane for panning the image, not the left. This is because the left preview pane is used to select the eyes to be treated. So use the **Navigate** button to centre the red eyes in the right preview window. You can obviously zoom in or out as necessary.

In the **Method** drop-down list, select the **Auto Human Eye** option as the correction method. This automatically selects the correction area using a circular selection and chooses settings appropriate to a human eye. If you want to know about the other options use the **Help** button.

In the left preview pane, automatically select the first eye to correct by clicking inside the red area of the eye. A circle appears around the selected area inside a square control box as shown in Fig. 9.11 above. The right preview pane displays the corrected eye.

Check that the circular selection is positioned and sized properly over the red area of the eye, if not just drag it to the correct position. You can even change the iris shape by dragging individual handles of the square control box. If necessary fine-tune the correction with the other settings. When you have done all the eyes click the **OK** button.

Manual Enhancement Tools

The manual tools we cover here are the ones with their own buttons on the Photo toolbar. These, and many others, can all be accessed from the **Adjust** menu. The first three are tools to correct camera lens deficiencies, which should be corrected before cropping the image.

Barrel Distortion Correction

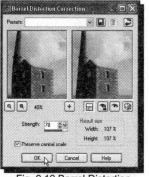

An image with barrel distortion has its sides bulging out at the centre, like a traditional beer barrel. Lines that should be straight are curved.

You adjust the **Strength** value until the distortion disappears. Look for lines in the image that are curved and adjust until they become straight, as with the chimney in Fig. 9.12. The image is re-sized as you adjust this value.

Fig. 9.12 Barrel Distortion Correction

Pincushion Distortion Correction

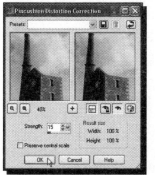

Pincushion distortion is the opposite, it has its sides curving in at the centre. Lines that should be straight are curved.

You adjust the **Strength** value until the distortion disappears. Look for lines in the image that are curved and adjust until they become straight, as with the chimney in Fig. 9.13. The image is re-sized as you adjust this value.

Fig. 9.13 Pincushion Distortion Correction

Fisheye Distortion Correction

An image with fisheye distortion looks a little bulbous. Straight lines are curved and the edges look compressed.

To make the correction, adjust the **Field of View** value until the distortion disappears.

If you play around with this tool on a normal photograph you can get some spectacular image distortion effects.

Fig. 9.14 Fisheye Distortion Correction

Fade Correction

We all know that photographs fade over time with exposure to light, especially sunlight. The dyes in a photograph fade, the colours become less vivid, and contrast is lost.

The **Fade Correction** tool can restore colour and contrast to faded photographic images. In Fig. 9.15 we are correcting an old school photograph which has seen far too much sunlight.

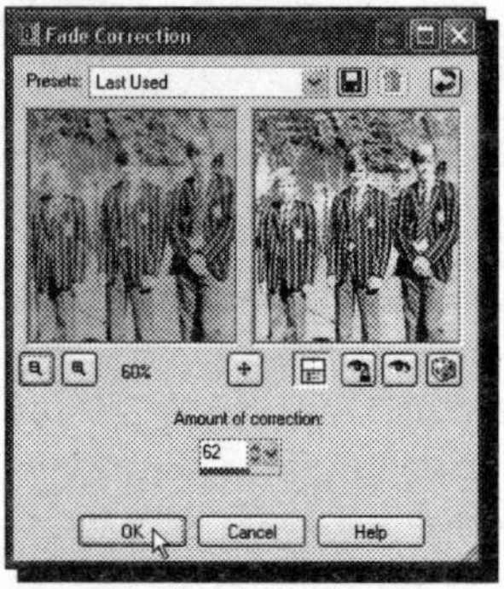

Fig. 9.15 The Fade Correction Dialogue Box

You set the **Amount of correction** value, starting at 45 and adjust it until the image looks the most natural. If you apply too much correction, highlight and shadow areas may lose detail and objects may blend together.

We must admit that we have usually found the automatic tools do such a good job with faded photographs that we very rarely need to use this tool. Your experiences may not be the same however.

Black and White Points

Sometimes the best way to correct a photo is to select those points that you know should be black or white and get PSP to shift all colours based on resetting these points to true black and true white. Hence the **Black and White Points** tool.

Fig. 9.16 The Black and White Points Dialogue Box

This dialogue box is similar to the Red-eye Removal box we saw earlier, in that you use the right preview pane for panning the image, not the left. This is because the left preview pane is used to select the colours. For each point that you want to correct, select the source point by clicking the colour's **Dropper** button, then click a colour in the left preview pane that you know should be the colour you are correcting (black, grey, or white).

You can also change a default colour by clicking the **Desired color** box and selecting a colour from the Color dialogue box that opens. To select a destination colour from the image window or the desktop, position the cursor over any **Desired color** box, press and hold the **Ctrl** key, move the cursor over the image or the desktop, and click a colour. To use a greyscale palette to select all destination colours, mark the **Balance to grey** check box.

To preserve the lightness of the source colour, mark the **Preserve lightness** check box, otherwise the lightness of the corrected image will match the target colour's lightness.

Like some of the other correction tools you will probably have to spend some time playing with the settings and colour selections before you get the best out of the Black and White Points command.

Manual Color Correction

Fig. 9.17 Using Selections

So far we have used the correction tools on the whole image, but for this example we want to change just the skin tones of the three boys, to give them back their tans. We used the **Freehand Selection** tool in the Add mode to select all their hands and faces as shown in Fig. 9.17.

Then we clicked the **Manual Color Correction** button on the Photo toolbar and panned and zoomed in to one of the faces, as shown in Fig. 9.18. We clicked the **Freehand**

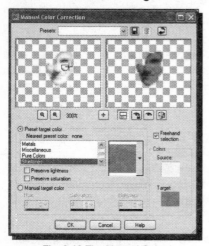

Fig. 9.18 The Manual Color Correction Dialogue Box

selection check box, and selected a small area of face in the left pane, as shown. PSP took an average of the colour inside the selection and showed it in the **Source Colors** box. We looked at the list of sample **Preset target colors** and selected 'Skintones'. Clicking the down-arrow to the right of this opened a window with a choice of 18 colour options. We chose one and it was

placed in the **Target Colors** box. Clicking the **OK** button completed the operation. If you select the **Manual target color** option you can enter a colour's **Hue**, **Saturation**, and **Lightness** (HSL) values to be very specific.

The **Preserve lightness** option preserves the lightness of the source colour in the corrected image, when checked. The **Preserve saturation** option preserves the saturation of the source colour in the corrected image, when selected. This is quite a powerful tool to play with.

Histogram Adjustment

You can use the **Histogram Adjustment** tool to adjust the contrast and colour balance of an image. It opens the Histogram Adjustment dialogue box, shown in Fig. 9.19. In this you can edit the luminance (lightness) and the red, green, and blue colour channels, one colour at a time.

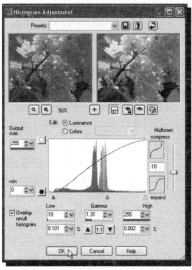

Fig. 9.19 The Histogram Adjustment Box

The graph in the Histogram Adjustment box displays how many pixels are at each value of the selected channel. The vertical axis represents the number of pixels, and ranges from zero pixels to the highest number of pixels in the graph. The horizontal axis represents the value from zero to 255 of the selected channel. When you change the histogram, the graph displays the adjusted histogram as red and the original histogram as grey.

This is a very complex tool which is really outside the remit of this book. If you want to know more about it, we suggest you study the several Help pages on it, or search for **histogram** on the Jasc Web site at:

www.jasc.com

Adjust HSL

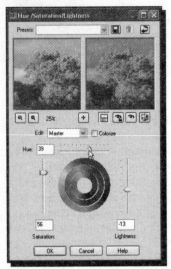

This tool shifts all the colours in an image and changes their strength and lightness. Dragging the **Hue** slider shifts all the pixels in an image around the colour wheel. Stop when the colours appear as you want them.

Dragging the **Saturation** slider adjusts the amount of grey in a colour. Drag it up to increase the saturation or down to decrease it, the level of grey increases as the saturation decreases.

Fig. 9.20 The Adjust HSL Box

Dragging the **Lightness** slider up will increase the image lightness, which increases the brightness of the image colours.

You can choose the colour range to adjust in the **Edit** drop-down list. To edit all colours simultaneously, as in Fig. 9.19, choose Master. To edit a specific colour range, choose between Reds, Yellows, Greens, Cyans, Blues, or Magentas. The colour rings in the middle of the box represent the colours in the image. The outer ring represents the original values and the inner ring the adjusted values.

The **Colorize** check box lets you quickly set the right-pane image to two-colour greyscale. You can then select a **Hue** and adjust the **Saturation** and **Lightness** values to 'colorize' the image.

If you know your way around the H, S and L numerical values, you can type them straight into their respective boxes. Every time a digit is placed, or removed, the whole dialogue box immediately updates.

JPEG Artifact Removal

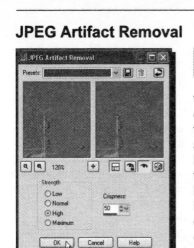

Fig. 9.21 Removing JPEG
Artifacts from an Image

JPEG, or **.jpg**, is a compressed image format used a lot on the Internet. When you convert a file to the **.jpg** format you can control the amount of compression. The higher the value, the smaller the file size produced, but at high compression values the image quality degrades. This can produce haloes, or colour leakage beyond the edges of objects, blocky areas with checkerboard effects in large areas of plain colours. These are known as JPEG artifacts, and can be seen in the left pane of Fig. 9.21.

The **JPEG Artifact Removal** tool can be used to help restore an image with such problems to its original appearance. Help, is the operative word here, as JPEG compression discards image information, so there are limits to how well the image can be restored.

Make sure the image has no selections, or the tool will not work, then open it by clicking its button on the Photo toolbar, shown above, or with the **A̲djust**, **Add/Remove N̲oise**, **J̲PEG Artifact Removal** menu command.

Try each **Strength** option and examine the image to see which setting works best. The worst artifact effects are usually around strong edges in the image, especially where they appear against the sky. So these are the first places to look.

Set the **Crispness** value to determine the amount of detail that is restored. Start with 50 and adjust until the image looks the most natural. Excessive crispness may produce fine dots in the image. A useful tool but it cannot work magic, once parts of an image are lost, they are lost!

Unsharp Mask

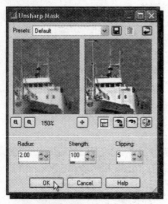

The last button on the Photo toolbar opens the **Unsharp Mask**, which in spite of its name, is another way in PSP to sharpen up an image, as shown here in Fig. 9.22. It sharpens the mid- to high-contrast edges in the image without enhancing noise, by locating adjacent pixels that have a difference in lightness values (that you specify) and increasing their contrast by an amount that you also specify.

Fig. 9.22 Using the Unsharp Mask to Sharpen an Image

As well as clicking the above Photo toolbar button, you can also use the **Adjust**, **Sharpness**, **Unsharp Mask** menu command to access this tool.

The **Radius** option sets the number of pixels to adjust around each edge. Values of between 0.5 and 2 seem to work best. The **Strength** option sets the amount of contrast to increase in the image's pixels. Increase this gradually from a low level until you get the optimum effect. **Clipping** sets the difference in lightness values that adjacent pixels must have before they are sharpened.

As with all of these tool dialogue boxes, clicking the OK button will fix the image with the current effect settings.

Retouching Photographs

There are several ways in PSP to retouch images to remove such things as scratches and blemishes. When you are doing this type of work it is safest to always work on a copy of your photographic image. Then, if it all goes wrong, you can always start again. Our example in Fig. 9.23 is part of a scan of a very old photograph. We will use several techniques to remove its very obvious blemishes.

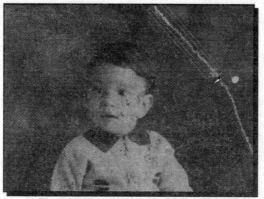

Fig. 9.23 An Image Ripe for Retouching

The Scratch Remover Tool

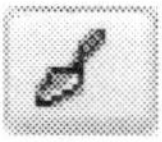

The large scratch is the most obvious blemish, but with PSP this is by far the easiest to rectify. On the Tools toolbar, probably hiding under the **Clone** tool, is the **Scratch Remover** tool button, shown here. As you might expect, this is used for removing scratches and lines from photographs, but only on the Background layer.

To use the tool, click its button, and select a **Width** and a **Selection boxes** shape for the tool in the Tool Options palette, shown in Fig. 9.24.

Fig. 9.24 The Scratch Remover Tool Options

Choose a width that is about 3 or 4 pixels wider than the scratch, so as not to lose image detail. Centre the cursor just outside one end of the scratch, then click and drag the bounding box over the scratch, as shown in Fig. 9.23 on the previous page. You should position the box so that the inner edges surround, but do not touch, the scratch. When the rectangle encloses the scratch, or part of it in our case, release the mouse button and that section of the scratch is removed. Just like magic.

Click the **Undo** button on the Standard toolbar if you are not happy and try selecting again but with a different tool width.

The Salt and Pepper Filter

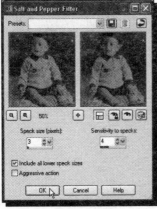

Fig. 9.25 Using the Salt and Pepper Filter

To try and remove the other blemishes automatically we could use the Salt and Pepper filter, opened with the **Adjust**, **Add/Remove Noise**, **Salt And Pepper Filter** menu command. This removes multiple-pixel black or white specks from an image, such as those caused by dust on film. It compares an area of pixels to the surrounding pixels and adjusts any areas that it considers to be specks to match the surroundings.

The **Speck size** option sets the minimum size, in pixels, of the largest speck that can be completely removed. **Sensitivity to specks** sets how different an area must be from its surrounding pixels to be considered a speck. It is usually best to select **Include all lower speck sizes** as it seems to produce better results that way. The **Aggressive** option is more likely to remove blemishes, but it can also blur some image features.

Using the Smudge Tool

 In the previous example, the automatic filter did not completely remove the blemishes from the photograph. We find the **Smudge** tool is the best tool to use for jobs like this, even though a little work is needed. This tool is on the default Tools toolbar, in the group on the ninth button down from the top.

It is a clever tool which you drag in small circles (as if you were using a rubber) over a blemish. It spreads colour and image details from the starting point and picks up new colour and image details as it moves.

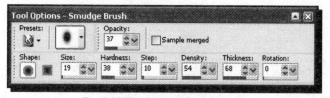

Fig. 9.26 The Smudge Tool Options

If you select the correct Tool Options, you can make blemishes blend in with the image background. We have found the settings shown in Fig. 9.26 to work well.

Fig. 9.27 Using the Smudge Tool

Applying Effects to Photographs

Paint Shop Pro has many special effects (or filters) that you can apply to your images, including 3D, artistic, geometric, illumination, reflection, and texture effects as can be seen in the listing in Fig. 9.28 below. The easiest way to explore and then apply them is with the Effect Browser, opened with the **Effects**, **Effect Browser** command.

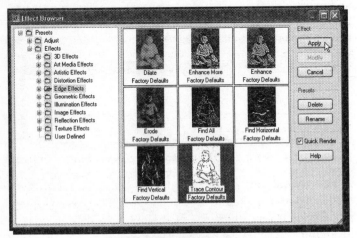

Fig. 9.28 The Effect Browser

The left panel gives you access to any Presets saved on your hard disc, and to all the tools in the Adjust and Effects menus. To preview the effects, click one of the folders (such as Edge Effects in the above figure).

To select an effect, click the thumbnail image in the right panel and then do one of the following. To apply the selected effect to the current image, click the **Apply** button. To open the effect's dialogue box click the **Modify** button, as long as it is not greyed out.

This is a superb feature of PSP 8, which really makes it easy to handle the hundreds of filters supplied with the package. Happy effecting!

10

Introducing Vectors

As we saw on page 65, vector images are object orientated and contain mathematical information on the shape, position, colour, etc., of all the objects making up the image. Vectors produce much smaller file sizes for most graphics, except photographs. They are also very easy to edit, reshape and change colour, since each object can be treated separately.

Why Use Vectors?

If you are working with mainly solid colour objects, manipulated text, or many small objects, once you have mastered the techniques, using vectors will save you time. Vector objects can be modified very easily, and can be re-sized or altered over and over again with no degradation in image quality. As long as you save your image as a **.Pspimage** file, you can modify its contained vector objects at any time in the future.

If you are working in any of the following areas you should seriously consider using vector objects:

Animations - You can make multiple copies of a complex object, or group, and reshape each copy to create different frames in an animation.

Designing logos - Create your logo using text and other objects grouped together. You can then change its content, size and colours whenever you like.

Web page interfaces - Ideal for creating different coloured versions of button sets, logos and interfaces for Web pages.

The Vector Tools

The tools you use to create and work with vectors are all located at the bottom of the PSP 8 Tools toolbar.

 Text tool - As we saw in Chapter 8 this is mainly used to create vector text, but it can also create raster text. We will not look at this again.

 Preset Shape tool - As we saw on page 175 this tool is used to draw both raster and vector objects such as rectangles, ellipses, etc., with line (foreground) and fill (background) colours and materials.

 Pen tool - In earlier versions of PSP this was known as the Drawing Tool. It is the key tool for working with Vectors, and is used to draw and edit single lines, freehand lines, Bezier curves, and point to point lines. This tool needs to be activated to use vector node functions (see later).

 Object Selection tool - This tool is used only on vector layers to select vector text and objects that you want to edit, move, place in a group, align, distribute or arrange on the canvas.

The Objects Menu - This in itself is not a tool, but it has many of the same options as the **Pen** and **Object Selection** tools (see page 25). All of its menu items are only available when a vector layer is active and a vector object is selected.

Some Definitions

Boring as it may seem we have to look at some PSP definitions of the parts that make up vector objects.

Object - An object is anything you create on a vector layer with the **Pen** or **Preset Shape** tool. Each object is represented by its own bounding box, as shown in Fig. 10.1. An object has properties you can control such as line style and fill colour. Each object contains one path made up of contours and nodes.

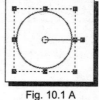

Fig. 10.1 A Circle Object

Path - An object contains one path. The path is all the contours in an object. The properties of the path are controlled by the object's properties. A path's direction flows from its start to its end point. The circle object in Fig. 10.2 has one contour and a closed path with a clockwise direction, as shown.

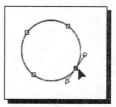

Fig. 10.2 A Circle in Node Edit Mode

Contour - A path contains at least one contour. A contour contains at least one line segment. A contour's direction flows from its start to its end point. A contour can also be open or closed. The contours in a path do not need to be connected. Some of a contour's properties

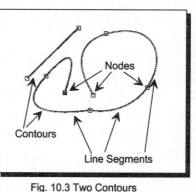

Fig. 10.3 Two Contours

are controlled by its object's properties (e.g. line style, fill colour, anti-aliasing). The shape of a contour is controlled by the type and location of its nodes.

Node - A contour contains at least two nodes. A node is a point on a contour that defines the contour's shape at that point.

Line Segment - The straight or curved line between two nodes is a line segment.

Creating Vector Shapes

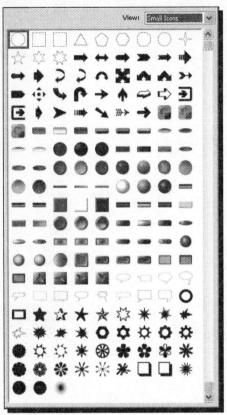

Fig. 10.4 The Shape List Drop-down Box

PSP 8 comes with a vast array of 'Preset' shapes for you to work with in your images. These are all shown in Fig. 10.4, and as we shall see, are very easy to place and work with.

First create a new blank image, of maybe 500 x 300 pixels with a white background.

Click the **Preset Shapes** tool button on the Tools toolbar, or if you can remember it, the **P** key on the keyboard, to activate the **Preset Shapes** tool. On the Tool Options palette, shown in Fig. 10.5 on the next page, select 'Star 2' from the Shape List and make sure the **Create as vector**, **Retain style**, and **Anti-alias** options are ticked as shown.

Many of the Preset shapes in the above listing have colours and other properties built into them. When the **Retain style** check box is ticked this is how they are placed in your image. If it is unchecked, the shape takes its colours from those in the Materials palette.

Fig. 10.5 The Tool Options Palette for Preset Shapes

Create a star shape by dragging the $^+\square$ pointer to get the shape you want. If you depress the **Shift** key while dragging,

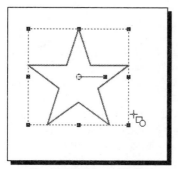

Fig. 10.6 A Selected Object

you can keep the height and width of the shape proportional. (This is how you draw squares and circles). To place the centre of the shape where you first click, right-click and drag the $^+\square$ pointer. Releasing the pointer will place the shape as a vector object on your image canvas, as shown in Fig. 10.6. Note that it is surrounded by a red dashed line box with red solid square 'handles' and a centre rotation handle, offset from the centre position. These handles allow you to change the shape and size of the object as a whole, and to rotate it around its centre.

Manipulating Shapes

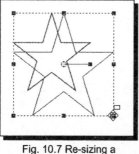

Fig. 10.7 Re-sizing a Vector Object

To re-size vector objects use either of the **Preset Shape**, or **Object Selection** tools to select it, as shown in Fig. 10.6. Move the pointer over a corner or edge handle and when it changes to a $\square$ shape, click and drag the handle, as shown in Fig. 10.7.

To keep the proportions the same, right-click and drag a corner handle.

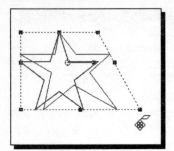

Fig. 10.8 Reshaping
Asymmetrically

To reshape a vector object **asymmetrically**, with the **Shift** key depressed, move the pointer over a corner handle and when it changes to a ✥ shape, click and drag the handle, as shown in Fig. 10.8.

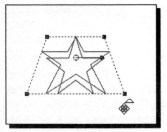

Fig. 10.9 Reshaping
Symmetrically

To reshape a vector object **symmetrically**, with the **Ctrl** key depressed, move the pointer over a corner handle and when it changes to a ✥ shape, click and drag the handle, as shown in Fig. 10.9.

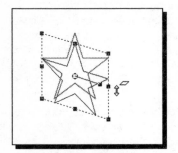

Fig. 10.10 Reshaping with
Shear perspective

To reshape a vector object with a **Shear** perspective, with the **Shift** key depressed, move the pointer over a side handle and when it changes to a ⇕ shape, click and drag the handle, as shown in Fig. 10.10.

You can also reshape a vector object with a '**Distort**' perspective, by holding down both the **Shift** and **Ctrl** keys, and moving the pointer over a handle, when it changes to a ✥ shape, click and drag the handle. We will let you find the shape this one produces.

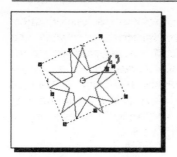

Fig. 10.11 Rotating
a Vector Shape Object

To **rotate** a vector object, first select it with the **Object Selection** tool, move the pointer over the centre rotation handle and when the pointer changes to a shape, click and drag the handle, as shown in Fig. 10.11.

To change the centre of rotation, press the **Ctrl** key while clicking and dragging the rotation pivot point to a new location.

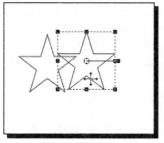

Fig. 10.12 Moving
a Vector Shape Object

To **move** a vector object, first select it with the **Object Selection** tool, then move the pointer over one of the shape lines and when the pointer changes to a ⊹ shape, click and drag the object to its new position, as shown in Fig. 10.12.

You can also have very fine control when moving vector objects. To move the object one pixel at a time, hold the **Shift** key down and press the ⇧, ⇩, ⇨, or ⇦ arrow keys.

Copying Vector Objects

As you might expect with PSP being a Windows program, you can cut, copy, and paste vector objects just like any other data. You first select the object and from the **Edit** menu, select **Cut** or **Copy**, or use the Standard toolbar buttons, as described on page 93. Both commands place the object on the clipboard, but **Cut** removes the original, while **Copy** leaves it intact.

Use the **Edit**, **Paste**, **As New Vector Selection** command, the **Paste vector data** button if you have placed it on your toolbar, or press **Ctrl+G**, to paste the contents of the clipboard as a vector object into the current vector layer. The new object is placed with a pointer arrow in it for you to drag to where you want in the image, as shown in Fig. 10.13. Just click the left mouse button to place it on your canvas as a selected object, as in Fig. 10.14 below.

Fig. 10.13

You can also use any of the other paste commands described on page 94, depending on where you want to place the object.

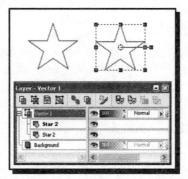

Fig. 10.14 An Object Pasted as a New Vector Selection

Fig. 10.14 shows that each object placed on a vector layer has its own entry in the Layer palette. You can click this to select the object in the image.

Working with Several Objects

When you have multiple vector objects on a layer in an image, there are several ways you can manipulate them together, such as grouping, aligning, distributing, positioning and arranging them. These commands are all available on the **Objects** menu, but first you must select each object.

To do this you use the **Object Selection** tool and with the **Shift** key depressed click the 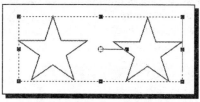 pointer on the path of each object you want to include in the group to manipulate.

A bounding box is placed around all the objects which are currently selected, as shown in Fig. 10.15.

Fig. 10.15 Two Objects Selected

You can then use the **Align**, **Distribute**, **Make Same Size** and **Arrange** commands, from the **Objects** menu to manipulate all the selected objects together.

Grouping Objects

When you select several objects, as discussed above, you can only manipulate them as one when they are actually selected. As soon as you click elsewhere in your image the group selection will be cancelled.

To keep several objects together you need to group them. Say you have made a cartoon character out of several different vector object shapes, you would group them so that you could manipulate your character as a whole. When objects are grouped, you can move, re-size, reshape, and change their lines and materials all at once, as shown in Fig. 10.16 below.

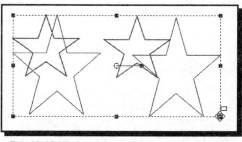

Fig. 10.16 Moving a Small Group of Two Objects

To create a group you first select all the objects to be included with the **Object Selection** tool, and then on the Tool Options palette, click **Group** as pointed to in Fig. 10.17, or use the **Objects**, **Group** command. Even if an object belongs to a group, you can still select it on the Layer palette and edit it individually.

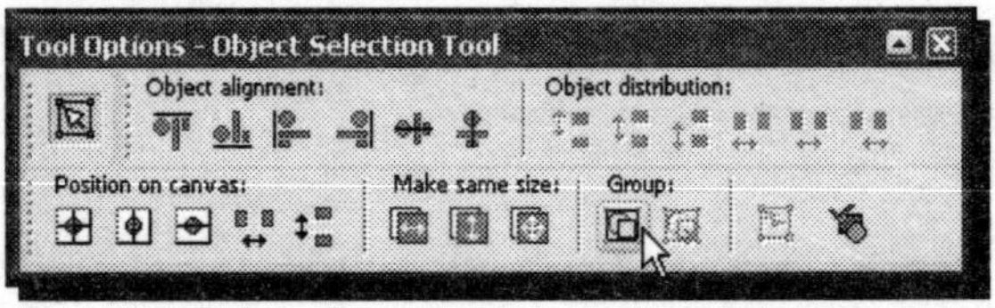

Fig. 10.17 The Object Selection Tool Options Palette

To ungroup all the objects in a group, select the group and use the **Objects**, **Ungroup** command, or click the **Ungroup** button on the **Object Selection** tool's Tool Options palette. To remove a single object from a group you open the Layers palette, select the object and drag it to another layer.

Object Properties

We mentioned earlier that every object has a set of properties. To see these, select the vector object with the **Object Selection** tool, and then on the Tool Options palette, click the **Properties** button ⬚, or use the **Objects**, **Properties** menu command. Both of these open the Property dialogue box, shown in Fig. 10.18 below.

Fig. 10.18 An Object with its Vector Property Box

This dialogue box gives you a very easy way to edit a vector object's properties, as you can change all the settings, and see the effect immediately in your object.

You can set the object's line options, such as **Stroke width**, **Join**, **Miter**, **Line style**, and **Anti-alias**. Just change these to see the resulting effects. If the **Stroke** check box is selected the shape will have a line outlining it. You can pick a colour for the line from the Material box by clicking in the colour box below. The **Fill** properties control the inside of the shape in a similar way. You clear the **Fill** check box to choose no fill.

In Fig. 10.18, on the previous page, we chose the 'Duotone bright green' gradient from the Materials box as the fill. This is a fun dialogue box, which we recommend you spend some time with.

Once you have your shape looking exactly how you want don't forget to save it. As long as you save your image as a **.Pspimage** file, you can modify its contained vector objects at any time in the future. This is the only file format that retains vector layers. With other file formats, such as **.jpg** or **.gif**, PSP converts all the layers to one raster image. Any vector objects are not lost, but you will no longer be able to edit them as vectors.

Of course if you won't ever need to edit your creation as a vector, you can also merge, or flatten, the vector layers (see page 146). Your image will then be a raster image and you will be able to use all the other tools on the Tools toolbar to further edit it.

Drawing Lines

 With PSP 8 you use the **Pen** tool to draw and edit lines and, if you like create custom shapes, in three different ways. You can draw straight lines, curved lines, and freehand lines, depending on the **Segment type** settings in the Tool Options palette.

Fig. 10.19 The Pen Tool Options Palette

To draw lines, set the foreground material style to the colour you want and the background material to transparent (in the Materials palette). Choose the **Pen** tool on the Tools toolbar, and on the Tool Options palette shown in Fig. 10.19, select **Create as vector**, and click the **Drawing Mode** button , followed by the **New** button . You can set the **Line style**, **Width**, **Join**, **Miter limit**, and **Anti-alias**.

Then select a **Segment type** to draw with depending on the type of line you want, as described in the following sections. With **Freehand** and **Line Segment** line types, mark the **Contiguous** check box to connect each node you draw to form one contour, or clear it to draw unconnected line segments or multiple contours.

Drawing with Straight Lines

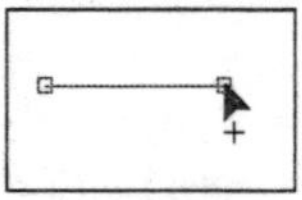

Click the **Line Segments** button on the Pen Tool Options palette. Click and drag the pointer from the line starting point to the location of the next node, then release the mouse button, as shown in Fig. 10.20. To

Fig. 10.20

extend the line just click, drag, and release again. Every time you do this you create another line segment between two nodes. If you hold the **Shift** key down as you drag, you can draw lines at fixed 45-degree increments. Whenever you want to start a new line, click the **New** button .

Curved and Straight Lines

Click the **Point to Point** button 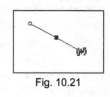 on the Pen Tool Options palette. Click and drag the pointer at the start point. When the direction of your line is correct, release the mouse button, as in Fig. 10.21. What you do next depends on the type of line you are drawing.

Fig. 10.21

To create a **straight line**, click where you want the next node. To add extra straight segments just click where you want their nodes to be. Fig. 10.22 shows 4 straight segments bounded by their 5 node points. The $\blacktriangleright_{END}$ pointer indicates the last node that was placed.

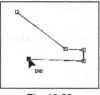

Fig. 10.22

To create a **curved line**, or Bezier curve, click and drag. When the curve is the right shape, release the mouse button. The shape of the curve is determined by the length and direction of each node's control arms, as shown in Fig. 10.23. To add extra curved segments just click and drag until each curved segment is correct. With a little practice this does get easier, we assure you.

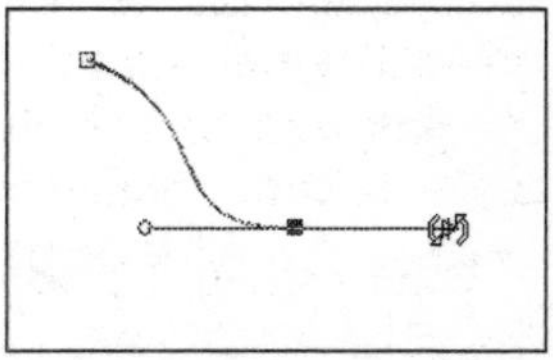

Fig. 10.23 A Bezier Curve

Drawing Freehand Lines

Click the **Freehand** button 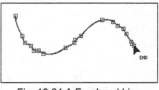 on the Pen Tool Options palette. Click and drag the cursor along the path you want the line to take and then release the mouse. A contour is drawn that matches the path, as in Fig. 10.24. As you can see, PSP places nodes along the drawn contour. You can control the spacing of these nodes with the **Curve**

Fig. 10.24 A Freehand Line

Tracking option on the **Pen** Tool Options palette. High values create smoother but less precise lines. Lower values create more nodes but more precise lines.

If ever you want to convert a raster image to a vector one, maybe to create cartoon characters for instance, you would have to 'trace' image lines as contours using this Freehand technique. It can be done, but it needs both practice and patience.

Don't forget that the **Pen** tool can create multiple contours in an object. If you don't click the **New** button 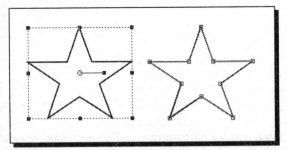 whenever you want a new contour, any separate line segments you draw will be one object.

Vector Nodes

In PSP you can also use the **Pen** tool to edit and manipulate the nodes of a vector object to control its overall shape. To explain how nodes work we need an object open. If necessary, create a new shape object, maybe a star like ours in Fig. 10.25. When an object is selected (with its bounding box around it) as soon as you click the **Pen** tool button the tool is put into **Edit mode** and the vector object displays as an outline with its nodes as hollow squares, as shown on the right in Fig. 10.25 below.

Fig. 10.25 An Object - Selected (Left) and in Node Edit Mode (Right)

In Edit mode you use the **Pen** tool to work on the nodes. If you click on a node it is selected and turns to solid red.

The pointer ▶ changes to a
▶⊕ shape and you can
drag the node to reshape
the object, as shown in
Fig. 10.26. When you let
the cursor go the node will
stay where it was dragged.

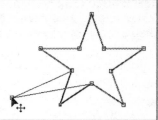

If you move the ▶ pointer
over the contour of the

Fig. 10.26 Dragging a Node

object it changes to a ▶~ shape
and you can then drag the whole
object to relocate it in your image,
as shown in Fig. 10.27.

Right-clicking the pointer on a
node opens the context menu
system shown in Fig. 10.28
below. Here the **Edit** menu
options are shown, which we shall
look at in a little more detail. The

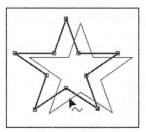

Fig. 10.27 Moving
an Object

Cut option removes a selected contour and places it on the

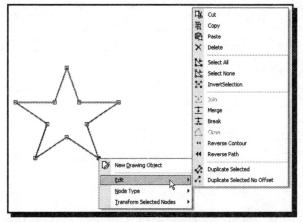

Fig. 10.28 The Right-click Edit Menu Options for a Selected Node

clipboard. **Copy** just places a selected contour on the
clipboard, and **Paste** places a contour from the clipboard
into the object. **Delete** just removes the selected nodes.

Select All will select all the nodes. **Select None** will deselect any selected nodes. **Invert Selection** will invert the selection of nodes by deselecting any selected nodes and selecting the rest.

Join lets you join two contours, **Merge** removes the nodes from a contour but keeps the line segments on each side, **Break** breaks a contour, and **Close** adds a line segment to close an open contour, **Reverse Contour** changes the direction of a single contour, **Reverse Path** changes the direction of all the contours in an object, **Duplicate Selected** pastes a copy of the selected contours on top of the originals with a 10 pixel offset, and **Duplicate Selected No Offset** pastes a copy of the selected contours on top of the originals.

More on Nodes

As we saw above, to make node selections you must have the **Pen** tool active and be in edit mode (click the **Edit Mode** button ▷ on the Pen Tool Options palette).

To select one node, you just click it with the **Pen** tool pointer. To deselect a node, click it with the **Shift** key depressed. To select multiple nodes, depress the **Shift** key and click each node in turn. You can also click and drag a rectangle over all the nodes you want selected. To select all the nodes on a contour, double-click one node. To select all the nodes in an object press **Ctrl+A** or use the **Select All** context menu command described above.

It is very easy to add a node to a contour. To do this, place the pointer over the contour where you want the new node. The pointer will change to a ▶ shape when it is over the contour. Pressing the **Ctrl** key will change the pointer to the ▶ shape and clicking this will add the new node.

If you are following this in PSP, you will notice that the pointer changes to the ▶ shape when a new node is added. If you press the **Ctrl** key with the pointer on a selected node you can then click to carry out a merge operation and remove the node but keep the line segments on each side.

Node Types

There are four different types of nodes, as we shall see later. The node type determines the 'behaviour' of the line segments before and after the node. To tell what type of node you have, place your cursor over it, and look on the status bar at the bottom of the screen.

It will look something like this, where 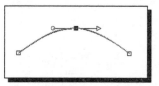 'Base Node' means the node is neither the start or the end point of the contour. 'Cusp, Line' gives you the node type and in this case shows it has lines before and after it. The (394.50, 377.69) entry shows the node's co-ordinates on the canvas.

Fig. 10.29 Node Type Menu

You can also find the node type by right-clicking the pointer on a node and choosing **Node Type** from the context menu that opens, shown in Fig. 10.28.

The current node and line segment types will be greyed out, as here in Fig. 10.29, which shows the **Node Type** context menu for the node whose status bar entry is shown above. It shows that the node is of Cusp type, with lines before and after it, rather than curves.

When they are being edited, nodes have up to two control arms coming from them, as shown in the following figures. The length and orientation of these arms determine the shape of the contour at the node. Basically you just drag their handles to get the line shape you want.

Fig. 10.30 Symmetrical Node

Symmetrical

The path is a smooth curve on each side of the node. The control arms are always equal in length and always maintain a straight line. If you adjust one arm it is mirrored in the other.

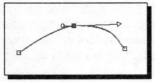

Fig. 10.31 Asymmetrical Node

Asymmetrical
Again the path is a smooth curve on each side of the node, but with differing curves on each side. The control arms move independently, and can have different lengths, but they always maintain a straight line.

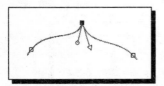

Fig. 10.32 A Cusp Node

Cusp
This type is used to define a sharp change of direction in the path. The control arms move independently and need not maintain any relation to each other. If there are line segments on both sides of the node, there will be no control handles. If there is a line segment on one side of the node, with a curved segment on the other, there will be one handle. This is then similar to the smooth node with the single control handle, but unlike the smooth node, the control handle's direction does not have to follow the direction of the line.

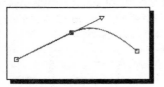

Fig. 10.33 A Smooth Node

Smooth
This type has a curve segment on one side of the node, and a line segment on the other. It allows a curve to bend seamlessly with a line. It has a single handle, on the curve side of the node, like a tangent, as in Fig. 10.33. The direction of the control handle is always the same as the direction of the line.

Like many other parts of this enormous package, you can read about this all you like, but it will only start to come together if you open PSP and try everything out. Not just our examples, for what they are, but try out all the combinations of everything.

As an example of how important node types are, try the following. Use the **Preset Shape** tool to draw a triangle or a star. Click the **Pen** tool button to open the tool in Edit mode and double-click on one of the nodes to select them all. Very simple stuff so far.

Now for the clever bit. Right-click on one of the selected nodes and choose **Node Type, Symmetric** from the context menu. This makes a tremendous change to the star, as shown in Fig. 10.34 below.

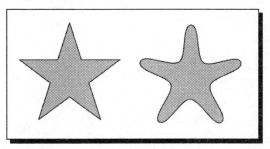

Fig. 10.34 A Star with Cusp Nodes (Left) and Symmetric Nodes (Right)

We almost have the start point here for a cartoon man. A few more nodes added, a few shape changes...

If you have read this far you may well want to try your hand at making vector cartoon characters. A good place to look is at **www.ronstoons.com**, as shown below.

Fig. 10.35 An Image from Ronstoons.com

Using Knife Mode

If you click the **Knife Mode** button 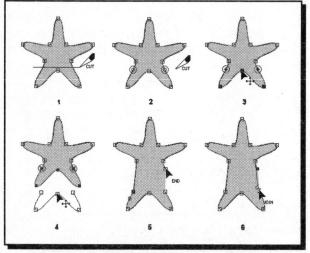 on the **Pen** Tool Options palette, you can cut a contour up as shown below.

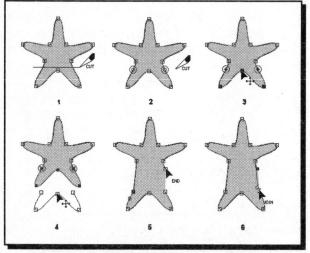

Fig. 10.36 Cutting a Contour using Knife Mode

You drag the knife pointer across the contour where you want to cut it, as in '1' above, the ⊛ markers in '2' show that PSP has cut the contour and added nodes to each cut end. In '3' we double-clicked a node to select all the nodes in the bottom contour and in '4' we dragged this to a new location.

Joining Contours

The last two stages of Fig. 10.36 show how easy it is to join contours, as long as they are in the same object. You simply drag the start or end node of one contour onto the start or end node of the other. When the pointer shows 'JOIN', as in '6' above, release the mouse button to complete the operation.

Hopefully you should now know your way around the vector tools of PSP. How much further you go will be up to you!

11

Using Scripts

With version 8, Paint Shop Pro has been equipped with the facility of using scripts, what we have always called macros. These are automated procedures that you can run time after time on any of your images. Most things you can do to an image can be included in a script, as we shall see.

Python Programming

PSP scripting is based on the powerful Python programming language, which is an interpreted, interactive, object-oriented programming language often compared to Perl, or Java. To find out more about this go to the following Web site:

http://www.python.org/

Fig. 11.1 A Composite of the Python Home Page

If you want to use Python to write scripts from scratch, you will need to get the documentation and look at tutorials on this Web site, as we do not have the space here. PSP includes a script recorder, which is all you really will need.

The Script Toolbar

Most of the scripting functions are accessed from the Script toolbar, alternatively you can use the **File**, **Script** menu.

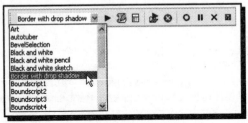

Fig. 11.2 The Script Toolbar

The **Select Script** button opens a drop-down list as shown above in Fig. 11.2, containing the scripts saved, by default, in PSP 8's Trusted and Restricted Scripts folders. The other Script toolbar buttons have the following functions:

Button ***Function***

 Run Selected Script - Runs the script displayed in the Select Script drop-down list.

 Edit Selected Script - Edit the script displayed in the Select Script drop-down list.

 Interactive Script Playback Toggle - Switches between Silent and Interactive mode when running scripts. When the button shows a border, it is set to Interactive mode, as here.

 Run Script - Opens and runs a script from any folder on your computer or a disc.

Stop Script - Stops the current script running.

Start Script Recording - Starts the recording actions to create a script.

 Pause Script Recording - Pauses recording of a script.

Cancel Script Recording - Cancels script recording.

Save Script Recording - Stops recording and saves the actions you have recorded.

Looking at a Script

As we saw in the last section, PSP has included quite a number of scripts with version 8. Before recording any of your own it's a good idea to have a look at some of these. Near the top of the list in Fig. 11.2 is a script called 'Border with Drop Shadow'. To see what it does, choose it in the **Select Script** box and click the **Edit Selected Script** button to open the Script Editor box shown here in Fig. 11.3.

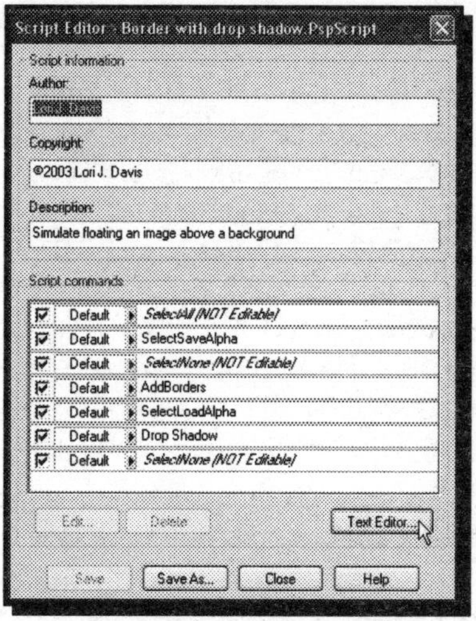

Fig. 11.3 The Script Editor

This shows who wrote the script and gives a **Description** of it, followed by a listing of the commands in the script. If these don't mean much to you worry not, the next figure will mean even less! Clicking the **Text Editor** button opens the script into your text editor, usually Notepad, as shown in Fig. 11.4.

Fig. 11.4 A Sample of Python Script Coding

Since scripts are text files they can be edited with any text editor. Python uses indentation to determine scoping, so be careful about mixing spaces and tabs. If you intend to hand write scripts you would be better using a Python aware editor. If not, just shudder and carry on below!

Running a Script

The 'Border with Drop Shadow' script contains 3 commands which involve dialogue boxes, shown by the lines which do not contain the text '[NOT Editable]' in Fig. 11.3.

Scripts can be run interactively or silently. When run silently all dialogue boxes are skipped and the commands in the script are executed automatically. In interactive mode all of the dialogue boxes are displayed, and you can change the settings in them, before they are executed. The **Interactive Script Playback Toggle** button 🔲 on the toolbar controls this. Clicking this button so that it has no dark border will set the script to run in silent mode. To run the macro, first open a favourite image, and then click the **Run Selected Script** ▶ Script toolbar button.

Fig. 11.5 The Result of Running the Script

This must be the easiest way to give an image a professional drop shadow effect. If you want to make changes to the border or drop shadow, click the **Undo** button , then toggle the **Interactive Script Playback Toggle** button , and run the script again, making any changes you want in the dialogue boxes that open.

Now your appetite is whetted we expect you will spend a few hours looking at the other built-in scripts. Have fun.

Beware of Viruses

Be careful if you get scripts from other people, or download them from the Internet, as Python is a full programming language, and can be used to execute malicious scripts. By default, PSP operates in a restricted execution mode which will not let it execute most of the **File** and **Export** menu options, which could potentially damage your PC setup.

When PSP was installed it included two specific folder sets for storing scripts. **Scripts-Restricted** for storing scripts that you need to be extra careful with, and **Scripts-Trusted** for the ones you are sure of. Make sure that you only place 'unknown' scripts in the **Scripts-Restricted** folder.

Recording a Script

Before starting to make your own script it is as well to work out exactly what commands and settings you want to include in it. Once the recording starts, the script recorder will record all the actions taken, so you don't want to be making mistakes at that stage.

As a useful exercise we will create a script that duplicates an open image and closes the original. You can then work on the duplicate without any danger of spoiling the original image. This is a very simple script, but it should demonstrate how it's done. The command sequence is:

1   **Window**, **Duplicate**
2   Select original image
3   **File**, **Close**
4   Select duplicate image

Make sure you have an image open and when you are ready to start recording, click the **Start Script Recording** button 🔘 on the Script toolbar. Carry out the above actions 1 to 4, one after the other. When you have finished recording, click the **Save Script Recording** button 🔳, which opens the Save As dialogue box shown here.

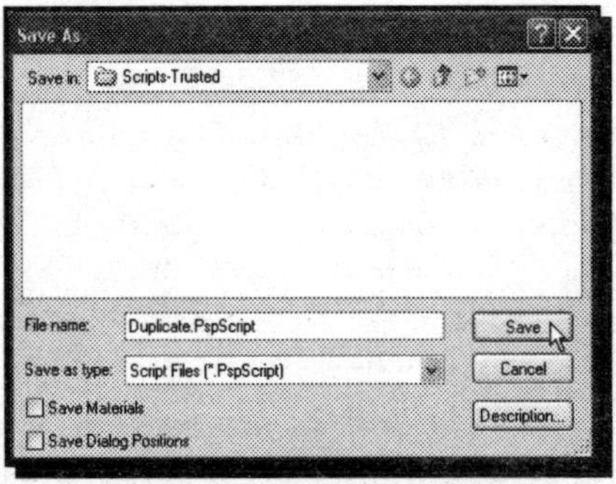

Fig. 11.6 Saving a Script

This box opens to the default Scripts-Restricted folder, but we have selected the Scripts-Trusted folder as the destination. The **Close** command will not run from the

Scripts-Restricted folder. Always be careful about placing scripts in the Scripts-Trusted folder, as they have full access to your system. In our case we know the source of the script and we know what it will do, so no problem.

Enter the name you want for your script in the **File name** box. Click the **Description** button to add your name, copyright information, and a brief description of the script, and finally click on **Save** to record the script.

Fig. 11.7 The Script Toolbar with the New Script

The next time you look in the **Select Script** drop-down list of the Script toolbar you should find your new script in the alphabetic list, as shown in Fig. 11.7 above. Just click the **Run Selected Script** button ▶ to duplicate your image.

That's really all there is to creating and running a PSP script. If you don't like the result, you can always undo the effect of a script by clicking the **Undo** button ② on the Standard toolbar.

BoundScripts

You may have noticed 9 scripts in the **Select Script** drop-down list of the Script toolbar with the unusual names Boundscript1 to Boundsript9. If you run any of these you only get the message box shown here.

Fig. 11.8 The Default BoundScript Message Box

If you name a script with one of these names, you can drag it onto a toolbar, a menu, or assign it a keyboard shortcut.

Batch Mode

PSP 8 has the facility for handling files in batch mode.

Running Batch Scripts

If you have a whole folder of image files that you want to apply the same modification to, you should first make a script that carries out the modification. Then use the new **File**, **Batch**, **Process** command. In the Batch Process dialogue box, you choose the files to be processed, the script to run, how and where the files should be saved and what names to give the resultant files. This is a very powerful command, so be careful with it.

The Batch Rename Process

You may also have noticed the new **File**, **Batch**, **Rename** command. This lets you rename groups of files with meaningful names and sequence numbers. You can rename an entire batch of photographs from your digital camera. For more details of this tool we suggest you go to the Help system shown below. There is even a 'movie' there for you to watch.

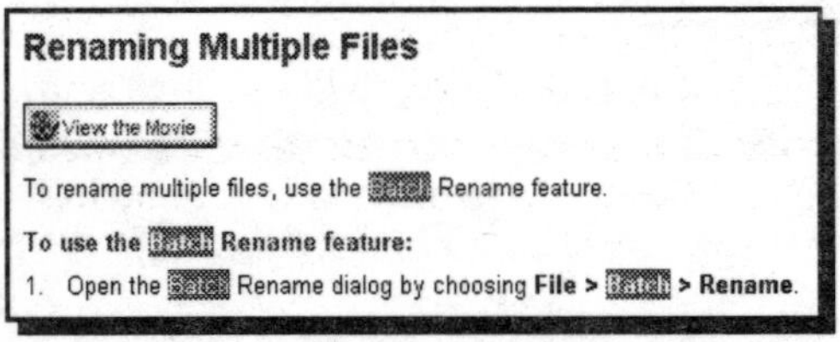

Renaming Multiple Files

[View the Movie]

To rename multiple files, use the Batch Rename feature.

To use the Batch Rename feature:

1. Open the Batch Rename dialog by choosing **File > Batch > Rename**.

Fig. 11.9 Part of the Help Page for Renaming Multiple Files

12

Customising Paint Shop Pro

We have seen the default PSP 8 user interface, shown below in Fig. 12.1 throughout this book, but there is no need for you to stick with this layout if you don't want to.

Fig. 12.1 The Default PSP 8 Workspace

Custom Workspaces

In PSP 8 pretty well everything is customisable. The 'Workspace' is made up of the layout, size and position of all the open palettes, toolbars, and images. PSP lets you to save any number of workspace arrangements, so once you have positioned your palettes and toolbars, as described in Chapter 3, you can save the workspace.

As well as the default workspace, there is one provided that duplicates the PSP 7 workspace. If you are upgrading from the previous version you may want to try this out.

Loading a Workspace

To load another workspace, use the **File**, **Workspace**, **Load** command, or the **Shift+Alt+L** shortcut, to open the Load Workspace dialogue box, shown below in Fig. 12.2. Select the workspace file you want and click on **Load**.

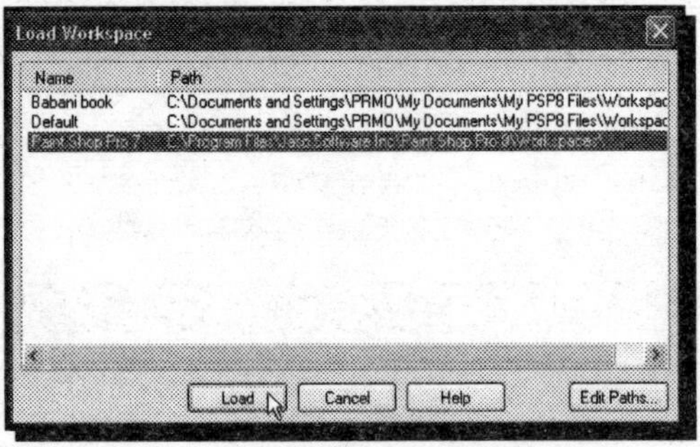

Fig. 12.2 Loading another Workspace

In our case we have only saved one workspace of our own, as can be seen above.

Saving a Workspace

When you have made any changes to your workspace, you should save the workspace, else the changes will soon get lost. By default, workspace information is saved in a **.PspWorkspace** file in the \My PSP 8 Files\Workspaces\ subfolder of your My Documents folder. Workspace files only reference the name and location of any open images saved, not the images themselves.

To save the current screen arrangement as a workspace, use the **File**, **Workspace**, **Save** command, or the **Shift+Alt+S** shortcut, type a **New Workspace Name** or accept an existing one to update it, and click the **Save** button.

General Program Preferences

🐾	General Program Preferences...
🔍	CMYK Conversion Preferences...
🖾	File Format Preferences...
📄	File Format Associations...
🗂	File Locations...
◆	Color Management...
🖥	Monitor Gamma...
💾	Autosave Settings...
🖙	Reset Preferences...

Fig. 12.3 The PSP
Preferences Sub-menu

Perhaps the first place to look when you want to customise the way PSP looks and operates is the **File**, **Preferences** sub-menu, shown in Fig. 12.3.

We will let you explore most of these on your own, but will point you first to the General Program Preferences dialogue box. To open this, you use the **File**, **Preferences**, **General Program Preferences** menu command. As you can see in Fig. 12.4 this contains 11 tabbed pages of settings for you to play with.

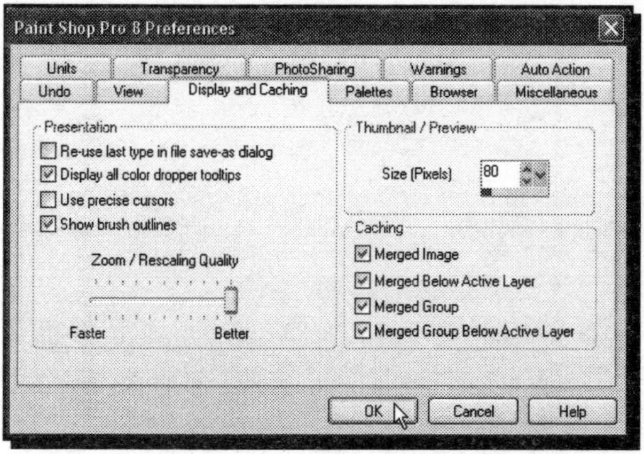

Fig. 12.4 The Display and Caching PSP Preferences

We suggest you work your way through these, but probably not too near bed time! The **Help** button is there whenever you need to know more about a setting or feature.

Once you have made all the changes you want, click the **OK** button to action them.

Customising Toolbars and Menus

When the Customize dialogue box is open, the whole PSP workspace changes to 'customise mode'. You can click and drag almost any menu command or tool to any other menu

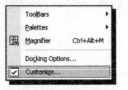

Fig. 12.5 Toolbars
Context Menu

or toolbar. You can add or delete commands from the Menu Bar, or buttons from the toolbars. There are two ways to open the Customize dialogue box. Either use the **View**, **Customize** main menu command, or right-click in the toolbar area and select **Customize** from the context menu shown in Fig. 12.5.

Fig. 12.6 The Customize Dialogue Box

Customising Toolbars

PSP 8 gives you total control over the toolbars you want to have open, and what buttons you have on them. You can add almost any command to a toolbar, add tools to palettes, add scripts to toolbars, and create your own toolbars from scratch. All the controls you need for customising your toolbars are on the Commands and Toolbars tabs of the Customize box, shown in Fig. 12.6.

To select which toolbars are displayed, click the Toolbars tab, and click in the check boxes of the toolbars you want to display, as shown in Fig. 12.7 below.

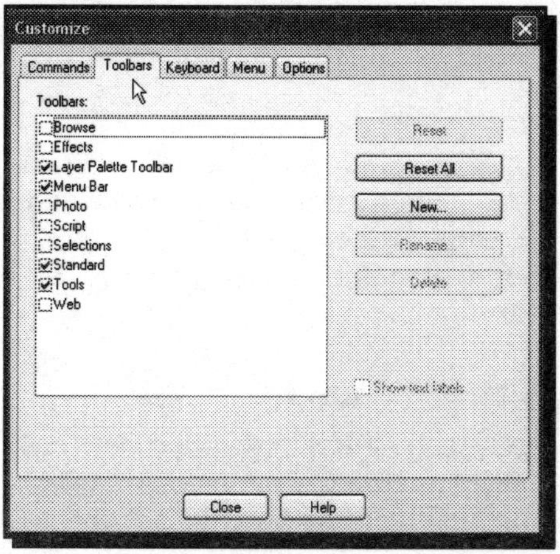

Fig. 12.7 Selecting Which Toolbars to Show

To add command buttons to a toolbar, first make sure the Commands tab is selected in the Customize dialogue box, as in Fig. 12.6 on the facing page. The **Categories** list includes all the menu items on the main menu, followed by the remaining categories you can work with. Selecting a category will open a list of **Commands** available in that category. In Fig. 12.6 we have started to place a **Load Workspace** button on the Standard toolbar. This command is in the **File** menu, so we selected File in the **Categories** list, and scrolled down the **Commands** list until the Load Workspace option is selected as in Fig. 12.6.

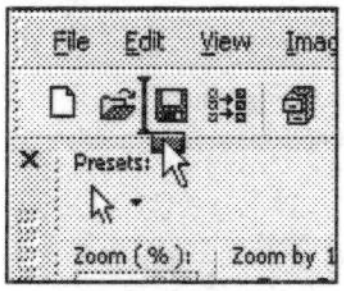

Fig. 12.8
Placing a
New Button

When you click the mouse button on the selected command, the cursor changes to a ⬚ shape. With the left mouse button depressed you can drag this anywhere in the PSP workspace. Try dragging it over the menus and toolbars, it changes to a ⬚ shape with an I bar, as shown in Fig. 12.8. Release the mouse button when this bar is where you want the new button to be.

Fig. 12.9
Context
Menu

To remove a button from a toolbar, click and drag it off the toolbars. The pointer will change to a 🔖 shape, you can then release the mouse button to 'delete' the tool button. Another way to do this is to right-click on the button you want to remove and choose **Delete** from the context menu that opens, as shown in Fig. 12.9.

To move a tool button from one place to another, on the same or a different toolbar, click on the button, and drag it. To copy a button, drag it to the new location with the **Ctrl** key depressed.

Creating a New Toolbar

It is just as easy with PSP 8 to create a new custom toolbar. To do this, click the **New** button on the Toolbars tab of the Customize dialogue box (see Fig. 12.7). Type a name for the new toolbar and click **OK**. A small empty toolbar will open in the middle of the workspace, as shown here. Move it to a blank area of the workspace so you can watch as you add tools, and drag the buttons you want to it, as described in the last section.

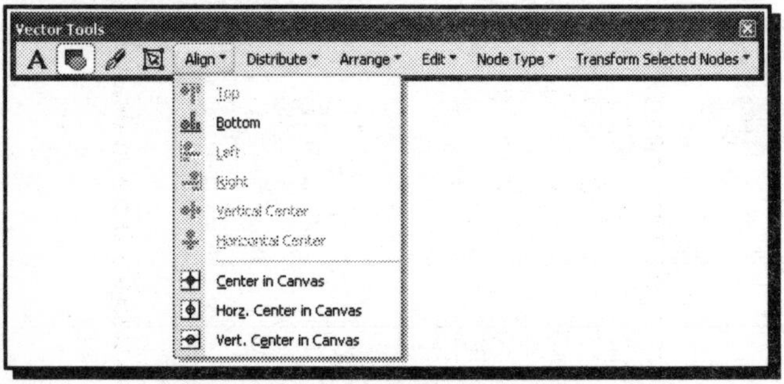

Fig. 12.10 A Custom Vector Tools Bar

If you spend much time using vector objects you may find the above toolbar makes life a little easier. The four buttons on the left were dragged from the Tools Commands list, and the others from the Objects Commands list. It took about three minutes to create.

If you want to add separators 📄 ✂ between buttons in your toolbar, right-click on the button in the toolbar to the right of where you want the separator and choose **Start Group** from the context menu that opens, as shown in Fig. 12.9. This is a 'toggle' command, so you remove them the same way.

When you have finished playing with your toolbars, clicking the **Close** button on the Customize dialogue box will make all your changes active. Don't forget to save your workspace though, it only takes a system crash to wipe out all your changes otherwise.

Customising Menus

All menu customisation procedures are also carried out in the Customize dialogue box. Either use the **View**, **Customize** main menu command, or right-click in the toolbar area and select **Customize** from the context menu. To select which menu is displayed in the Customize workspace, click the Menu tab, as shown in Fig. 12.11 below.

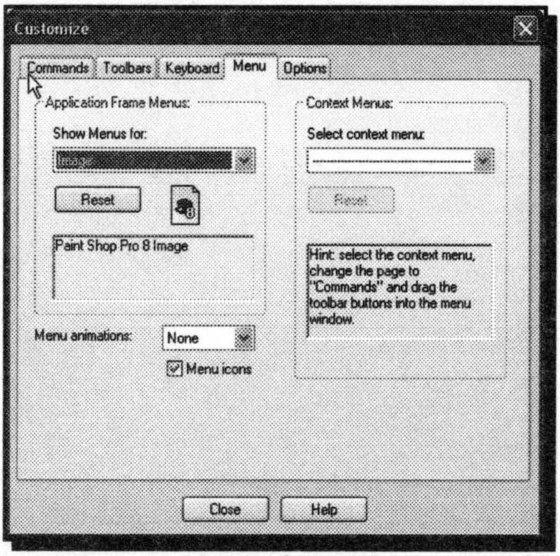

Fig. 12.11 Selecting Which Menu System to Customise

In the **Application Frame Menus** box, select an option from the **Show Menus for** drop-down list.

Default is the menu that displays when no images are open in PSP.

Image is the menu that displays when an image is open.

Browser is the menu that displays when the Browser is the active window.

You add commands and separators to a menu from the Commands tab of the Customize dialogue box in exactly the same way you add buttons and separators to a toolbar.

You also remove items from a menu in exactly the same way you remove buttons from a toolbar.

If you have problems customising your menus, you can always reset them to the factory default settings by first selecting the menu you want to reset from the **Show Menus for** list on the Menus tab, shown in Fig. 12.11, and then clicking the **Reset** button.

Creating New Menus

This is as easy as creating a new toolbar. On the Commands tab, scroll down in the **Categories** pane until you find New Menu, and click on it. Drag the New Menu item from the **Commands** pane, shown in Fig. 12.12, to wherever you want it on the menu bar.

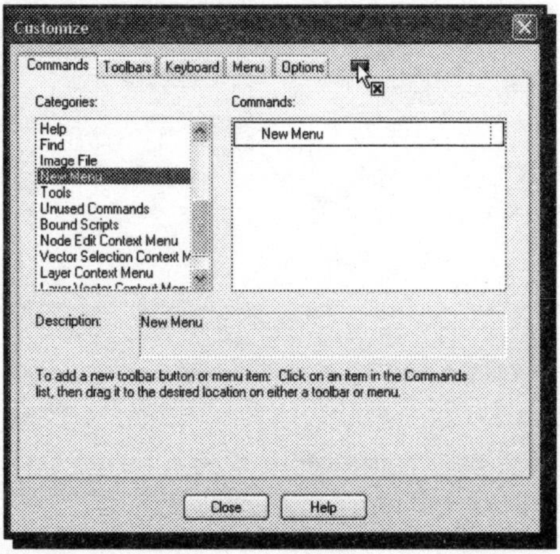

Fig. 12.12 Starting to Create a New Menu

We wanted to make it easier to access the PSP palettes so we renamed the 'New Menu' item by right-clicking on it, selecting **Menu Text** from the context menu, shown in Fig. 12,13, and typing **&Palettes** into the Rename Menu Item dialogue box. In case you were wondering, we wanted to assign a shortcut to the menu, so we could access it using the **ALT+P** shortcut. That is why we placed the ampersand (&) before the letter **P**.

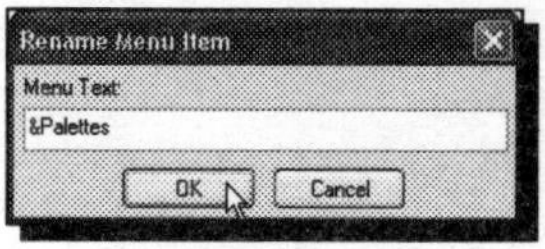

Fig. 12.13
Context
Menu

Fig. 12.14 Renaming
The New Menu

It's just a case then of dragging the commands you want onto the new menu, in the same way as adding toolbar buttons described before.

If you want to add sub-menus, drag another New Menu item to the menu, rename as above, and then add commands to it.

Fig. 12.15 Our Completed
New Palettes Menu

When you are finished, click the **Close** button on the Customize dialogue box and the customised menu will be part of the main PSP menu, and will work just like any other menu. Our completed Palettes menu is shown in Fig. 12.15.

Assigning Shortcut Keys

If you have the time and energy, you can assign your own keyboard shortcuts to menu commands and tools from the Keyboard tab of the Customize dialogue box, shown in Fig. 12.16 on the next page.

In the **Set Accelerator for** drop-down list, select either
Browser or Default. Browser if you want the shortcut to work
with the Browser, and Default if it is to work in PSP's main
workspace.

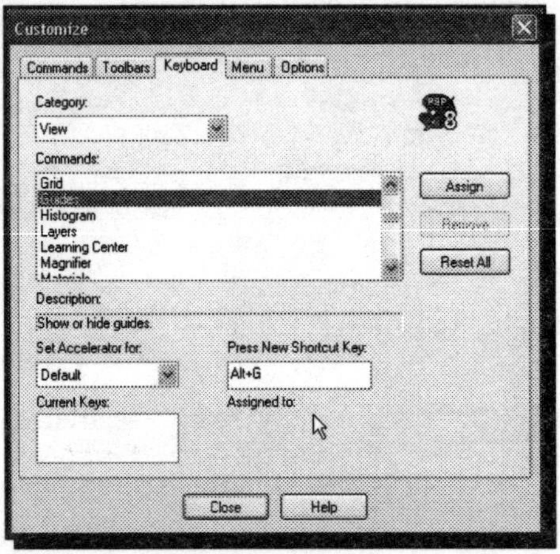

Fig. 12.16 Assigning a Keyboard Shortcut

In the **Category** drop-down list, select a category. In the
Commands list, which is arranged alphabetically in this box,
select a command name. If a shortcut is already set to that
command, it is shown in the **Current Keys** box. You can if
you like change this, but it is probably better not to.

Click in the **Press New Shortcut Key** field and 'action' the
new keyboard shortcut you want to assign to the command
you have selected. It will be placed in the box for you, and if
the shortcut is already assigned it will tell you so. In which
case just action another shortcut. When a shortcut is
available, the **Assigned to:** part of the box will be empty as
pointed to in Fig. 12.16 above. Here we are assigning the
Alt+G shortcut to the **View**, **Guides** menu command.

When you are happy with your settings, clicking **Assign**
will associate the new shortcut to the selected command.
Then click **Close** to leave the Customize dialogue box.

Resetting Preferences

With PSP 8 it is fairly easy to reset most parts of the program to their original factory settings. To reset application preferences, use the **File**, **Preferences**, **Reset Preferences** menu command to open the following box.

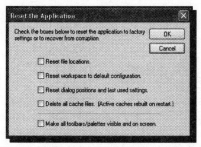

Fig. 12.17 Resetting PSP to Default Settings

Most of the options in this box are self-explanatory, so need no comment. The **Delete all cache files** option lets you delete the files PSP saves on your computer to improve its performance. It is as well to action this command every now and then, as cache files can become corrupted if your machine hangs. This was especially true for the earlier versions of PSP 8. As usual, click **OK** to action the choices.

Resetting Toolbars

You can reset any of PSP's toolbars in the Toolbars tab page of the Customize dialogue box, shown in Fig. 12.7. It is very easy to 'destroy' all your toolbar customisation. To reset all the toolbars just click the **Reset All** button. To reset a specific toolbar, select it in the **Toolbars** list and click the **Reset** button.

Resetting Menus

You can reset menus to the factory default settings by first selecting the menu to reset from the **Show Menus for** list on the Menus tabbed page of the Customize dialogue box, shown in Fig. 12.11, and then clicking the **Reset** button.

Resetting Tool Presets

Most of PSP's tools can use Presets, which are scripts that define the behaviour, properties, or settings for the tool. Most tools have, either in their dialogue boxes, or on their Tool Options palette, a **Default** Preset - the out-of-the-box or factory settings, obtained by clicking the **Reset to Default** button ⬛.

PSP File Locations

As we have seen in earlier chapters, by default, all new files you create with PSP 8 are saved in the appropriate folder of your My Documents folder, which with us is:

C:\Documents and Settings\PRMO\My Documents\My PSP8 Files

Most default program files are stored in the appropriate folder in the PSP 8 program folder, which with us is:

C:\Program Files\Jasc Software Inc\Paint Shop Pro 8

Editing File Locations

You can control where PSP looks for and saves important files on your computer. To change file locations use the **F**ile, **Pref**erences, **File L**ocations command to open the File Locations dialogue box, shown in Fig. 12.18.

Fig. 12.18 The File Locations Dialogue Box

The **File types** list gives the file types that you can change file locations for. In our example this is set for Workspaces files, looked at earlier in the chapter.

Save To Folder 🖳 Sets the folder for PSP to save new files of this type.

Scan Subfolders 🗂 Sets PSP to search any sub-folders inside this folder.

Enable Directory 🗂 Sets PSP to search for this type of files in this folder.

To set PSP to look elsewhere on your PC, click the **Add** button and either type in the location address, or click the **Browse** button and find it the easy way.

The folder at the top of the **Workspace folders** list will be searched and loaded first. You can use the arrows in the top right of the dialogue box to move a folder up or down the list of folders.

13

Optimising Web Images

We have said several times throughout this book, that you should keep your image files in the **.PspImage** format. This is because it supports all of the program's powerful features, such as layers, alpha channels, grid and guide settings, etc. While you are working on them that is fine, but then, depending on what you are going to do with them, you may have to save them in a different format. As far as we know, only PSP 8 can use **.PspImage** format files.

Saving Images for the Internet

When saving files for use on the Internet, whether for sending with an e-mail or putting on a Web page, there are two main considerations. The quality of the image and its file size. The quality should be as high as possible and the file size as small as possible. As the size of an image file increases, it takes more time to download. So you need a file format that reduces the image size most efficiently while keeping the quality as high as possible.

Web File Formats

There are only three file formats used on the Internet for images, and only two of these are in general use.

JPEG or .jpg - The standard format for compressing photographic images for Web sites. It supports 24-bit (16 million) colours and uses 'lossy' compression that discards data to reduce the file size.

GIF or .gif - You use this format to compress line art and images with areas of similar colours, such as logos and buttons. GIF files support 8-bit (256) colour and use lossless compression, which retains the original image data and reduces the file size by storing patterns of pixels.

PNG or .png - This is the latest format for Web use. It compresses most image types efficiently, supports up to 24-bit (16 million) colours and uses lossless compression. However it is not in standard use, as most browsers cannot handle all its features.

The JPEG Optimizer

To save an image as a **.jpg** file, you should use the PSP JPEG Optimizer, opened with the **File**, **Export**, **JPEG Optimizer** command, or its toolbar button 🖼, and shown in Fig.13.1 below.

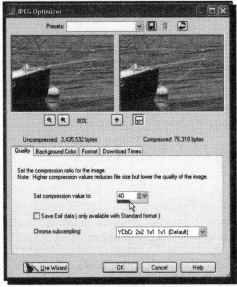

Fig. 13.1 The JPEG Optimizer

The first page, or Quality tab, lets you **Set the compression value to** an optimum. You set a value in this box and watch the right-hand display panel above. If the image has not deteriorated, increase the value until it starts to 'go off'. This usually happens between compression values of 25 and 40, depending on the image. As you increase the compression value you can watch the **Compressed** file size, which will fall. The optimum setting is the smallest file size with the minimum of image degradation.

The Background Color tab lets you set the background colour of your Web page. If the original image has any transparent sections they will be blended with the selected colour, as JPEG images cannot have transparency.

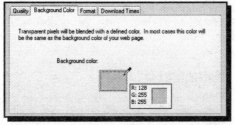

Fig. 13.2 Choosing a Background Colour

You select the colour by clicking in the colour box and choosing from the Color dialogue box that is opened. Or you can move the pointer over an image in the workspace and select a colour by clicking the **Dropper** tool that opens.

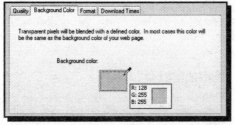

Fig. 13.3 The Format Tab

The Format tab lets you choose how your image will be built up on the Web page. The usual choice is **Standard**.

The Download Times tab just gives an indication of how long the image will take to download with different transmission rates.

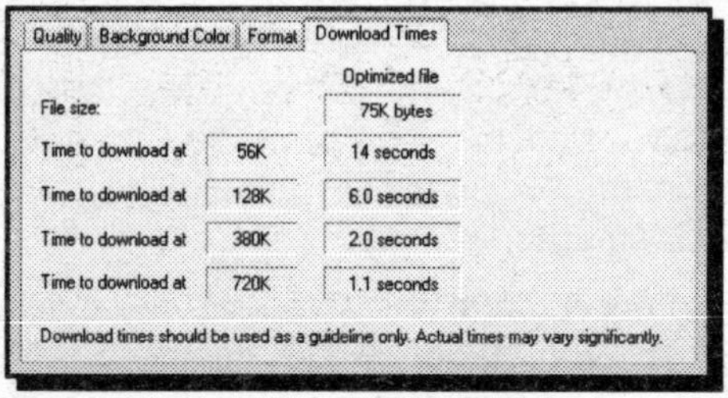

Quality	Background Color	Format	Download Times	
			Optimized file	
File size:			75K bytes	
Time to download at	56K		14 seconds	
Time to download at	128K		6.0 seconds	
Time to download at	380K		2.0 seconds	
Time to download at	720K		1.1 seconds	

Download times should be used as a guideline only. Actual times may vary significantly.

Fig. 13.4 The Download Times Tab

When you have finished, clicking **OK** opens the Save As dialogue box for you to save a copy of the image as a **.jpg** file. The original file remains open and unchanged.

The GIF Optimizer

To save an image as a **.gif** file, you should use the PSP GIF Optimizer, opened with the **File**, **Export**, **GIF Optimizer** command, or its toolbar button 🔳, and shown in Fig.13.5 on the facing page.

The Transparency tab lets you choose a colour in the image that will be transparent to Web browsers in the final GIF file. This way a square image can look like a circular one on the Web page, if the area outside the circle is made transparent.

If you don't want your **.gif** file to have a transparent background, select **None**. If you do want one, as with our logo example, select either **Existing image or layer transparency** (if your image has no coloured background), or **Areas that match this colour** as in Fig. 13.5. With the latter, select the colour by moving the pointer over your image in the workspace and clicking the **Dropper** tool on the background colour. Adjust the **Tolerance** setting when the area you want to be transparent contains pixels that are close in colour but not exactly the same.

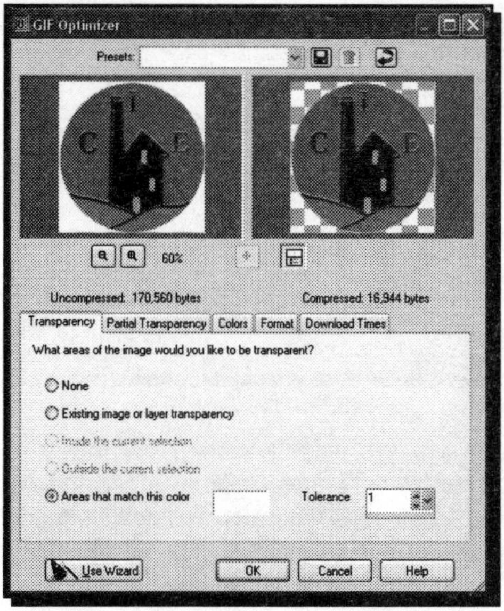

Fig. 13.5 The GIF Optimiser - Transparency Tab

On the Partial Transparency tab, we usually select **Use full transparency for pixels below** 5% **opacity**, and **Yes, blend with the background colour** as shown below.

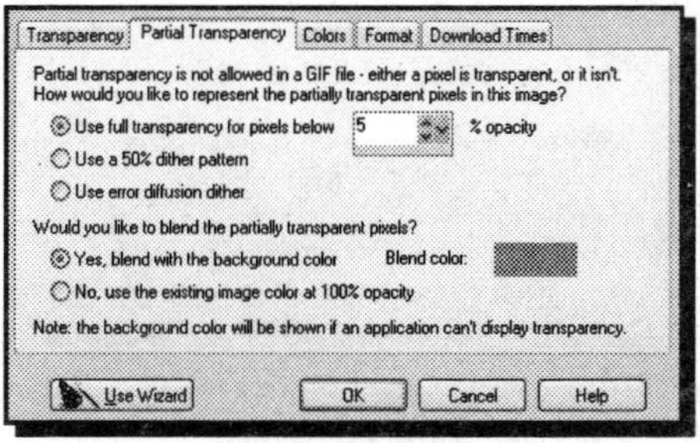

Fig. 13.6 The Partial Transparency Tab

Click on the **Blend color** box to choose the dominant colour of your Web page background. If you want the current foreground or background colour, right-click and choose the appropriate colour box from the lower left, bottom panel of the dialogue box. This is an important step for getting good transparent GIFs - if you don't select this colour carefully, you may have a fringe around your image, because part of the transparent GIF process blends the colours from the image into the background colour.

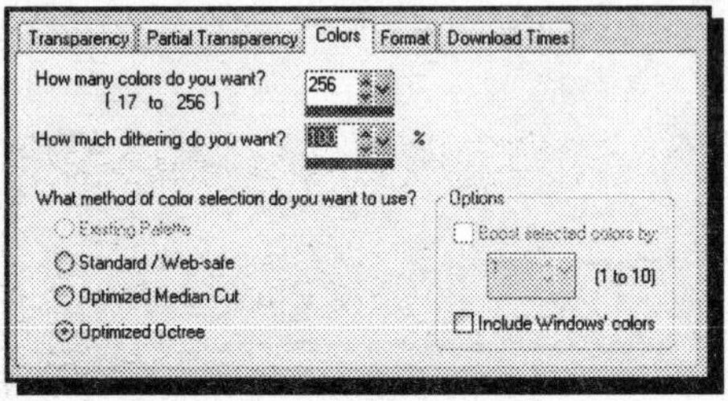

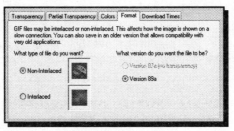

Fig. 13.7 The Colors Tab

In the Colors tab, we usually leave **How many colours do you want?** set to 256 and **How much dithering do you want?** set to 100%. For the colour selection method, we use either **Optimized Median Cut** or **Optimized Octree**, whichever looks better in the right pane.

Fig. 13.8 The Format Tab

On the Format tab, select **Non-interlaced** if you want the image to load one line at a time, starting from the top down. Select **Interlaced** if you want the image to display incrementally in several passes, with detail being added each time. This is a personal choice.

The Download Times tab just gives an indication of how long the image will take to download with different transmission rates, as in Fig. 13.4. When you have finished, clicking **OK** opens the Save As dialogue box for you to save a copy of the image as a **.gif** file. The original file remains open and unchanged.

The PNG Optimizer

To save an image as a **.png** file, you should use the PNG Optimizer, opened with the **File**, **Export**, **PNG Optimizer** command, or its toolbar button ▦, and shown in Fig. 13.9 below.

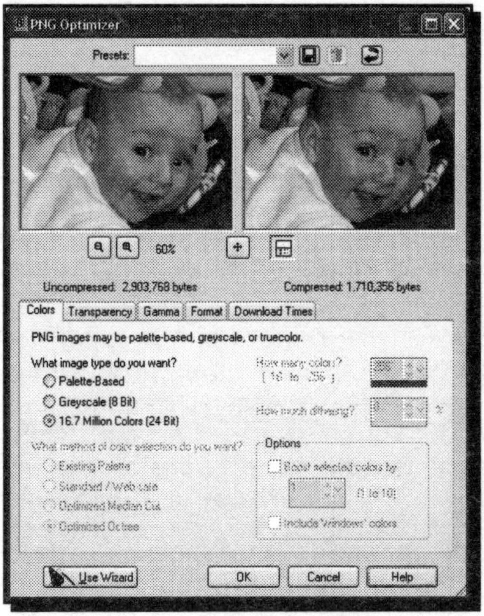

Fig. 13.9 The PNG Optimizer

The Colors tab lets you select a colour depth for the PNG image created. If the original is a drawing or logo you could choose **Palette-Based**, which can have up to 256 colours, you can then choose the method of colour selection, number of colours, and amount of dithering, as with the GIF Optimizer. The images in this book were created as **Greyscale** in this Optimizer. For a photograph you would choose **16 million colour (24 Bit)**, which would create a larger image but of much better quality than an 8 Bit image.

The Transparency tab sets what will be transparent. You can control this by making a selection in the image before opening the Optimizer.

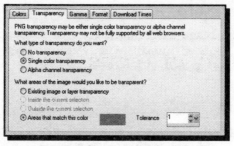
Fig. 13.10 The Transparency Tab

No transparency saves the image without any. **Single color transparency** sets one colour as transparent. You then need to select either **Existing image or layer transparency** (if your image has no coloured background), or **Areas that match this color** as above. With this option, select the colour by moving the pointer over your image in the workspace and clicking the **Dropper** tool on the background colour. Adjust the **Tolerance** setting when the area you want to be transparent contains pixels that are close in colour but not exactly the same. **Alpha channel transparency** uses the image's alpha channel transparency and is available only for Greyscale or 24 Bit images.

If the original image has a selection, the **Inside the current selection** option makes everything transparent within that selection. **Outside the current selection** makes everything transparent outside the selection.

On the Format tab, as in Fig. 13.8, select **Non-interlaced** if you want the image to load one line at a time, starting from the top down. Select **Interlaced** if you want the image to display incrementally in several passes with detail being added each time.

The Download Times tab just gives an indication of how long the image will take to download with different transmission rates, as in Fig. 13.4.

When you have finished, clicking **OK** opens the Save As dialogue box for you to save a copy of the image as a **.png** file. The original file remains open and unchanged.

14

Glossary of Terms

Adobe Acrobat
A suite of applications to create and view PDF files.

Aliasing
In graphic design, aliasing occurs when a computer monitor, printer, or graphics file does not have a high enough resolution to represent a graphic image or text. An aliased image is often said to have "jaggies".

Alpha channel
A special 8-bit greyscale channel that is used for saving a selection.

Anti-alias
The blending of pixel colours on the perimeter of hard-edged shapes, to smooth undesirable edges or jaggies.

Application
Software (program) designed to carry out a certain activity, such as word processing, or image editing.

Baud rate
The speed at which a modem communicates.

Bevel
Adding a bevelled effect to a graphic image gives the image a raised appearance by applying highlight colours and shadow colours to the inside and outside edges.

Bezier
The term used to describe the way in which software like PSP uses anchor points and control handles to create curved shapes.

Bitmap Image   A graphic image stored as a specific arrangement of screen dots, or pixels. A graphic which is defined by specifying the colours of dots or pixels which make up the picture. Also known as raster graphics. Common types of bitmap graphics are GIF, JPEG, and TIFF.

Bounding Box   A function in PSP vector graphics that describes a rectangular shape just large enough to contain all elements of a design or illustration.

Brightness   The relative lightness or darkness of the colour, usually measured as a percentage from 0% (black) to 100% (white).

Broadband   A communications systems in which the medium of transmission (such as a wire or fibre-optic cable) carries multiple messages at a time.

Browse   A button in some Windows dialogue boxes that lets you view a list of files and folders before you make a selection. Also to view Internet Web pages online.

Browser   A program, like Internet Explorer, that lets you view Web pages. Also the PSP application that lets you easily view and handle the images on your PC.

Button   A graphic element in a dialogue box or toolbar that performs a specified function. Also known as an icon.

Byte   A unit of data that holds a single character, such as a letter, a digit.

Camera-ready copy	Final publication material that is ready to be made into a negative for a printing plate. May be a computer file or actual print and images on hard copy.
CD-ROM	Read Only Memory compact disc. Data can be read but not written.
Character	Any letter, figure, punctuation, symbol or space.
Click	To press and release a mouse button once without moving the mouse.
Clip art	Ready-made artwork sold or distributed for 'clipping and pasting' into publications. Available in hard-copy books, and in electronic form, as files on disc.
Clipboard	A temporary storage area of memory, where text and graphics are stored with the Windows cut and copy actions.
CMYK	Represents the colours Cyan-Magenta-Yellow-Black. In print design, colours are defined as a percentage of each of these 4 colours.
Colour Cast	A colour cast changes the hue (colour) of a selected part of an image while keeping the saturation and brightness intact.
Colour Correction	The act of correcting for and eliminating an unwanted colour cast.
Configuration	A general purpose term referring to the way your computer is set up.
Contrast	The degree of difference between light and dark areas in an image.

Extreme lights and darks give an image high contrast. An image with a wide tonal range has lower contrast.

Control Handle

A handle that extends from a node point that is used to create a curved shape in a path. Both the length and angle affect the shape achieved. The length will affect the depth of the curve and the angle will affect the angle at which the path exits from the anchor point.

Cropping

The act of discarding unwanted detail around the edge of a picture. Cropping in this way permanently discards the detail from the file and reduces file size.

Default

The command, device or option automatically chosen. Also known as factory setting, or out of the box setting.

Desktop Publishing

A process for creating camera-ready and plate-ready artwork on a personal computer.

Device driver

A special file that must be loaded into memory for Windows to be able to address a specific procedure or hardware device.

Device name

A logical name used by your system to identify a device, such as LPT1 or COM1 for the parallel or serial printer.

Dialogue box

A window displayed on the screen to allow the user to enter information.

Digital Photography

The process of recording images using a digital camera, or a conventional camera with a digital adapter, it records on a disc or on microchip which can then be downloaded directly to a computer in tiff, jpg, pict or eps format.

Dingbat typeface

A typeface made up of non-alphabetic marker characters, such as arrows, asterisks, encircled numbers.

Directory

An area on disc where information relating to a group of files is kept. Also known as a folder.

Display adapter

An expansion board that plugs into a PC to give it display capabilities.

Dithering

In order to convert a full-colour graphic image to one of 256 colours, computers must simulate the colours it cannot display. They do this by dithering, which is combining pixels from a 256-colour palette into patterns that approximate to other colours.

Document

A file produced by an application program, such as Paint Shop Pro.

Domain

A group of devices, servers and computers on a network.

Domain Name

The unique name of an Internet site, for example www.microsoft.com, which allows you to reference them without knowing their true numerical address.

Double-click

To quickly press and release a mouse button twice.

Download

To transfer to your computer a file, or data, from another computer.

DPI   Dots Per Inch - a resolution standard
                    for laser printers.

Drag   To move an object on the screen by
                    pressing and holding down the left
                    mouse button while moving the
                    mouse.

Drive name   The letter followed by a colon which
                    identifies a floppy or hard disc drive.

Drop Shadow   A drop shadow gives an image depth
                    by creating a shading offset behind a
                    selected image.

DVD   Digital Versatile Disc; a type of optical
                    disc technology. It looks like a CD but
                    can store greater amounts of data.

Effect   See Filter.

E-mail   Electronic mail - A system that allows
                    computer users to send and receive
                    messages electronically.

EPS (EPSF)   Encapsulated Postscript File. A
                    vector-based, computer graphics file
                    format developed by Adobe Systems.

FAQ   Frequently Asked Questions - A
                    common feature on the Internet,
                    FAQs are files of answers to
                    commonly asked questions.

Feathering   Smoothing the edge of a graphic
                    image gradually, making the edge
                    look a little blurred.

Filename   The name given to a file. In Windows
                    95 and above this can be up to 256
                    characters long.

Filter   Used in PSP to enhance images by
                    applying complex alterations based
                    on the colour values of individual

pixels compared to those surrounding them. Also known as an Effect.

Folder

An area used to store a group of files, usually with a common link. Used to be known as a directory.

Font

A graphic design representing a set of characters, numbers and symbols.

Freeware

Software that is available for downloading and unlimited use without charge.

Function key

One of the series of 10 or 12 keys marked with the letter F and a numeral, used for specific operations.

Gamma Adjustment

An adjustment that makes the tonal distribution lighter or darker. A Gamma Adjustment may be made to a monitor, a scanner or to an image during the scanning or image editing process.

GIF

Graphics Interchange Format, a common standard for images on the Web.

Gigabyte

(GB); 1,024 Megabytes. Usually thought of as one billion bytes.

Glow

The opposite of a shadow in that it creates a surrounding highlight of an image.

Gradient

A gradual transition of colours. Many metallic images are gradients.

Graphic

A picture or illustration, also called an image. Formats include GIF, JPEG, BMP, PCX, and TIFF.

Graphic Design	A way of communication with visual elements and information to present an idea or concept.
Graphic Designer	The person who puts Graphic Designs together, many of whom now use computers, drafting and illustration techniques and other tools to create with.
Graphics card	A device that controls the display on the monitor and other allied functions.
Greyscale	An application of black ink (for print) or the colour black (for the screen) that simulates a range of tones. Greyscale images have no hue (colour).
GUI	A Graphic User Interface, such as Windows, the software front-end meant to provide an attractive and easy to use interface.
Halftone	A printed picture that uses dots to simulate the tones between light and dark.
Hard copy	Output on paper.
Hard disc	A device built into the computer for holding programs and data.
Hardware	The equipment that makes up a computer system, excluding the programs or software.
Help	A Windows system that gives you instructions and additional information on using a program.
HSB	Hue, saturation, brightness. Based on the human perception of colour,

the HSB model describes three fundamental characteristics of colour.

HTML

HyperText Markup Language, the format used in many documents on the Web.

Hue

The colour reflected from or transmitted through an object, such as red, green or blue. It is measured as a location on the colour wheel and is expressed as a degree between 0 and 360 on that wheel.

Hyperlink

A segment of text, or an image, that refers to another document on the Web, an intranet or your PC.

Hypertext

A system that allows documents to be cross-linked so that the reader can explore related links, or documents, by clicking on a highlighted symbol.

Icon

A small graphic image that represents a function or object. Clicking on an icon produces an action. Also known as a button.

Image

See graphic.

Insertion point

A flashing bar that shows where typed text will be entered into a document.

Interface

A device that allows you to connect a computer to its peripherals.

Interlace

Storing partial data from a single graphic image in multiple sequences. The purpose of interlacing is to have a partial image initially appear on screen rather than having to wait for the image to appear in its entirety.

Internet	The global system of computer networks.
ISP	Internet Service Provider - A company that offers access to the Internet.
JPEG / JPG	Joint Photographic Experts Group, a popular cross-platform format for image files. JPEG is best suited for true colour photographic images.
Kern	To squeeze together characters, for a better fit of strokes and white space. In display type, characters usually need to be kerned because the white space between characters at large sizes is more noticeable.
Kilobyte	(KB); 1024 bytes of information or storage space.
Landscape	(Orientation) - A page or layout that is wider than it is tall.
Layers	A function in PSP that allows the user to work with multiple levels in an image.
LCD	Liquid Crystal Display.
Leader	A line of dots or dashes to lead the eye across the page to separated copy.
Leading	(Pronounced "led-ding"). The space between lines of type, traditionally measured baseline-to-baseline, in points. Text type is generally set with one or two points of leading; for example, 10-point type with 2 points of leading. This is described as 10/12, read ten on twelve.

Line art	Black-and-white artwork with no grey areas. Pen-and-ink drawings are line art, and most graphic images produced with desktop publishing graphics programs can be treated as line art. For printing purposes, positive halftones can be handled as line art.
Line segment	The straight or curved line between two vector nodes.
Links	The hypertext connections between Web pages.
Log on	To gain access to a network.
Lossless	Image compression techniques that don't remove detail as they reduce file size.
Lossy	An image compression technique that removes detail as it reduces file size.
Mask	A function within image editing software that allows the user to restrict their image edits to only a part of the image.
Megabyte	(MB); 1024 kilobytes of information or storage space.
Megahertz	(MHz); Speed of processor in millions of cycles per second.
Menu	A list of available options in an application.
Menu bar	The horizontal bar that lists the names of menus.
MIPS	Million Instructions Per Second; measures speed of a system.

Modem	Short for Modulator-demodulator. An electronic device that lets computers communicate electronically.
Moiré patterns	(Pronounced "mwa-ray") - Irregular plaid-like patterns that occur when a bit-mapped image is reduced, enlarged, displayed, or printed at a resolution different from the resolution of the original.
Monitor	The display device connected to your PC, also called a screen.
Mouse	A device used to manipulate a pointer around your display and activate processes by pressing buttons.
Multimedia	The use of photographs, music and sound and movie images in a presentation.
Multitasking	Performing more than one operation at the same time.
My Documents	A folder that provides a convenient place to store documents, graphics, or other files you want to access quickly.
Network	Two or more computers connected together to share resources.
Node	A point on a vector contour that defines the contour's shape at that point.
Noise	A term used to describe the occurrence of pixels within an image that contain random colours.
Object	Anything you create on a vector layer in PSP, it is a single item that can form part of a vector image.

Online	Having access to the Internet.
Opacity	A characteristic of image editing software, such as PSP. By adjusting opacity to a percentage of less than 100%, the user can paint a colour onto an image and allow some of the image beneath to show through.
Operating system	Software that runs a computer.
Page	An HTML document, or Web site.
Parallel port	The input/output connector for a parallel interface device. Printers are often plugged into a parallel port.
Path	The location of a file in the directory tree, or The shape of a vector element in an illustration. A path, on its own will not show until it has a stroke (line weight) and/or fill (colour attribute) assigned to it.
PDF	Portable Document file. A proprietary format developed by Adobe Systems for the transfer of designs across multiple computer platforms.
Peripheral	Any device attached to a PC.
Photo CD	A proprietary format developed by Eastman Kodak for storing photographic images on a compact disc.
Pica	A measurement used in typography for column widths and other space specifications in a page layout. There are 12 points in a pica, and approximately 6 picas to an inch.
Pixel	A picture element on screen; the smallest element that can be

	independently assigned colour and intensity.
Plug-and-play	Hardware which can be plugged into a PC and be used immediately without configuration.
Plug-in	Additional software to expand the capabilities of PSP. Plug-ins are available from Adobe and other sources, to perform many specialised tasks.
PNG	Portable Network Graphics format, generally pronounced "ping". PNG is used for lossless compression and displaying images on the web. It supports images with millions of colours and produces background transparency without jagged edges.
Point	A measurement used in typography for type size, leading, and other space specifications in a page layout. There are 12 points in a pica, and approximately 70 points to an inch.
Port	The place where information goes into or out of a computer, e.g. a modem might be connected to the serial port.
PostScript	A page-description language (PDL), developed by Adobe Systems for printing on laser printers.
Program	A set of instructions which cause a computer to perform tasks.
RAM	Random Access Memory. The computer's volatile memory. Data held in it is lost when power is switched off.

Refresh

To update displayed information with current data.

Registered file type

File types that are tracked by the system registry and are recognised by the programs you have installed on your computer.

Registry

A database where information about a computer's configuration is deposited. The registry contains information that Windows continually references during its operation.

Re-sample

A function available in image editing that allows the user to change the resolution of an image.

Re-size

A function available in image editing software. Re-sizing an image is possible to any percent but there is a high quality penalty to pay if the image is scaled above 150% or below 50%. The quality loss shows by decreased image sharpness.

Resolution

The crispness of detail or fineness of grain in an image. Screen resolution is measured in dots by lines (eg., 640 x 480); printer resolution is measured in dpi (e.g., 300 dpi).

RGB

Red Green Blue - The colours used by a computer monitor to create colour images on the screen. When all three colours are combined over each other the colour of light is white.

Saturation

Also called chroma, is the strength or purity of the colour. Saturation represents the amount of grey in proportion to the hue and is

	measured as a percentage from 0% (grey) to 100% (fully saturated).
Screen saver	A moving picture or pattern that appears on your screen when you have not used the mouse or keyboard for a specified period of time.
Script	A type of program consisting of a set of instructions to an application or tool program. Also known as a macro.
Scroll bar	A bar that appears at the right side or bottom edge of a window.
Shareware	Software that is available on public networks and bulletin boards. Users are expected to pay a nominal amount to the software developer.
Shortcut	A link to any item accessible on your computer or on a network, such as a program, file, folder, disc drive, Web page, printer, or another computer.
Software	The programs and instructions that control your PC.
Stroke	The printing line that is applied onto an object's path.
SVGA	Super Video Graphics Array; it has all the VGA modes but with 256, or more, colours.
System files	Files used by Windows to load, configure, and run the operating system.
Thumbnail	A small version of a graphic image.
TIFF	Tag Image File Format - a popular graphic image file format.

Toggle	To turn an action on and off with the same switch.
Tool	A PSP function used to carry out a certain type of operation.
Toolbar	A bar containing buttons giving quick access to commands.
TrueType fonts	Fonts that can be scaled to any size and print as they show on the screen.
Typeface	A series of fonts. For example, the typeface Arial contains the fonts Arial, Arial Bold, Arial Italic and Arial Bold Italic.
TWAIN	An image capture interface for Windows and Macintosh systems. Many cameras and most scanners can use this type of connection.
Unsharp Masking	An important function that allows the user to add apparent clarity via electronic means. Unsharp masking is considered the most sophisticated sharpening method because it sharpens without the undesirable graininess that appears with other sharpening methods.
Upload/Download	The process of transferring files between computers. Files are uploaded from your computer to another and downloaded from another computer to your own.
URL	Uniform Resource Locator, the addressing system used on the Web, containing information about the method of access, the server to be accessed and the path of the file to be accessed.

USB

Universal Serial Bus - an external bus standard that enables data transfer rates of 12 Mbps.

Vector Graphic

A graphic image drawn in shapes and lines, called paths. Images created on PSP's vector layers are vector graphics.

Virus

A malicious program, downloaded from a web site, e-mail or disc, designed to wipe out information on, or take control of, your computer.

Web

A network of hypertext-based multimedia information servers. Browsers like Explorer are used to view any information on the Web.

Web Page

A document, usually HTML, that is accessible on the Web.

White space

In designing publication, the areas where there is no text or graphics.

WIA

Windows Image Acquisition - enables imaging programs, such as PSP to communicate with imaging devices like digital cameras and scanners. WIA is built on the Microsoft Still Image Architecture that was introduced in Windows 98 to provide support for imaging devices.

Appendix A

Keyboard Shortcuts

The following is a list of PSP's Quick Keys and other keyboard shortcuts, many require you to press two keys. For example, **Ctrl+A** means hold down the Ctrl key and press the letter A.

File Menu

Ctrl+B	Browse through images on disc
Ctrl+F4	Close this image
Ctrl+Delete	Delete this image file from the disc
Ctrl+N	Create new image
Ctrl+O	Open an existing document
Ctrl+P	Print the active document
Ctrl+S	Save the active document
F12	Save the active document with a new name
Ctrl+F12	Save a copy of the active document with a new name
Shift+Alt+D	Deletes a previously saved workspace
Shift+Alt+L	Loads the current workspace
Shift+Alt+S	Saves the current workspace

Edit Menu

Delete	Clear the selection or image
Ctrl+Shift+Z	Show the command history for the current document
Ctrl+C; Ctrl+Insert	Copy the selection from the current layer into the clipboard
Ctrl+Shift+C	Copy the current merged image
Ctrl+X; Shift+Delete	Cut out the selection and put it into the clipboard

Ctrl+V; Shift+Insert	Paste data in clipboard as new image
Ctrl+L	Paste the clipboard contents into the current document as a new layer
Ctrl+E	Paste data in the clipboard into the current image as a new selection
Ctrl+G	Paste vector data in clipboard into the current image as a new vector selection
Ctrl+Shift+E	Paste data from clipboard into the current image using the background colour as transparent
Ctrl+Shift+L	Paste data from clipboard into the selected area.
Ctrl+Alt+Z Shift+Alt+Backspace	Redo the last command
Ctrl+Y	Repeat the last action
Ctrl+Z Alt+Backspace	Undo the last command

View Menu

Shift+A	Edit the current document using all available screen space
Ctrl+Shift+A	View the current document full screen (Press <Esc> to exit preview mode)
Ctrl+Alt+G	Show Grid
Ctrl+Alt+M	Show or hide the Tool Magnifier window
F11	Show or hide the Brush Variance palette
F7	Show or hide the Histogram palette
F8	Show or hide the Layers palette
F10	Show or hide the Learning Center palette
F6	Show or hide the Materials palette
F9	Show or hide the Overview palette
F3	Show or hide the Script Output palette
F4	Show or hide the Tool Options palette
Ctrl+Alt+R	Shows/hides rulers

Ctrl+Shift+G	Snaps position to the grid
Shift+Alt+G	Snaps position to the guides
Num plus	Zoom in by 1 Step (Increases the apparent size)
Num sub	Zoom out by 1 Step (Decreases the apparent size)
Ctrl+Alt+N	View the image normally, with no zoom factor

Image Menu

Shift+R	Crop Tool: Use to eliminate or crop areas of an image
Ctrl+Shift+1	Decrease the number of colours to 2
Ctrl+Shift+2	Decrease the number of colours to 16
Ctrl+Shift+3	Decrease the number of colours to 256
Ctrl+Shift+4	Decrease the number of colours to 32K
Ctrl+Shift+5	Decrease the number of colours to 64K
Ctrl+Shift+6	Decrease the number of colours to a value you select
Ctrl+I	Flip image
Shift+I	View details about the current image
Ctrl+Shift+8	Increase the number of colours to 16
Ctrl+Shift+0	Increase the number of colours to 16 million (24 bit)
Ctrl+Shift+9	Increase the number of colours to 256
Ctrl+M	Apply mirror to image
Shift+P	Edit the palette for the current picture
Shift+O	Load a palette from disc, and apply to the current image
Shift+S	Change the size of the image
Ctrl+R	Apply rotation to image

Adjust Menu

Shift+B	Adjust brightness and/or contrast
Shift+G	Apply gamma correction to the image
Shift+M	Adjust the brightness of the highlights and shadows
Ctrl+Shift+H	Adjust the image while viewing the histogram
Shift+E	Equalize the relative brightness of the current image
Shift+T	Stretch the contrast of the current image so that all possible values are used
Shift+U	Adjust the red, green, and/or blue
Shift+L	Colorize the image

Layers Menu

Shift+K	Invert the current mask or adjustment layer
Shift+Y	Make a new mask that obscures the entire layer

Selections Menu

Ctrl+Shift+F	Place the current floating selection into the image
Ctrl+F	Convert the current regular selection into a floating selection
Ctrl+Shift+S	Create a new selection from the current mask channel
Ctrl+Shift+B	Create a Raster Selection from a Vector Selection
Ctrl+Shift+M	Keep the selection marquee from appearing on the image
Ctrl+Shift+I	Invert the current selection area
Ctrl+H	Feather the existing selection
Ctrl+Shift+P	Promote a floating selection to a new layer
Ctrl+A	Select entire image
Ctrl+D	Remove the current selection

Window Menu

Shift+D	Duplicate the current image
Ctrl+W	Fit the window to the image
Shift+W	Open another window for the active document

Help Menu

Shift+F1	Display help for clicked on buttons, menus and windows
F10	Show or hide the Learning Center palette

Unused Commands

Ctrl+K	Edit the closest mask layer
F2	Hide the palettes
Ctrl+Num plus	Magnify Window Zoom In
Ctrl+Num sub	Magnify Window Zoom Out
Ctrl+Shift+F6	Resets materials to solid black and white
Ctrl+Shift+T	Show all toolbars
Ctrl+Alt+F6	Swaps foreground and background materials in the Materials palette
Ctrl+Alt+V	View the image through the current mask

Tools

C	**Clone Brush:** Use to create brush strokes that duplicate part of an image.
R	**Crop Tool:** Use to eliminate or crop areas of an image.
D	**Deform Tool:** Use to rotate, resize, skew, and distort layers or images.
J	**Dodge Brush:** Use to bring out details in areas that are in shadow.
E	**Dropper Tool:** Use to select active foreground and background colours.

X	**Eraser Tool:** Use to replace colours in image with background colour or transparency.
F	**Flood Fill Tool:** Use to fill an area with a colour, pattern, or gradient.
L	**Lighten/Darken Brush:** Use to increase or decrease lightness (affects HSL value).
M	**Move Tool:** Use to move a layer or selection marquee.
O	**Object Selection Tool:** Use to select, move, resize, reshape, and rotate vector objects.
B	**Paint Brush:** Use to paint strokes on a raster layer.
A	**Pan Tool:** Use to pan large images.
V	**Pen Tool:** Draws lines, polylines, point to point, and freehand
I	**Picture Tube Tool:** Use to paint with pictures.
P	**Preset Shape Tool:** Use to draw shapes as raster or vector objects on raster or vector layers.
S	**Selection Tool:** Use to create selections of precise shapes.
T	**Text Tool:** Use to create raster or vector text on raster or vector
Z	**Zoom Tool:** Use to zoom in and out of images.

Appendix B

File Types and Default Folders

Folder	File Format - Description
Brushes	**.PspBrush** - Brushes & Brush Tips. Previous version brushes MUST BE CONVERTED to work in PSP 8
Bump Maps	**anything** - Used by Balls and Bubbles filter
CMYK Profiles	Stored preferences for how PSP handles conversion from RGB to CMYK
Deformation Maps	**.PspDeformationMap** - Saved deformed meshes used by Mesh Warp tool
Environment Maps	**.PspEnvironmentMap** - Used by Magnifying Lens and Balls and Bubbles filters
Gradients	**.PspGradient** - Previous version gradients (**.jgd**) can be used without conversion
Masks	**.PspMask** - Previous version masks (**.msk**) can be used without conversion
Palettes	**.PspPalette** - Saved collection of colours for an image. Previous version palettes (**.pal**) can be used without conversion

Patterns	**anything** - PSP 8 supports all image types as Patterns, including **.bmp**, .**psp**, .**pspimage**, .**jpg**, .**gif**
Picture Frames	**.PspFrame** - Previous version picture frames (**.pfr**) can be used without conversion
Picture Tubes	**.PspTube** - Previous version picture tubes (**.tub**) can be used without conversion
Preset Shapes	**.PspShape** - Previous version preset shapes (**.jsl**) can be used without conversion
Presets	**Preset_xxx.yyy.PspScript** xxx = name of effect yyy = user name for preset Previous version presets MUST BE CONVERTED to work in PSP 8
Print Templates	**MIPTemplate._.PspScript** - Saved page layouts for printing
Quick Guides	**.html** - Short, quick, tutorials in html format, with their supporting images
Sample Images	**anything**
Scripts-Restricted	**.PspScript** - Most scripts, except those that save or delete files, or perform other system-altering tasks
Scripts-Trusted	**.PspScript** - Scripts you KNOW are safe; all scripts which save or delete files, or perform other system-altering tasks
Selections	**.PspSelection** - Previous version selections (.sel) can be used without conversion

Styled Lines	**.PspStyledLine** - Previous version styled lines (.sld) can be used without conversion
Swatches	**Swatch._.PspScript** - Materials you can save to use again
Textures	**anything** - PSP 8 supports all image types as Textures, including **.bmp**, **.psp**, **.pspimage**, **.jpg**, **.gif**
Workspaces	**.PspWorkspace** - This file stores information about PSP, including ruler, grid and guide information; menu, palette, and toolbar settings, location, and docking status; browser window position (if open); full screen edit mode status; and open images, including scroll bar locations and zoom levels.

Appendix C

Supported File Formats

Format	Description	Support
AFX	AutoFX	Read only
BMP	Windows Bitmap	Read/Write
BRK	Brooktrout Fax	Read/Write
CAL	CALS Raster	Read/Write
CDR	CorelDraw Drawing	Read only
CGM	Computer Graphics Metafile	Read only
CLP	Windows Clipboard	Read/Write
CMX	Corel Clipart	Read only
CUR	Windows Cursor	Read only
CUT	Dr. Halo	Read/Write
DCX	Zsoft Multipage Paintbrush	Read only
DGN	MicroStation Drawing	Read only
DIB	Windows DIB	Read/Write
DRW	Micrografx Draw	Read only
DWG	AutoCAD Drawing	Read only
DXF	Autodesk Drawing Interchange	Read only
EMF	Windows Enhanced Metafile	Read/Write
EPS	Encapsulated PostScript	Read/Write
FPX	Flashpix	Read/Write
GEM	Ventura/GEM Drawing	Read only
GIF	Compuserve Graphics Interch.	Read/Write
HPGL	HP Graphics Language	Read only
IFF	Amiga	Read/Write
IMG	GEM Paint	Read/Write
JP2	JPEG 2000	Read/Write
JPG	JPEG – JFIF Compliant	Read/Write
KDC	Kodak Digital Camera File	Read only
KFX	Kofax	Read only
LBM	Deluxe Paint	Read/Write
LV	Lazer View	Read only
MAC	MacPaint	Read/Write

MSP	Microsoft Paint	Read/Write
NCR	NCR G4	Read/Write
PBM	Portable Bitmap	Read/Write
PCD	Kodak Photo CD	Read only
PCT (PICT)	Macintosh PICT	Read/Write
PCX	Zsoft Paintbrush	Read/Write
PDF	Portable Document File	Read only
PGM	Portable Greymap	Read/Write
PIC (Lotus)	Lotus PIC	Read only
PIC	PC Paint	Read/Write
PNG	Portable Network Graphics	Read/Write
PPM	Portable Pixelmap	Read/Write
PSD	Photoshop	Read/Write
PSP	Paint Shop Pro Image	Read/Write
RAS	Sun Raster Image	Read/Write
RAW	Raw File Format	Read/Write
RLE	Windows or CompuServe RLE	Read/Write
SCT	SciTex Continous Tone	Read/Write
SGI/RGB	SGI Image File	Read/Write
SVG	Scalable Vector Graphics	Read only
TGA	Truevision Targa	Read/Write
TIF	Tagged Image File Format	Read/Write
WBMP	Wireless Bitmap	Read/Write
WMF	Windows Meta File	Read/Write
XBM	X Windows Bitmap	Read/Write
XPM	X Windows Pixmap	Read/Write
XWD	X Windows Dump	Read/Write
WPG	Wordperfect Bitmap/Vector	Read/Write

Appendix D

Colour Models

The following information on colours and colour models is from the Paint Shop Pro 8 help system. Hopefully you will find it useful as a reference.

When you apply ink to paper, the colours you see result from the light that the ink reflects. Computer monitors use emitted light rather than reflected light - the colours we see result from light emitted from the screen.

To describe how colour is produced or perceived, we use colour models. Computer monitors display colours by producing varying amounts of red, green, and blue light - the RGB colour model. Human eyes perceive colour by its hue, saturation, and lightness levels - the HSL colour model. With Paint Shop Pro you can select colours using either the RGB or HSL colour model. You can also output images using the CMYK (Cyan, Magenta, Yellow, Black) model, which is used for high-end printing applications.

Selecting the colour model: RGB is the default colour model. Paint Shop Pro uses your preferred colour model (RGB or HSL) whenever colour values are displayed, such as with the Dropper tool. When you select colours from the Jasc Color Picker, you are able to enter RGB or HSL values regardless of your preference setting. The colour model used to display colour values on-screen has no effect on how colours are printed. Choose a colour model preference that is easier for you to use.

The RGB Model

All colours on your computer screen are created by mixing red, green, and blue light in varying proportions and intensities. When these primary colours are mixed in equal proportions, they create yellow, cyan, and magenta. Adding all the colours together creates white.

Each primary colour (red, green, and blue) is assigned a value from 0 (none of the colour present) to 255 (the colour at full strength). For example, pure red is produced by combining a red value of 255, a green value of 0, and a blue value of 0. Yellow is a combination of a red value of 255, a green value of 255, and a blue value of 0. Setting all three values to 255 produces white; setting all three values to 0 produces black. When all three colours are set to the same value (such as 120, 120, 120), the result is grey.

The HSL Model

The HSL model is based on how the human eye perceives colour using the characteristics of hue, saturation, and lightness. Each characteristic is assigned a value from 0 to 255. The three characteristics are described as follows:

Hue - The colour reflected from an object, such as red, yellow, or orange. Each hue value is assigned based on its position on the colour wheel. On the Jasc Color Picker's Color wheel, colours are assigned counter-clockwise from the top. Red is at the top (value 0) and as you move around the wheel the colours go through orange, yellow, green, blue, purple, and back to red.

Saturation - The purity or vividness of the colour. Saturation represents the amount of grey in the colour, from 0 (entirely grey) to 255 (fully saturated colour).

Lightness - The perceived amount or intensity of light in the colour. Lightness ranges from 0 (no light, or black) to 255 (total lightness, or white). At 50 percent lightness, or a value of 128, a colour is considered pure.

For example, pure red has a hue of 255, a saturation of 255 (100 percent) and a lightness of 128 (50 percent). For pure blue, the hue is 170, saturation is 255 and lightness is 128.

The CMYK Model

The CMYK model is based on the fact that ink on paper both absorbs and reflects light. As white light strikes the ink, part of the colour spectrum is absorbed and part is reflected back to your eyes (resulting in the colour you see).

In this model, the primary colours cyan (C), magenta (M), and yellow (Y) combine in varying proportions to produce a variety of colours. When the three colours are combined, they produce black. Because impurities in the ink make it difficult to produce a true black, a fourth colour, black (K), is added.

Combining inks in this way is called four-colour process printing. It is used by printing services and high-end colour printers.

Although you cannot create images in Paint Shop Pro using the CMYK model, you can produce colour separations that can be printed on CMYK printers. There are two ways to do this: You can split the images into CMYK channels or you can print colour separation pages.

CMYK channels are simply four separate greyscale images that represent the percentage and location of cyan, magenta, yellow, and black in the image.

When you print CMYK separations, Paint Shop Pro prints a separate greyscale page for each primary colour. You can then use these pages as "colour plates" to give to a printing service.

Understanding Colour Depth

Colour depth, also called bit depth, refers to the number of colours each pixel (and therefore its image) can display. As the colour depth increases, the number of colours an image can display increases. Each pixel's colour information is stored in a certain number of computer bits - from 1 bit to 24 bits. In a 1-bit image, each pixel can display only one of two colours (black or white). In a 24-bit image, each pixel can display one of 16 million colours (2^{24} or 2 colours for each bit). Images with a colour depth of 16 million colours look best because they contain the most colours, but they also require the most memory to store and edit.

In Paint Shop Pro, you can create 2 colour (1-bit), 16 colour (4-bit), greyscale (8-bit), 256 colour (8-bit), and 16 million colour (24-bit) images. Many of Paint Shop Pro's effect and correction commands work on 16 million colour images only. Therefore, it is best to create most images using 16 million colours. After you finish working on an image, you can decrease its colour depth and save it in another format.

Computer monitors also have a colour depth that is determined by the monitor's capabilities as well as the selected colour setting. If you display an image with a higher colour depth than the monitor can display, the image will have some colour distortion. Some file formats limit the number of supported colours so that images display correctly on a variety of monitor types. For example, GIF images, a popular format for the Web, contain up to 256 colours (8-bit depth).

The number of colours actually used in an image is usually less than the colour depth. For example, in a 16 million colour image, the image is capable of displaying that many colours but may only use say 50,000 colours.

Appendix E

Blend Modes

These blend modes are common to both layers and the Paint and Flood Fill tool brush options. In PSP 8 several of the blend modes have been enhanced and may not be compatible with other applications. Use the Legacy blend modes for compatibility with other applications such as Photoshop and older versions of PSP.

Blend Mode	Result
Normal	Displays pixels of underlying layers based on the opacity of pixels on the selected layer. If data is fully opaque, no pixels show through. As the opacity decreases, more pixels from underlying layers show through.
Darken	Displays pixels in the selected layer that are darker than the underlying layers. Pixels lighter than the underlying layers disappear.
Lighten	Displays pixels in the selected layer that are lighter than the underlying layers. Pixels darker than the underlying layers disappear.
Hue	Applies the hue of the selected layer to the underlying layers (without changing the saturation or lightness).
Hue (Legacy)	Applies the hue of the selected layer to the underlying layers

	(without affecting the saturation or lightness).
Saturation	Applies the saturation of the selected layer to the underlying layers (without affecting the hue or lightness).
Saturation (Legacy)	Applies the saturation of the selected layer to the underlying layers (without affecting the hue or lightness).
Color	Applies the hue and saturation of the selected layer to the underlying layers (without affecting the lightness).
Color (Legacy)	Applies the hue and saturation of the selected layer to the underlying layers (without affecting the lightness).
Luminance	Applies the luminance (or lightness) of the selected layer to the underlying layers (without affecting the hue or saturation).
Luminance (Legacy)	Applies the luminance (or lightness) of the selected layer to the underlying layers (without affecting the hue or saturation).
Multiply	Combines the colours of the selected layer with the underlying layers to produce a darker colour. Multiplying any colour with black produces black. Multiplying any colour with white leaves the colour unchanged.
Screen	Lightens the colours of underlying layers by multiplying the inverse of the selected and underlying layers.

The result is a colour that is the same or a lightened version of the selected layer.

Dissolve

Randomly replaces the colours of some pixels on the selected layer with those of the underlying layers to create a speckled effect. The selected layer's opacity determines the number of pixels replaced; the lower the opacity, the more pixels that are replaced.

Overlay

Combines the Multiply and Screen blend modes. If the colour channel value of underlying layers is less than half the maximum value, the Multiply blend mode is used. If the colour channel value is greater than or equal to half the value, the Screen blend mode is used. The Overlay blend mode shows patterns or colours of the selected layer while preserving the shadows and highlights of underlying layers.

Hard Light

Combines the Multiply and Screen blend modes. If the colour channel value of the selected layer is less than 128, the Multiply blend mode is used. If the colour channel value is greater than or equal to 128, the Screen blend mode is used. In general, use the Hard Light blend mode to add highlights or shadows.

Soft Light

Combines the Burn and Dodge blend modes. If the colour channel value of the selected layer is less than 128, the Burn blend mode is used. If the colour channel value is greater than or equal to 128, the

Dodge blend mode is used. In general, use the Soft Light blend mode to add soft highlights or shadows.

Difference

Subtracts the selected layer's colour from the colour of the underlying layers.

Dodge

Lightens the image by having the lightness values of the colours in the selected layer lighten the colours of underlying layers. Light colours produce the most lightening; black has no effect.

Burn

Darkens the image by having the lightness values of the selected layer reduce the lightness of underlying layers.

Exclusion

Creates an effect similar to but softer than the Difference blend mode.

Index

Companion Discs

COMPANION DISCS are available for most computer books written by the same author(s) and published by BERNARD BABANI (publishing) LTD, as listed at the front of this book (except for those marked with an asterisk).

There is no Companion Disc for this book

To obtain companion discs for other books, fill in the order form below, or a copy of it, enclose a cheque (payable to **P.R.M. Oliver**) or a postal order, and send it to the address given below. **Make sure you fill in your name and address** and specify the book number and title in your order.

Book No.	Book Name	Unit Price	Total Price
BP		£3.50	
BP		£3.50	
BP		£3.50	
Name .... Address		Sub-total	£.............
		P & P (@ 45p/disc)	£.............
		Total Due	£.............
Send to: P.R.M. Oliver, West Trevarth House, West Trevarth Nr Redruth, Cornwall, TR16 5TJ			

PLEASE NOTE

The author(s) are fully responsible for providing this Companion Disc service. The publishers of this book accept no responsibility for the supply, quality, or magnetic contents of the disc, or in respect of any damage, or injury that might be suffered or caused by its use.